SUCCESS FOR ALL

About the University of Nevada, Reno

Inspired by its land grant foundation, the University of Nevada, Reno, serves the economic, social, environmental, and cultural needs of the citizens of Nevada, the nation, and the world (Northwest Accreditation Report 2016).

The University was established in 1864, the year of the state's admission into the Union. Classes were first offered by the University in 1874 in Elko as a preparatory high school. In 1885, the University was moved to Reno, near the center of the state's population (University of Nevada, Reno General Catalog). The 1886 register of the University of Nevada referenced that the State Constitution in Section I of Article XI, declares that, "the Legislature shall encourage by all suitable means the promotion of intellectual, literary, scientific, mining, mechanical, agricultural and moral improvement."

Within the University of Nevada, Reno, twelve schools and colleges offer undergraduate and graduate majors. Graduate-level training and research, including a number of doctoral-level programs, further the University's mission to create scholarly activity. The University is classified by the Carnegie Foundation for the Advancement of Teaching as a Comprehensive Doctoral (institution) with medical and/or veterinary medicine. This designation indicates that the University awards doctoral degrees in the humanities, the social sciences, and in science, technology, engineering and mathematics (STEM) disciplines as well as medicine. The University also offers professional education in other health professions, business, education, engineering, public policy, and social work (University of Nevada, Reno General Catalog, 2017).

SUCCESS FOR ALL

PROGRAMS TO SUPPORT STUDENTS THROUGHOUT THEIR COLLEGE EXPERIENCE

Edited by
MELISA N. CHOROSZY,
THEODOR M. MEEK,
JAMES BEATTIE,
and REEMA K. NAIK

UNIVERSITY OF NEVADA PRESS *Reno & Las Vegas*

University of Nevada Press | Reno, Nevada 89557 USA
www.unpress.nevada.edu

Cover art by University of Nevada, Reno
Cover design by David Ter-Avanesyan
All photos are by the author unless otherwise indicated.

LIBRARY OF CONGRESS CATALOGING-IN-PUBLICATION DATA
Names: Choroszy, Melisa N. (Melisa Nancy), 1949- editor. | Meek, Theodor M., editor. | Beattie, James, 1973- editor. | Naik, Reema K., 1995-editor.
Title: Success for all : programs to support students throughout their college experience / Melisa N. Choroszy, Theodor M. Meek, James Beattie, Reema K. Naik.
Description: Reno ; Las Vegas : University of Nevada Press, [2020] | Includes bibliographical references and index. | Summary: "This book provides an overview of the research, services and programs at the University of Nevada, Reno and Truckee Meadows Community College that support student success in undergraduate and graduate programs"—Provided by publisher.
Identifiers: LCCN 2019055443 (print) | LCCN 2019055444 (ebook) | ISBN 9781948908580 (paperback) | ISBN 9781948908597 (ebook)
Subjects: LCSH: University of Nevada, Reno. | Truckee Meadows Community College. | College students—Services for—Nevada—Reno. | College student development programs—Nevada—Reno. | Academic achievement—Nevada—Reno. | Study skills—Nevada—Reno.
Classification: LCC LB2342.93.N3 S83 2020 (print) | LCC LB2342.93.N3 (ebook) | DDC 378.1/90979355—dc23
LC record available at https://lccn.loc.gov/2019055443
LC ebook record available at https://lccn.loc.gov/2019055444

The paper used in this book meets the requirements of American National Standard for Information Sciences — Permanence of Paper for Printed Library Materials, ANSI/NISO Z39.48-1992 (R2002).

FIRST PRINTING

Manufactured in the United States of America

Contents

Part III—Success Through Outreach

Part IV—Success Through Tutoring

Part V—Success Through Undergraduate Research

Part VI—Success with the UNRSOM

An Introduction to Success

Chancellor Thom Reilly, Ph.D.

The chancellor is appointed by the Board of Regents to serve as chief executive officer for the Nevada System of Higher Education (NSHE). He supervises the eight NSHE presidents and ensures the Board of Regents polices are implemented throughout the system. As chancellor, he is the System liaison with the governor, state legislators, and other public officials and community leaders. Dr. Thom Reilly was appointed by the Board to serve as NSHE's chancellor starting August 2017. Prior to his appointment, he served as director of the Morrison Institute for Public Policy at Arizona State University, where he also was a professor in the School of Public Affairs. He currently is a Fellow of the National Academy of Public Administration and professor emeritus at San Diego State University.

The success of Nevada's students pursuing higher education is a prerequisite for a robust state economy. The opportunity for individuals to pursue higher education brings many personal gains, including social mobility, increased job security, and a higher income, among others; however, the benefits of higher education are not limited to the individuals who earn degrees and certificates. Our state benefits from a more educated populous by having citizens with higher discretionary income, healthier lives, lower rates of poverty and crime, and reduced reliance on federal and state social services.

The pursuit of higher education has always been a public good from which our entire community derives benefit. Because of this, post-secondary leaders have a civic responsibility to give each of our students the maximum opportunity to succeed in their educational endeavors. For our certificate and degree-seeking population, we measure success as the student earning their desired credential.

Whether for the recent high school graduate with aspirations to become an engineer, a first-generation student with the dream of becoming a doctor, a returning adult with the desire to pursue a second career, or an individual seeking a certificate of value to enrich their current work opportunities, the success of our students remains a strategic goal of the Nevada System of Higher Education. We are acutely aware that many students can be worse off economically if they drop out before receiving a diploma than if they have not started college at all.

To build a culture of success within our system, institutions must meet students where they are, provide the needed academic support and a positive learning environment as well as foster innovation. Our future will require that graduates be equipped with critical thinking, logic, and reasoning skills, as well as creativity and innovation to challenge the status quo, as past solutions may not solve future problems.

Despite our intentional and deep commitment to student success, there is no silver bullet. Student success is a strategic goal not only because it is the right thing to do, but because we have not yet reached our success potential. Today, too many underrepresented ethnic minority students still do not graduate on time, if at all. Higher education remains a financial challenge for many of our low-income students, and the stress of college affordability causes many students to leave without a degree or certificate to show for it. Housing and food insecurity, transportation, mental health, and childcare are among just a few of the factors that influence a student's ability to be successful. While our graduation rates continue to improve, our work is not yet done. Nevada's institutions must, and do, remain committed to the continuous improvement of success. To maintain accountability, each institution set aggressive student success goals to be achieved by 2025. All institutions have made it a goal to increase their graduation rates, some by more than double.

The programs and services outlined in this book detail just some of the critical work being done in our system to promote student success—especially for our African American and Latino students. In this collection, you will see that the Nevada System of Higher Education is committed to the success of every student. I hope that you will take this book and make notes on what may work for your institution. Consider what is possible for your institution to start now. Discuss with your campus community the programs that may take additional human and financial capital to implement, but would be worthwhile ventures. By no means is our work perfect, but I invite you to engage, enjoy, and emulate, should you choose, the outstanding work taking place in our system.

Foreword

Shannon Ellis, Ph.D.

Shannon Ellis was appointed vice president for Student Services in 1998. Reporting directly to the president, Ellis serves as lead administrative officer and provides leadership for the Division of Student Services, which includes enrollment services, student life, services and student success services.

At this University, a student is a success if they graduate with a bachelor's degree in four years. Somewhere along the way, it became acceptable and even necessary for students to graduate in six or more years; it was a travesty that those of us leading and teaching in higher education allowed that to happen. There was a myth that all our students were working more than part-time jobs. No one could ever prove that. Even if it was true, why weren't we doing the math for those students to demonstrate that the longer it takes, the more it costs? At Nevada, for every year you delay graduation beyond four years, it costs a student (or their parents or those providing loans and scholarships) a minimum of $35,000, maximum $58,000 per year. Each year, our budget and analysis professionals provide me with figures along those lines, and every year the figures go up. The numbers are comprised of lost full-time wages with benefits, increases in tuition, cost of living and compounded debt.

Faculty yearn for the days when students would spend their time in college poking around various courses, exploring ideas, professions, theories and practices with the great curiosity of a scholar. While that still occurs, things are so different now from when many of them were in school. The social contracts states made with their schools in the 60s, 70s and even early 80s have been broken. Without state support, tuition has soared; many students no longer have the luxury to explore the life of the mind even at the value that public higher education continues to offer, especially as compared to private schools.

Even with the push to help students graduate in four years, there are plenty of opportunities for students to explore the things that we hope students will engage with inside and outside the classroom. In our most recent survey of Nevada graduates, 92 percent of students told us their coursework had the greatest impact on their critical thinking. They also valued their development of clear and effective writing skills as well as the ability to think independently and creatively. These skills also represent the hallmarks of a successful student. Outside the classroom, student surveys around campus engagement confirm student appreciation of the impact of community service and ability to understand issues pertaining to diversity, equity, and the globe—more keys to defining a successful student at the University of Nevada, Reno.

Critically, our students find jobs in their chosen fields. If that is an indicator of success in this increasingly career-driven educational system, then that further defines how we could perceive student success. While it can rankle the psyche of the scholars committed to the life-of-the-mind, it is a reality most of us face whether recruiting students, retaining students, or working hard to get them across the stage at commencement.

Every institution's leaders and educators should be very vocal about what consists of student success: it sets clear expectations. It prioritizes curricular offerings over things less likely to help a student graduate. It puts the focus on the right things while allowing for exploration, deep thinking, part-time jobs and internships, study abroad and a lot of fun along the way. Four years go by quickly, but they offer plenty of time to achieve a college degree with all the breadth and depth of knowledge necessary to create a life of meaning.

Introduction to Success at TMCC

Karin Hilgersom, Ph.D.,
President of Truckee Meadows Community College

When she transformed into a butterfly,
the caterpillars spoke not of her beauty, but of her weirdness.
They wanted her to change back into what she always had been.
But she had wings.

Dean Jackson

During my second week teaching the first of many community college courses, and after two years teaching freshmen at the University of Oregon, I recall a remark from a woman in class, easily ten years my senior to my twenty-three. While polite, she was brutally frank when she shared with the entire *Interpersonal Communication* class that she did not think it wise for me to expect that she and her classmates practice the ten specific communication skills discussed in the text. Doing so, in her words, was an act akin to taking a bird and breaking its wing. She went on to explain that she learned the value of cultivating one's true nature, often outside of the norm, from her time at Rajneeshpuram, a commune in Northern Oregon. I recall taking in the remark cautiously, with a good deep breath, a tad amazed at the confidence and clarity that she portrayed. We quickly became academic friends and although I continued to expect that students learn specific communication tools, her lessons positively shaped my pedagogy, my view of student success, and seeded my vision of community colleges as a transformative institutional setting.

Student success at Truckee Meadows Community College (TMCC) is appropriately measured by certificate and degree completion. We are proud to exceed national benchmarks when we count annual completions. And yet student success at TMCC is so much more; success for our diverse student population can be amorphous. We are in the "business" of cultivating true natures so that students learn to fly professionally, academically, and even personally. As Sonny Ramaswamy, president of the Northwest Regional Accrediting Agency, recently explained:

> Student success is defined by student learning and achievement that occurs as a result of the educational programs, experiences, and support offered by the college such that students accomplish their current and future academic, personal, and professional goals. (Sonny Ramaswamy, NWCCU President, The Beacon, 9/6/2019)

For over three decades, I've observed shifting perspectives in how we measure and view student success in higher education. I am pleased that Ramaswamy expands the discussion to include broadly defined *personal* goals. In contrast, the past decade has relied heavily on quantitative, aggregated data that is helpful and correct, but when one considers the complexities of the lives of community college students, the data may not access underlying truths. Perhaps an overemphasis upon accountability, data has led to arbitrary deadlines, and to a growing extent, a hint of shame when educators fail at targets. Furthermore, disappointment among faculty and students young enough to qualify as "digital natives" often occurs when performance targets are fueled by traditions that are literally more than a hundred years old.

Old assumptions about *how* and *what* people ought to be learning, and how fast, have moved to the forefront of the discourse like birds with broken wings. I worry that, as educators, we continue to be satisfied by the completion of requirements, often accelerated, in a global economy that responds less to the completion of requirements and instead values skilled and talented people who are great learners and agents of change. Has the numbers game of the past decade, a narrative which has strengthened the institutional story, subsumed a more brilliant narrative about the cultivation of skill, talent, and potential experience unique to each community college learner?

Community college learners succeed for reasons that cultivate in them resiliency, but also fragility; hope, and yet some despair. Many community college students arrive having already experienced marriage, jobs, job loss, births, traumas, wealth, poverty, aging parents, terrible parents, religious devotion, and even cults. Some have children with special needs, spouses who have abused them, and learning disabilities undiagnosed until well into adulthood. Many have talent—so much talent—as writers, painters, mechanics, and public speakers. Many do not believe in their talent, or lack confidence in subjects long forgotten or never learned in K-12; intermediate Algebra is a typical concern. Many *are* fresh out of high school, and these eighteen-year-olds often enjoy the companionship of their older colleagues. Most students enjoy the diversity of ages, socioeconomic status, ethnic diversity, and the fascinating stories shared during class discussions; such discussions also deepened the classroom experiences for me during my teaching career.

It has been more than three decades since I became part of the important work of community colleges. During that time, I've seen many positive changes (and some unfortunate ones, too). The emphasis on outcomes and assessment as a way to reflect on our productivity as educators has been difficult but beneficial. Faculty and students are changing as well, and the effects of the internet and mobile devices cannot be overstated. Faculty are changing the way class time is structured, dedicating less time to lectures that can be offered on YouTube, thus providing more time for discussion and activity designed to reach the peaks of Bloom's taxonomy—synthesis and evaluation. Community colleges have gained widespread acceptance and decent support from state and local governments. We are the envy of workforce training in numerous technical professions (too many to list here) and many of our compassionate students make wonderful healthcare providers. We continue to transfer thousands of students to universities. We do all of this with faculty who love teaching.

I remain optimistic that a nuanced discussion which defines student success in richer ways will rule this era of public higher education, and in doing so, acknowledge and honor the complexities of our students, including their enormous capacity for transformation and TMCC's capacity for cultivating positive change in each one of them.

Introduction to Success at UNR

Marc A. Johnson, Ph.D.,
President of the University of Nevada, Reno

For the past decade, the University of Nevada, Reno, has stressed the value of creating a "culture of student success" on our campus. It has become a rallying cry for our faculty and staff, and has spurred our student body to greater graduation rates, retention rates, involvement in our community, and professionally productive and personally enriching careers once they depart our institution.

But what does "student success" really mean? Perhaps first and foremost, "student success" should be considered a defining challenge for any institution of higher learning. If our public universities are to succeed in the twenty-first century, it is imperative we dramatically demand more of ourselves. We must make every effort to ensure that services, programs, and research opportunities in the student realm become thoroughly intertwined with an institution's vision and mission. When we identify, support, and actualize student success-centered services and programs, we are finding a catalyzing alignment with institutional purposes and goals that will inevitably lead to higher student achievement, and will give our students their best opportunity for success in a highly competitive and quickly changing world.

We are fortunate on our campus to have people who not only have helped advance our student success mission, but who have written comprehensively, insightfully, and poignantly about the broader implications of student success. *Access for All: Expanding Opportunity and Programs to Support Successful Student Outcomes at the University of Nevada, Reno* previously examined the programs and strategies created by our University to support first-generation and other underrepresented groups. This new work, written by Melisa Choroszy, Theo Meek, James Beattie, and Reema Naik—all key contributors in propelling our Division of Student Services forward among the nation's vanguard—makes a timely and important view of what our institution has done in its efforts to create a "culture of completion" through a "culture of student success" for all of its students.

These are goals we must never lose sight of, particularly as it relates to the most important form of human capital a college campus can ever have—its students.

PART I

Success Beyond the Traditional Classroom

Student success extends beyond the traditional classroom setting. A critical complement to the attainment of professional goals is participation in our curricular and co-curricular programs, activities, and organizations. Some programs begin serving students as early as middle school for college readiness, while others serve students later in their college career and enhance their educational experience. This section highlights how the Davidson Academy prepares bright, young minds from middle school to the time they graduate from the program and enter college, how students who are in community college define success, and how STEM programs can take the next steps in creating certification programs that students earn while reaching their degree. In addition, the section reveals how different programs at the University of Nevada, Reno, help students academically, financially, physically, and mentally.

CHAPTER 1

Home Means Nevada

Students from Across the Country Attend Davidson Academy

COLLEEN M. HARSIN, M.A., MSW

Colleen M. Harsin, M.A., MSW, is the director of the Davidson Academy, a unique public school designed to serve profoundly gifted middle and high school students located on the University of Nevada, Reno campus. She earned her bachelor's degree in Psychology at the University of Idaho, followed by a master's degree in Psychology and a master's degree in Social Work. Both master's degrees were completed at the University of Nevada, Reno.

Introduction

Since the beginning of the 2006–2007 academic year, the University of Nevada, Reno campus has been home to the Davidson Academy, a one-of-a-kind public middle and high school for profoundly gifted students. This small school designed to educate some of nation's brightest students started because Nevadans were thinking big. While there are other selective public high schools in the United States (Finn and Hockett), the Davidson Academy is the only public middle and high school specifically designed for students who perform at the upper extreme of the intellectual continuum. Often described as "profoundly gifted," these students are at the 99.9th percentile of the population as measured by intelligence, as well as, aptitude or achievement tests.

Thinking Big and Giving Back

Educational software entrepreneurs Jan and Bob Davidson led the charge for finding and serving exceptionally bright students who needed the opportunity to learn at a level in tune with their abilities. Highly able students without the opportunity to experience meaningful academic challenges are at risk of underachievement and disengagement from learning (Reis and McCoach). The Davidsons realized that supporting student learning beyond what was offered to students as standard grade-level material was critical to fostering an ongoing love of learning and persistence through challenges. Providing educational opportunities for highly intelligent young people is an investment in the future of those individuals, and ultimately, the future of our country. In 1997, after selling Davidson & Associates, their educational software company ("Mission Goals"), they were determined to "give back" to education in ways that stood to make a positive difference for our nation's brightest young people, who were too often underserved in a regular school setting. In 1999, The Davidson Institute for Talent Development was established in Nevada as a 501c(3) private operating foundation with the mission "to recognize, nurture and support profoundly intelligent young people and to provide opportunities for them to develop their talents to make a positive difference" ("About Us").

It is no secret that the public education system has room for improvement in addressing the needs of our brightest students (Cloud; Colangelo et al., Vols. I–II). It can also be said that private elementary and secondary education options are not consistently prepared to address the needs of exceptionally bright students (Davidson and Davidson). This leads to several questions about educational opportunities for highly-able young people (Assouline et al., Vol. I; Assouline et al., Vol. II). Who is focusing on the needs of the students who are ahead of their peers in terms of their learning? What happens to students who do not have the opportunity to learn to the extent of their abilities? What can be done to support exceptionally bright so that they may thrive? With solid research in place, what can be done to put pedagogy into practice?

The Davidsons summarized what they learned from their investigations into these and other questions, pulling together the stories they learned from parents, educators, and experts, and published their call to action, *Genius Denied: How to Stop Wasting Our Brightest Young Minds* (Davidson and Davidson). In parallel, throughout the development and implementation of successful programs and services offered by the Davidson Institute for Talent Development ("Davidson Institute"), families of exceptionally bright young people increasingly asked the Davidsons about starting a school. While many families were clear that they were most interested in having such a school in their own backyard, so to speak, the Davidsons believed that such an endeavor was best built in the Davidson Institute's backyard, Northern Nevada.

Educational Opportunities in Nevada

The local landscape for proposing a new educational option turned out to be quite favorable. The Davidson Institute for Talent Development continued to grow. Families of profoundly gifted young people from all over the country were increasingly showing interest in an educational option designed for their children. The Davidsons' commitment to education, profoundly gifted young people, and Nevada set the stage for breaking the mold on current public education for these students. Converging interests in raising the bar for education in Nevada drove important discussions about how to maximize opportunities for these students and set a nationwide example. University of Nevada, Reno leadership played a vital role in making this vision a reality. Initially embraced by President John Lilley, the dynamic and supportive University leaders which followed have continued to be invaluable to the success of what is now the Davidson Academy.

In 2005 Nevada legislative action in support of a "university school for profoundly gifted pupils" made providing public education specifically designed for students at the upper extreme of the intellectual continuum a reality. Opened in 2006 with thirty five students, Davidson Academy is a public, special purpose school, located on a university campus where students are placed in classes based on ability rather than age-based grade level. By definition, a university school for profoundly gifted pupils is not a charter school, not affiliated with a school district, and not funded by a university. The mission and location of the school provide the opportunity for profoundly gifted students to be educated in a manner that aligns with their abilities and interests, and provides access to advanced rigorous curriculum across all subject areas. Distributive school account (DSA) funding is provided consistent with the formula established for public school in Nevada to receive per-pupil funding (Profoundly Gifted Pupils; University Schools for Profoundly Gifted Pupils). The Davidsons also remain committed to funding the school in order for it to continue to progress. In 2019 the Davidson Academy remains a unique public school with over 150 students attending middle and high school in the Jot Travis Building on the University campus, and over thirty students attending classes via the online campus. The Academy's program of distance education was authorized via NRS 388C.130 as of the 2015 Nevada legislative. Ideally, by setting a legislative precedent and making the school public, other states may be in a better position to follow in providing aspects of this model, if not the model in its entirety.

Mission, Goals, and the Role of the University of Nevada

"The mission of the Davidson Academy is to provide profoundly gifted young people an advanced educational opportunity matched to their abilities, strengths and interests" ("Mission & Goals"). The synergy of the Academy with the University campus and community contributes greatly to the overall optimal match between highly-able students and their educational environment.

The Davidson Academy addresses educational and social-emotional needs of local and national students at the upper extreme of the intellectual continuum, who are often overlooked and underserved in schools ("National Statistics"). Approximately 40 percent of the students at the Reno campus originally lived outside Northern Nevada, and moved with their families in order to access the Academy. This influx of students moving to Northern Nevada from different parts of the country brings varied experiences and interests to bear, adding to the college-like atmosphere of the Academy. This increased diversity enhances opportunities for students to learn from one another in meaningful ways. Recognizing that not everyone is in a position to move to Reno as a family, the full-time online campus opened beginning with the 2017–2018 school year ("Online School"). This is yet another way that students stand to benefit from interacting with intellectual peers from all over the country.

A multi-dimensional working relationship with the University is an inherent element of the success of the Davidson Academy. Between the Reno and Online campuses, there are no fewer than twenty one staff members who graduated from University of Nevada, Reno. This includes seventeen staff members who earned their bachelor's degrees, fourteen who earned their master's degrees, and three who earned their doctoral degrees. Eleven Academy instructors have either previously taught at the University, or are currently teaching there while also teaching a course at the Academy. In addition, the Reno campus employs at least a dozen Honors Program students each semester to oversee study hall and lunch periods at the Academy, as well as chaperone Academy students under age 16 to and from their University classes.

Mutual benefits are apparent in the context of day to day operations, as well as the goals identified by the Academy during the initial accreditation process for the school ("Mission & Goals"), conducted by Northwest Accreditation Commission (NWAC) and later subsumed under Cognia, the current accrediting organization ("Cognia").

Seven Identified Goals of the Davidson Academy

1. "To provide a Personalized Learning Plan (PLP) that appropriately challenges each student's abilities, allowing him or her to engage in learning opportunities at a pace and depth consistent with the student's knowledge, skills and personal motivations."

All Academy students participate in a dynamic advising process that places them in rigorous core courses based on demonstrated abilities. In the context of a dual-enrollment agreement with the University of Nevada, Academy students academically and socially ready for university courses may enroll in them as part of their PLP advising process. Approximately one-third of Reno campus students take one or more classes at the University of Nevada each semester. These range from 100-level elective courses to 400-level math, science, philosophy, and computer courses; all in the context of the students' PLPs. Students graduating from the Academy often have demonstrated success in 200 and 300 level courses, or higher, which helps increase the likelihood of them being considered as competitive and compelling applicants at post-secondary institutions of interest to them. Students' high school credits are tracked to ensure that their graduation criteria are being met by their traditional graduation age. Some students graduate early, but most choose to stay and maximize the benefits of the Academy and the University before moving on to their post-secondary plans.

2. "To allow students the opportunity to develop their talents and skills at an advanced level and be supported by teachers, professors and other experts in their fields of interest."

Academy students who progress to an advanced level in a particular area of interest often enjoy competitions to further develop their expertise. Academy instructors support and coach students on these endeavors, as do qualified parent volunteers and University professors. Davidson Academy students have developed competitive teams for a number of events, including but not limited to, Academic World Quest, DECA, MATHCOUNTS, Speech & Debate, Science Bowl, and Science Olympiad. These teams have had successful competitions at local, state, and in many cases, national levels. Access to aspects of the University raises the ceiling for all Academy students. Experience in courses of interest, including advanced and University courses, prepares them for lab and other research opportunities on campus for which they become qualified. Some Academy students even contribute to publications with University students and professors. In addition, Academy students enjoy the benefits of special events and experiences at the University, including spending time with Discover Science series speakers prior to the public speaking engagements they do on campus ("Discover Science Lecture Series").

3. "To provide students an opportunity to learn with intellectual peers."

While there are a plethora of rigorous in-depth options available for academic study, particularly in the online environment, what is often missing is access to intellectual peers within a similar age range. Learning with students who are near one's age and who share similar intellectual capabilities allows students to express, explore, and to be themselves in developmentally appropriate ways. Academy students often report that the Academy experience is the first time they have really been challenged in an academic environment, as well as the first time they felt they could really be themselves. Students at the Academy are placed by ability, not age, so there is typically a two- to three-year age span in any given class. Class sizes are also relatively small, approximately fifteen students, which facilitates coursework focused on critical thinking and expression, consistent with the upper levels of Bloom's Taxonomy so often sought after for bright students: analyzing, evaluating, and creating (Bloom, 1956). As students approach high school graduation age, they are well prepared to be active participants in University courses as well.

4. "To provide students a learning environment that fosters integrity, personal responsibility, conscientious citizenship, understanding and an appreciation of individual differences, along with respect for others."

The Davidson Academy Core Values (respect, responsibility, integrity, leadership, balance, and the pursuit of knowledge) guide all aspects of the Academy. Safety and inclusion are paramount to the Academy experience. Academy students and families have formed a community that generally looks out for one another, while also seeking ways to benefit the larger community. Whether they came to the Academy from another school in the area or from another state, students and their families tend to embrace the opportunities afforded by being part of a larger campus at University of Nevada, Reno. Several parents of students work at the University, and it is also an exceptional draw for Academy graduates as well. Responsibility as good neighbors on campus is essential to the success of the Academy. The privilege of accessing University courses and other benefits depends in large part upon the maturity and overall readiness of Academy students, including strengths consistent with these core values.

5. "To provide students guidance in identifying and developing their unique talents and abilities counseling for the college application process, procurement of scholarships, and access to professional areas of interest and career counseling."

The Academy provides a proactive counseling model in which students meet on a regular basis with their counselor in order to establish rapport and to determine how best to incorporate school counseling and related services for each individual student. In the context of each student's PLP, interests are discussed with student services staff members, and options for exploring them are considered. In addition to school counselors, several staff members comprise a student services team. The college application process is supported by a certified college counselor, as well as an outside professional consultant. Scholarship opportunities are encouraged and guidance is provided for relevant searches. Students and parents have access to an online college planning tool that houses resources and information to support the college applications process from start to finish, and rising seniors kick off the summer before their senior year with a Common Application Boot Camp hosted by Academy counselors. The three-day seminar gets them started on completing the Common Application, as well as identifying a smart list of colleges and universities to which they plan to apply. Simultaneously, they refine their selection criteria and develop a game plan for their summer application activities. The University has been supportive of this process as well, by making sure a representative from the Office of Prospective Students meets with students considering the University of Nevada. National Merit Finalists are honored with a signing day when committing to the University.

6. "To encourage students to develop their talents, abilities and leadership skills in positive ways while in pursuit of knowledge."

The pursuit of knowledge extends beyond Academy classrooms. All clubs at the Academy are initiated by students, for students. Davidson Academy students at the Reno campus have initiated or maintained clubs focusing on various areas of interest for the current school year: art, baking, Bionicle toys

(Lego), business, chess, Chinese, computers, creative writing, dance, drama, electronic music, engineering, filmography, French, future physicians, Green Earth Community Knowledge Organization (GECKO), India, Japanese, LGBT+, math, microbiology, poetry, running, science, Science Bowl, Science Olympiad, Spanish, speech and debate, strategic games, stitching, and world affairs. Online campus students have initiated or maintained clubs focusing on art, creative writing, chess, games, math, and Spanish. The Academy has a vibrant student council with elected officers for the Reno and Online campuses. Student Council is primarily responsible for running various student events and activities, including community meetings, dances, fundraisers, and spirit week activities. Additional leadership opportunities include student-led seminars for elective credits. Interested students propose an elective course they wish to lead, including syllabus and materials, for consideration by the Academy curriculum team. Exceptional options are then made available as elective courses led by the students and supported by qualified adults as needed. Examples include aviation, computer programming, genealogy, rock climbing, vocal ensemble, and many more over the years.

7. "To engage parents in the learning process and provide opportunities for understanding and nurturing their children."

Consistent with the mission of the Davidson Institute for Talent Development and the programs and services that led to the creation of the Academy, providing information, resources, and support for parents is essential for successful students. Surveys are done at least annually, and parent feedback is incorporated as much as possible. Fortunately, reaching disengaged parents has not been a problem for the Academy. Parents of students attending the Academy are engaged and committed to addressing the needs of their children. Opportunities to address this goal include orientation sessions, guest speakers, and individual meetings and check-ins. Parents are involved in the Personalized Learning Plan process with their students. They also have access to the student information system, PowerSchool, to access current information on their children's classes, grades, attendance information, and teacher comments. The Academy uses Blackboard K-12 as the learning management system for online classes, as well as the central depository for information including policies and procedures, counseling and advising information, college planning resources, and community service referrals. Weekly electronic newsletters go out to parents that include updates and information pertinent to them and their students, and the Online campus holds quarterly town hall meetings during which parents can meet online as a group with the Director. Parent volunteers make a significant positive difference at the Academy in myriad ways. Fundraising for an Educational Opportunities Fund to assist with education costs for students who may not otherwise be fully able to participate in academic activities such as competitions that involve registration fees and travel expenses is a major benefit to the Academy community. Parent volunteers serve as club advisors for students, as well as coaches, teachers, and mentors in areas of interest and expertise. They create a welcoming community for families who are new to the school and the surrounding area. From the Davidson Academy perspective, it is clear that focused parent engagement maximizes student opportunities. at the Academy.

Student Successes

Being part of a small school with graduating classes of approximately twenty, students really get to know one another during their time at the Academy. Many of them remain close with one another, regardless of distance. Social media is frequented by photos and comments about shared experiences as several of them meet up for spring breaks or take part in one another's weddings. The Reno campus serves as a gathering place for alumni on break from college, with many of them stopping by the school before they even get home from the airport. However, just as with any group, all is not well all the time. In such a case, there is a solid sense of support and understanding among Academy alumni that is endearing.

Davidson Academy graduates have attended, or are attending, as many as seventy five different undergraduate institutions, and many have gone on to graduate schools as well. A total of 19 percent of Academy graduates have chosen to attend University of Nevada, Reno for their undergraduate studies. A subset of these, 4 percent of all Academy graduates, have been selected for the BS-MD program at the University of Nevada, Reno School of Medicine (UNRSOM). Other leading undergraduate options include Stanford University (6 percent) and MIT (4 percent), followed by UC Berkeley and University of Chicago (3 percent each), Harvard University, Princeton University, Washington University in St. Louis, and University of Rochester (2 percent each).

For Academy alumni attending the University of Nevada, Reno, several factors make it a top choice among post-secondary options. Given that most

UNR campus students have taken University classes by the time they graduate from the Academy, there is the direct benefit of having those credits already in the bank, so to speak. The University of Nevada, Reno as a National Merit Scholarship sponsor institution provides an exceptionally lucrative option for National Merit Scholarship program finalists to attend. These factors are particularly true for those students accessing the BS-MD program. Students are familiar with what the University has to offer, and recognize the opportunity to conduct meaningful research prior to pursuing graduate studies. As a Tier 1 University, students have access to a breadth and depth of knowledge across academic majors that is truly impressive. Davidson Academy alumni have chosen to major in various subject areas, including neuroscience, biochemistry, engineering, philosophy, veterinary medicine, and computer science, among others. Some graduate comparatively early based on the University credits earned while in high school, and others stay for the generally expected four years in order to further explore options or perhaps add a second major or a minor area of study.

One student named Jessica lived in Reno prior to attending the Davidson Academy. She graduated in 2010 and entered into the BS-MD program at UNRSOM. Staying in Reno was initially a difficult decision, as she had always planned to attend college out of state and had offers for admission to schools she had dreamed of attending. However, Jessica is very clear about not regretting the decision to stay in Reno, and is not sure where she would be without the experiences she was afforded by doing so. As a National Merit Finalist with many courses completed prior to high school graduation, including organic chemistry, Jessica was able to continue with outside activities she enjoyed, including maintaining friendships with Academy students. She reported that Academy and BS-MD program prepared her exceptionally well for the success she is enjoying now, completing her residency in internal medicine and pediatrics.

Another student, from the Class of 2014, sees success as where he is currently, having found a passion for research in interventional radiology. He is also in the BS-MD program, in his second year in medical school. He indicated that the Davidson Academy and his access to university classes while in high school resulted in him feeling prepared for what came next, more so than other undergraduates entering the program with him. He reported that the Academy fostered academic rigor, critical thinking across subject areas, and provided teachers who are excellent at provoking thought and encouraging discussion. Well-developed writing skills have been very beneficial for him throughout his post-secondary experiences. Another important aspect of the Academy is that it can be a humbling experience. Realizing that there is always someone smarter in any given area, and having a perspective of this early on in his education provided the student with a sense of relief at not having to be the best all the time. It also enhanced his awareness of the need to collaborate effectively with highly-able peers.

One student just returned from a field course in Malta on migration in the Mediterranean. She graduated from the Academy in 2009; a member of the first graduating class with seven other students. She will be finishing her M.A. in conflict analysis and resolution at George Mason University this spring. Prior to her graduate work, she spent two years in her hometown in Montana working as a victim advocate for the sheriff's office providing systemic support across three rural counties. This was preceded by two years at Corrymeela in Northern Ireland, as assistant to the executive director of the long-standing peace and reconciliation center. The student's undergraduate studies were completed at Bennington College. Bennington provided a passion-driven education where students design their own academic plan with no set majors or minors. She reports that Bennington helped to reform her vision of success to include attending to people's words and voices, thereby creating a deep connection. She recognizes that she loves small communities and thrives best in them. The group of true peers she encountered at the Academy who shared an investment in education were foundational for her. She is confident in her ability to find meaningful work and to overcome obstacles that are inherent in life.

Another student completed their B.A. in bioengineering and a second major in business economics and management at California Institute of Technology following her graduation from the Davidson Academy in 2010. She is currently working on her doctorate in bioengineering at Stanford University, focusing on research in optogenetics (light sensitive proteins put into the brain to control neural activity) and applications in translational research and therapy. She is most interested at this time in the treatment of depression and anxiety, as well as basic research. The importance of its potential impact on humanity is what drives her to get up in the mornings and gives her energy. She extolls the many benefits of having intellectual peers at the Academy who were excited about science and math, showed drive and ability to pursue their studies, engaged in relevant conversations, and broadened her worldview and her appreciation of science and math. In addition, she reports connecting with University professors and access to advanced courses as being critical to her success. She expressed thankfulness for being nurtured as a younger student in an encouraging environment that fostered both passion and confidence.

One student from the Class of 2013 is two years into his doctoral program in philosophy at Princeton University, following his undergraduate work in a dual degree program with Columbia University and Sciences Po, in France. He earned a B.A. in social science with an emphasis in Middle Eastern law, as well as a dual major B.A. in philosophy and political science. Graduated *summa cum laude*; thought he would go into U.S. foreign policy, wanted his finger in the pulse of the world, but found more and more that his true love was philosophy. He finds it fun and interesting to do, and absolutely loves teaching it. The best part is seeing that 'lightbulb moment.' The Academy helped Ian develop a strong work ethic, challenged him from a young age, fostered development of a set of skills, and encouraged perseverance. It made college much more manageable. He appreciates his English teachers at the Academy who really taught him how to write clearly and do in-depth analysis, which is the foundation of his academic success. He made connections with key peers; his best friends are from high school and fit in well with new friends he has made since that time. According to him, "The Academy changed my life."

The Academy is generally successful in accomplishing its mission to provide profoundly gifted young people an advanced educational opportunity matched to their abilities, strengths and interests. The brief snapshots provided here are a small sample of Academy alumni experiences. Others can be accessed in an alumni video on the Davidson Academy's press site. Students sharing their perspectives about the Academy experience are also available in monthly newsletters for prospective students on the school website.

What's Next for the Davidson Academy?

Thinking big and focusing on continuous improvement from the base of all endeavors undertaken by the Davidsons. It is anticipated that Davidson Academy Online campus enrollment will exceed that of Reno campus enrollment in the next few years and grow exponentially in the next decade. An ongoing commitment to the Reno campus is at the base of the intended expansion of online services for those students whose families are not in a position to move to Nevada for the Academy. This includes working with the University of Nevada on access to 365 Learning for Online campus students who are ready for university classes, as well as creating in-person summer experiences on campus.

The Online campus staff continues to build and offer online courses that are unparalleled in terms of the quality of content, live session engagement, and rigor. In 2018, the Davidson Academy won the Blackboard Catalyst Award for Teaching and Learning, as well as, recognizing innovation and excellence in an online learning environment ("Online School"). As a new member of the Abdul Latif Jameel World Education Lab (J-WEL) at Massachusetts Institute for Technology (MIT), the Davidson Academy actively contributes to J-WEL collaboratives ("MIT J-WEL") that function to ensure that the Academy is well-prepared to remain at the cutting edge of online and in-person secondary education. This is also an excellent opportunity to give back to education, as participants share mutually beneficial information. In addition, online campus staff will continue to attend and to present at national online learning conferences, such as Blackboard World, the Digital Learning Alliance Conference, and the International Association for K-12 Online Learning (iNACOL) Symposium, to facilitate continuous improvement of the online learning environment.

In the interest of outreach for the Reno campus and the Online campus, the Davidson Academy is committed to further development of processes and activities to identify and recruit an increasingly diverse student body. The Academy is also contracting with experts in gifted education to compile existing Academy student and program data in ways that inform continuous improvement and stand to have a positive impact on the larger field of education.

The Davidson Academy is committed to serving Nevada and exploring mutually beneficial opportunities with the University well into the future. With all that the Academy and the University have to offer one another and the larger community, it is anticipated that this successful relationship will continue to develop in the best interest of all stakeholders, including profoundly gifted young people.

REFERENCES

"About Us." Davidson Institute. 2019. https://www.davidsongifted.org/About-Us/

Assouline, S., Colangelo, N., VanTassel-Baska, J., & Lupkowski-Shoplik, A., editors.

A nation empowered: Evidence trumps the excuses holding back America's brightest students, vol. 2. Iowa City, IA: The Belin-Blank Center, 2015.

Assouline, S., Colangelo, N., & VanTassel-Baska, J., with Sharp, M. *A nation empowered: Evidence trumps the excuses holding back America's brightest students* vol. 1. Iowa City, IA: The Belin-Blank Center, 2015.

Bloom, B. S., Englehart, M. D., Furst, E., Hill, W. H., & Krathwohl, D. R. *Taxonomy of educational objectives, handbook J: cognitive domain.* New York: McKay, 1956.

Cloud, J. "Failing our geniuses: In U.S. schools, the highest achievers are too often challenged the least." *Time*, August 2007, pp. 40–47.

"Cognia." *Cognia.* 2019. https://www.cognia.org/.

Colangelo, N., Assouline, S., & Gross, M. U. M. *A nation deceived: How schools hold back America's brightest students* vol. 1. Iowa City, IA: University of Iowa, 2004.

Colangelo, N., Assouline, S., & Gross, M. U. M., editors. *A nation deceived: How schools hold back America's brightest students* (vol. 2). Iowa City, IA: University of Iowa., 2004.

Davidson Institute. 2019. https://www.davidsongifted.org/.

Davidson, J., & Davidson, B. with Vanderkam, L. *Genius denied: How to stop wasting our brightest young minds.* New York: Simon & Schuster, 2004.

"Discover Science Lecture Series: College of Science." University of Nevada, Reno. 2019. https://www.unr.edu/science/discover-science.

Finn, C. E., Jr., & Hockett, J. A. *Exam schools: Inside America's most selective public high schools.* Princeton, NJ: Princeton University Press, 2012.

"Massachusetts Institute of Technology (MIT) Abdul Latif Jameel World Education Lab." Massachusetts Institute of Technology, 2019. https://jwel.mit.edu/.

"Mission & Goals." Davidson Academy. 2019. http://www.davidsonacademy.unr.edu/About-Us/Mission-Goals.

"National Statistics—Why our Nation Needs to Educate our Gifted and Talented Youth" Davidson Institute. 2019. http://www.davidsongifted.org/Search-Database/entry/A10398.

"Online School." Davidson Academy. 2019. http://www.davidsonacademy.unr.edu/Online.

Reis, S., & McCoach, B. "The underachievement of gifted students: What do we know and where do we go?" *Gifted Child Quarterly*, vol. 44, no. 12, 2000, pp. 3–9.

CHAPTER 2

The Shapes and Sizes of Success at Community Colleges

ELENA BUBNOVA, M.A.

As the associate vice president of Truckee Meadows Community College (TMCC), Elena Bubnova, M.A. oversees institutional research, marketing, web services, and is a member of the executive leadership team at the College. She has done extensive work in enrollment management, institutional research, outcomes assessment, marketing, and communications. Elena has over twenty years of experience in higher education and held various positions at the University of Nevada, Reno (UNR), Nevada System of Higher Education System Office, and TMCC. She has an unwavering passion for community colleges and helping students from all walks of life succeed. In addition to her leadership role, she has taught as an adjunct language professor at UNR and now teaches at TMCC.

The emergence of the new economy redefined the role of a community college as a critical mechanism for responsive and accessible training for the modern workforce. The diverse and complex skills required for careers in specialized fields like allied health, advanced manufacturing, and many others (for which community colleges train students) is at an all-time high. As educational costs continue to climb, community colleges are becoming the primary access point to higher education not only for first-generation, low-income, under-represented, and minority students (the typical student population served by community colleges), but also for a growing number of traditional students who are priced out of four-year institutions. Indeed, the community college of today is a melting pot of students from every stratum of society with diverse goals, interests, and abilities. Students served by community colleges include high school students taking college classes, traditional students, first-generation students, low-income, academically under-prepared students, adults coming back for retraining, homemakers reentering the workforce, English as a Second Language (ESL) learners, working adults upgrading their skills, and community members taking classes for personal enrichment. At no other point in history has the mission of the community college been as critical as it is today. The multidimensional community college mission includes workforce development, transfer, basic skills training, and community education—pathways that are equally important with each of their own unique outcomes, time frames, and measures of success. All of these students enter a community college at different points in their educational journeys, with different levels of readiness, trajectories, and goals. The length of time it takes to get to their own finish line varies depending on how many classes they take each semester. Life happens to all college students, but community college students have to juggle school, work, and family obligations to a greater extent than their university peers. The overwhelming majority of community college students attend school part-time and take longer to complete their certificate or degree program. In fact, 72 percent of Truckee Meadows Community College (TMCC) students are enrolled part-time because they are working full-time to support themselves and their families as they work toward completing their educational goals.

The diversity of those goals—and of community college students—the variety of training and programs offered at community colleges, and the flexibility and modular structure of learning experiences paint a rich and colorful picture of student success. However, the measure of that success is based on university-oriented performance metrics that fail to take into account the reality of the community college: its mission, structure, goals, and student population. The most-frequently used measures of institutional and student success is the graduation rate of full-time, first-time, degree-seeking students. This measure, as defined by U.S. Department of Education Integrated Postsecondary Education Data Systems (IPEDS), assesses the percentage of students new to college who graduate with a degree or certificate within 150 percent of the allotted time for degree completion (three years for an associate level credential). The IPEDS graduation rate is widely used by many educational organizations to determine a college's ranking, and by lawmakers and others who allocate funding. Yet, this measure focuses on only a small subset of the student population that is served by community colleges.

At TMCC, the three-year IPEDS graduation rate for the freshman class of 2014 is 28 percent. Granted, this measure only quantifies the success of the new, full-time, degree-seeking students in that freshman class.

However, it omits the successes of so many students who are also a part of the community college: part-time students, students who were seeking short-term skills certificates, those seeking to acquire basic skills, homemakers reentering the workforce, high school overachievers who wanted to get their feet wet by taking college courses, community members taking classes for fun, and students who are still enrolled due to their studies taking longer than three years (most of TMCC's allied health programs, for example). All of these students were served by TMCC, all were successful at reaching their goals, but none are captured in the conventional student success metric. If we expand the definition of success for full-time students beyond those who graduated with an associate's degree or certificate of achievement to include students who transferred to another institution, those who are still enrolled, students who earned a short-term skills certificate or acquired life skills (as evidenced by completing thirty or more credits with us), that same three-year success rate for the new, full-time, degree-seeking freshmen class of 2014 increases by nearly double, to 66 percent. Yet, even allowing for these additional successes, 66 percent does not tell the whole story.

If we take this one step further and include part-time students in the performance measure, the student success picture acquires yet another

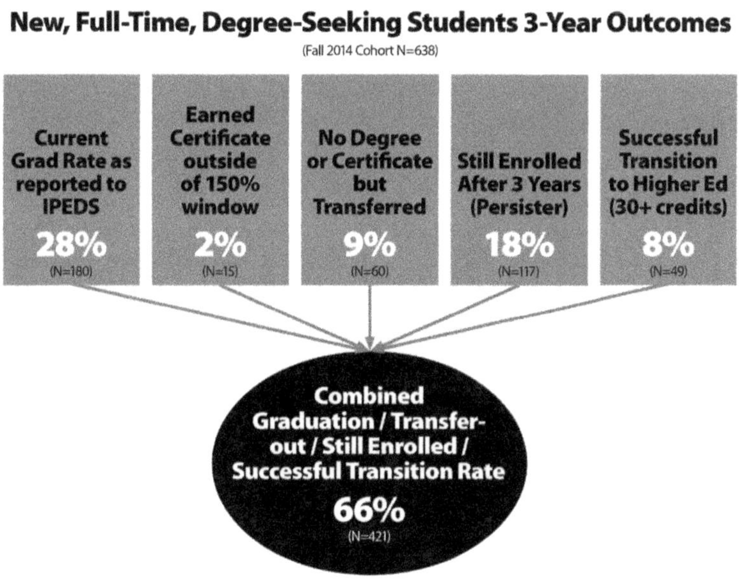

dimension. Many part-time students earn degrees and certificates, transfer, continuously enroll, earn short-term skills certificates, and acquire life-skills within three years of matriculation. When accounting for all these factors, 41 percent of part-time students in the 2014 freshman class at TMCC achieved a successful outcome within the same three years. The IPEDS graduation rate fails to capture this 41 percent success rate among part-time students; a substantial number of student successes that remain invisible under conventional reporting methods.

Additionally, it is worth noting that recently, in recognition of the limitations of traditional graduation measures, efforts have been made to assess more accurately and completely the success of part-time and transfer student populations. Initiatives, such as the Student Achievement Measure (SAM), and the new metrics that make up Voluntary Framework of Accountability (VFA) project by American Association of Community Colleges (AACC), are welcome alternatives to the conventional measures of student success because they recognize the longer time it takes part-time and transfer students to achieve their degree or certificate. These measures reflect the many unconventional paths community college students take to achieve their goals.

How student success is defined at a community college is diverse and varied—it truly comes in different shapes and sizes. To tell the story of student success at community colleges requires putting all the puzzle pieces—transfer, workforce training, life skills, ESL, etc.—together. Only then can one appreciate the multi-dimensional picture of student grit, perseverance, and achievement.

CHAPTER 3

Creating Credential Milestones for Student Success

J. KYLE DALPE, PH.D.

J. Kyle Dalpe, Ph.D., has worked in higher education for more than twenty two years supporting student access and success. During the past sixteen years in various positions of leadership at Truckee Meadows Community College, he has gained insight into Nevada's emerging workforce needs brought about by many new-to-the-region companies. Dalpe is currently working as the dean of Technical Sciences, heading the Applied Technology Programs—Advanced Manufacturing (robotics and automation), Drafting, Construction Management, Architectural Design, Welding, Machining, HVAC, Unmanned Aerial Systems, Diesel, Automotive and Apprenticeships—as well as the Computer Information Technology, Criminal Justice and Law/Paralegal Programs. He regularly works with industry partners to develop new programs, and with the state to provide support to the college and its students to maintain a pipeline of trained talent. Recently, he worked with faculty to create a four-year degree program in Cyber-Physical Manufacturing to support expanding local workforce needs.

Creating Credential Milestones

A key component to student success is getting students to the finish line. In many cases, with unemployment at 3.8 percent and employers constantly looking to fill vacancies, the finish line is no longer at the four-, or even two-year, degree mark (Bureau of Labor Statistics). Many students are looking for short-term programs to gain a needed skill and enter the workforce. The reason why they seek these credentials is quite simple—employers are demanding credentials to build their workforce. In response to this demand, prudent educational institutions have developed a pipeline of educational milestones over the past decade to provide additional outcomes for students.

In the realm of career and technical education (CTE), there are many options for credentials outside the traditional one-year certificate and two-year associates degree. In fact, employers are looking for students who have a particular skill set often defined by competencies over traditional academic milestones. It appears many students have figured this out. We hear stories of how students take two or three classes, six to nine credits, and get a job making close to six figures in fields such as cybersecurity, automotive, and air conditioning technology. As an educational institution, how should we design curricula to meet these needs? The key is conversations with employers.

However, we should begin with a few definitions. At community colleges, we have historically awarded two-year degrees at the sixty-credit mark (or thereabouts) and thirty-credit certificates of achievement. However, more recently, colleges have been developing and awarding "skills certificates" that range from nine to thirty credits. When these programs of study are stacked, students can move from a skills certificate to a certificate of achievement to an associates degree and gain a credential along the way. However, to truly stack, credits in the associate degree should include those credits in the certificate of achievement, and the credits in the certificate of achievement should include those in the skills certificate. By designing programs this way, students completing an associates degree have at least two milestones along the degree path that result in credentials and are thus not taking extra classes.

Depending on where students live, these short-term credentials may lead them to robust career opportunities. Nationally, 53 percent of jobs require "middle skills"—those competencies that require more than high school, but less than a four-year degree (National Skills Coalition). In the State of Nevada, this number is 51 percent of jobs. Going forward, the projections will stay about the same through 2024, with the nation decreasing to 48 percent but certain states like Texas increasing (National Skills Coalition).

Creating these stackable credentials is often not as complicated as one might think. Most colleges have existing certificates of achievement and associates degrees. To create skills certificates and other milestones, a selection of class credits from the existing certificate and degree programs should be determined and matched with an industry-recognized test to develop the short-term training program. But again, employers are key.

Employer engagement is tricky at times because business owners are so busy and often do not have sufficient time to think through what they need in employees. At times, difficulty arises just getting job descriptions of upcoming job postings. However, two ways that short-term programs can be developed are as follows:

First, faculty and administrators should engage employers at least once each semester by discipline in an advisory council format. For example, automotive industry business owners might be invited to a lunch meeting in which they can share industry trends, talk about upcoming staffing needs, help the institution with ideas for new areas of study, and provide feedback on their perceptions of the skills of recent graduates they have employed (non-specific to provide confidentiality). These meetings are good forums to gather industry trends for all programs. However, employers may be hesitant to share information in a group setting (pay scales, number of employees, etc.).

As employers may be reticent to share in public settings, the second option might be one-on-one meetings with employers, especially those who are doing the hiring. Larger businesses will have a human resources department, training managers, and recruiters while smaller establishments might have a sole proprietor. Engaging employers in one-on-one conversations can help determine the best approaches for individual employers, but can also allow for common themes to emerge related to the industry. Many times an employer has come to a meeting and said that his/her business will have five vacancies in the upcoming year. Five vacancies is not a high enough number to develop an academic program or to justify the continuance of an existing program. However, if four employers indicate that they will need similar numbers, it conveys that twenty vacancies will be available and can offer a reasonable opportunity for some programs.

Training students on the skillsets that employers will need is of paramount import. Individual meetings are highly impactful to determine the skillsets needed by individual employers as well as industries. To begin, college faculty and administrators should show the employer existing programs and course offerings complete with curriculum. Despite living in a digital era, these program sheets should be printed for the employer to be able to check off, circle, or otherwise notate which content within each program and class fit their needs as skills for employees. The final list can then be utilized to purposefully and intentionally create a program of study that fits employer needs and will prepare students for jobs in that sector.

For example, an institution of higher education might have a program in advanced manufacturing that includes a certificate (thirty credits) and degree (sixty credits) programs. The certificate should stack into the degree, so an employer can begin reviewing the two-year program as the degree is all-inclusive of the course in the program of study. The employers (this should be done with more than one) can quite literally circle and select classes in the degree program that include the skills needed in the employer's business. College faculty and administrators will most likely need to share course outcomes (which may not be included in course descriptions). With a sixty-credit program, there should be approximately twenty different options for courses. The employer may only choose a few, (e.g. five for illustration purposes) that are needed for their level one technician. These five classes or fifteen credits could then become the basis for a skills certificate in that specific discipline.

The above example is somewhat simplified; however, it illustrates a possible example of a process that can be used to develop new programs that exactly meet the needs of employers while providing students with a credential along the way to a traditional degree program completion. This framework can provide a milestone of a skillset while providing an avenue to a credential that allows for immediate employment while students continue to pursue the next level of post-secondary education.

Where does this leave four-year programs? Interestingly, employers are looking for credential milestones to get employees started (less than thirty credits) as their workforce expands, but also continue to encourage employees to stack credentials all that way to a four-year degree program. For this reason, educational institutions need to ensure employers are looped in with program development to design stackable credentials that are targeted to the economic environment in which students will find entry-level employment and advance with additional training.

REFERENCES

Bureau of Labor Statistics Data. 2019. *Bureau of Labor Statistics.* Accessed March 16, 2019. https://data.bls.gov/timeseries/lns14000000.

"United States' Forgotten Middle." *National Skills Coalition*, February 6. 2017. Accessed March 14, 2019. https://www.nationalskillscoalition.org/state-policy/fact-sheets.

CHAPTER 4

Financial Aid

Fostering Student Success

JOSE QUIROGA, MA

Jose Quiroga is the loan coordinator/financial aid advisor at the University of Nevada, Reno. He has over ten years of experience working in higher education, seven of which have been in financial aid administration. Jose has served as a faculty member of the Western Association of Financial Aid Administrators' Sister Dale Summer Institute. He is currently pursuing a Ph.D. in Educational Leadership.

Introduction

The purpose of financial aid has historically focused on increasing access through awarding grants, scholarships, and loans. Financial aid, however, can also promote student success through encouraging persistence, degree completion, and financial literacy. Promoting student success requires a commitment to align financial aid incentives with characteristics of student success.

At the University of Nevada, Reno (UNR), the Financial Aid and Scholarships Office aligns financial aid policy and practices to promote student success before college, during college, and after graduation. The rest of this chapter will be dedicated to three innovative programs and practices at UNR that seek to improve student success.

Before College: The Pell Dual Enrollment Experiment

Throughout higher education, low-income and first-generation (LIFG) students are overall less likely to persist and graduate. One way to affect student success for low-income and underrepresented students is to form a connection with a postsecondary institution before they are of traditional college age. Dual enrollment programs have shown promise in increasing graduation rates (Allen & Dadgar, 2012). However, student funding remains an issue because federal student aid is only available to high school graduates or those with an equivalent degree. For many LIFG students and their families, paying for college classes out of pocket is financially impossible. Through the Pell Dual Enrollment program, low-income students at UNR have been able to participate in college-level courses while completing high school requirements with no out-of-pocket expenses.

The Pell Dual Enrollment Experiment

In 2016, UNR applied for and received approval from the Department of Education to participate in the Pell Dual Enrollment program as part of a Pell Experiment Site Initiative (PESI). As one of only forty four postsecondary institutions invited to participate, qualifying students enrolled in dual-credit at UNR are able to receive Pell grants. UNR used institutional funds to pay for all other registration costs not covered by the Pell grant, as well as books, course materials, and transportation to the University.

UNR's dual enrollment program is focused on engineering, which has been identified as a workforce area of need for the State of Nevada. Students in this program take 12 credits of college classes at UNR during their senior year in high school which count toward both their high school degree and toward an engineering bachelor's degree. Through a mixture of core and engineering-specific classes, students are able to earn college credit and obtain experience on a university campus before graduating from high school.

The Financial Aid Office, Upward Bound, and Enrollment Services at UNR have worked closely together in order to best create a program that would positively affect student success. A team of financial aid advisors, enrollment staff, and Academic and Opportunity Support counselors collaborated to provide the best environment for participants. Enrollment services registered students in classes, ensured degree eligibility, and coordinated transportation solutions for students. The Financial Aid Office processed financial aid applications, administered federal and institutional funds, and completed all required reporting to the U.S. Department of Education. The Upward Bound Programs provide individualized academic counseling and group tutoring services tailored for the rigorous college course content the PESI students encounter.

> The college transition was fairly easy for me. What made it easy was the preparation/guidance that was given during the [Pell Dual Enrollment] orientation. The on-campus resources are phenomenal. They will be your best friend if you are struggling in a class. There is [*sic*] always people there to help you.
>
> —Freshman student

The Students

UNR partners with four high schools in the Washoe County School District to identity rising seniors who qualify for this program. In order to qualify, rising seniors must be University admissible with a 3.0 grade point average in their academic core courses, place into Math 126—college-level Pre-Calculus 1 based on ACT/SAT or ACCUPLACER scores, be declared as an Engineering major, and meet the low-income qualification as defined by eligibility for a Federal Pell Grant at half-time enrollment status.

> [The dual enrollment program] gave me the option to fit in somewhere else. I was able to get ahead in school and get excited about college. PESI helped me overcome some fears and give me an education about how to exist on campus. PESI will help get rid of a majority of college jitters of how to fit in with other college students.
>
> —Freshman student

Results

To date, three cohorts (thirty one students total) have participated in the UNR Pell Dual Enrollment program. Fall to spring retention rates for participants are considerably higher than the general population. Though it is a small pilot program, the Pell Dual Enrollment experiment is showing encouraging results that may help change federal policy. Furthermore, it is making a significant difference in the lives of participants. Table 1 shows high retention within the dual enrollment program. It also shows a high matriculation rate into the University and fall-to-fall retention of participants during their freshman year at UNR. The table also includes ethnicity information for students, showing that participants are not only low-income (demonstrated through Pell-eligibility) but overwhelmingly come from underrepresented ethnic backgrounds in higher education.

> Going through the [Pell Dual Enrollment] program, I was able to gain a tremendous amount of college experience. It really prepared me for the rigor of academics in college and helped me to excel my first year of college. I had so much college experience that as a freshman I was able to join a fraternity, attain a student worker job, and study abroad in Thailand while still maintaining a strong GPA. I am so grateful I was able to be a part of such an amazing program.
>
> —Sophomore student

TABLE 1. Dual Enrollment PESI Results. University of Nevada, Reno Pell Experimental Site Initiative (PESI) Data

Year	Cohort	Ethnicity	PESI Fall to Spring Retention	UNR PESI Matriculation	UNR Fall to Fall PESI Retention
2016	8	12.5% Asian 87.5% Latinx	100%	100%	87.50%
2017	11	18% Black 82% Latinx	91%	100%	*
2018	12	8% White 92% Latinx	*	*	*
Total	31	3% Asian 3% White 7% Black 87% Latinx	95% (18 of 19)	100% (31 of 31)	87.5% (7 of 8)

During College: 30 to Complete

Challenge

Federal financial aid eligibility maxes out at twelve credits per semester. In other words, a student enrolled in more than twelve credits does not receive any additional Pell grants, or other federal aid. This policy has the unintended consequence of encouraging low-income students to limit their enrollment to only twelve credits per semester. Enrolling in more classes increases tuition costs without increasing federal financial aid eligibility. At UNR, a typical bachelor's degree consists of 120 credits, which would require a student to enroll in fifteen credits per fall and spring semester in order to graduate in four years. For low-income students who count on every dollar to live, delaying graduation may be the only way to pay for school.

30 to Complete

UNR, along with all other Nevada System of Higher Education (NSHE) institutions, has adopted an initiative to encourage students to enroll in fifteen credits per semester or thirty credits per year. This cross-departmental initiative uses a mixture of advising, marketing, and financial aid policy. The UNR Financial Aid Office requires students to enroll in fifteen credits per semester to receive institutional grants and scholarships.

> There have been several semesters in which I considered taking less credits in order to have a more flexible schedule, but ultimately decided to take fifteen since the funding from that scholarship is essential to paying my tuition. Without this requirement, I may have taken an extra semester in addition to my four years.
>
> —Junior student

Creating the fifteen-credit per semester standard for institutional grants and scholarships is an important step to promoting student success. We know that some students are not able to meet these requirements for a variety of reasons. Non-traditional students may have outside commitments that prevent a fifteen-credit load. Students in certain majors may have a degree plan that only requires twelve credits during a given semester. To accommodate the unique needs of our students, UNR created an appeal process to explain why they are unable to take fifteen credits and still receive institutional grants and scholarships. Through the appeal process, students can plan to make a plan to take thirty credits during the academic year between fall, spring, and summer semesters.

> The thirty to Complete has been very helpful for me. I am going into my senior year of college and I only need a few more classes to graduate. thirty to Complete has provided me with assurance that I will have the financial aid that I need to pay for my classes, as well as the flexibility I need to focus on other things such as internships and lab work.
>
> —Senior student

Results: NSHE Data on student success at 15 credits per semester

After Graduation: Loan Debt Letter

Challenge

Forty eight percent of student borrowers either do not know or incorrectly estimate the amount they have borrowed and 28 percent incorrectly believe they have no federal loans at all which is a good indicator that students are not grasping their borrowing or how to track their loans from entrance counseling (Akers and Chingos 1). This could lead to over-borrowing, lower degree attainment, and potentially student loan default. 94 percent of student borrowers do not understand their loan repayment terms and 54 percent of student borrowers did not try to estimate the monthly repayment amount as part of their most recent loan procurement which means as they are accepting their upcoming year's loans, they are not considering what they already currently owe for their previous years of borrowing. Students are borrowing blindly. (Inceptia Webinar; Student loan Borrower Survey: LendEDU & Student Loan Debt in the U.S. Global Financial Literacy Excellence Center)

Student Indebtedness Debt Letter

> What I liked about the Student Loan Indebtedness Letter was that it had a lot of important information in one place [. . .] which made me realize that I should start paying some of my loans off while still in school to keep the interest from accumulating. This letter definitely helped me be more proactive in managing my student loans."
>
> —Junior student

Beginning in the summer of 2018, the UNR Financial Aid Office piloted a debt letter sent to students who have borrowed federal loans at the University. The letter included the student's current amount of federal loans borrowed, what percentage of their overall federal loan eligibility they have used, estimated monthly repayment amounts, and multiple resources to help the student make financial choices in college and beyond.

The purpose of the indebtedness letter is to increase student awareness of their debt, to lower student indebtedness, and to help them plan for their future after graduation. Some states have required colleges and universities to send this type of letter to their students. Although Nevada does not currently require an annual letter, the Nevada Money Mentors and Financial Aid Office teamed up to pilot a letter to the students at UNR in Spring 2018.

Results

One measure of success of the indebtedness letter is the increasing student engagement with financial literacy. In the 17–18 academic year, student participation roughly doubled to over 2,500 students taking part in financial wellness programs. These included one-on-one coaching sessions, attending presentations, and interactive financial literacy games. Another measure of how successful students are after graduation is whether they are able to repay their federal student loans. The University's cohort default rate (a measure of students who have defaulted on their federal loan

TABLE 2. 3-year cohort default rates by federal year

	UNR	National	Public	Public 4-year	Nevada
FY2015	5.1%	10.8%	10.3%	7.1%	15.3%
FY2014	5.1%	11.5%	11.3%	7.5%	14.6%
FY2013	5.2%	11.3%	11.3%	7.3%	12.7%

repayment in the last three years) is not yet available to take into account the effects of the indebtedness letter. However, for the latest available year (2015) the cohort default rate was 5.1 percent. This rate measures favorably among higher education institutions.

Conclusion

The UNR Financial Aid and Scholarships Office will continue to work to align its policies and practice with student success. Through the Pell Dual enrollment program, low-income students are able to prepare for college. The 30-to-Complete program encourages enrollment that will allow students to graduate on-time. Financial literacy programs like the indebtedness letter help students make decisions to be successful after college. All of these innovative programs require cross-campus collaboration to be successful. The UNR financial aid office is not content with only administering financial aid; we actively seek to be a partner in promoting student success.

REFERENCES

Allen, D., & Dadgar, M. "Does dual enrollment increase students' success in college? Evidence from a quasi-experimental analysis of dual enrollment in New York City". *New Directions for Higher Education*, vol. 2012, no. 158, 2012, pp. 11–19.

Akers, Elizabeth. J., and Chingos, Matthew M. "Are College Students Borrowing Blindly?" Brown Center on Education Policy at Brookings Institution. December 2014. https://www.brookings.edu/wp-content/uploads/2016/06/Are-College-Students-Borrowing-Blindly_Dec-2014.pdf.

Attewell, P., and Monaghan, D. "How many credits should an undergraduate take?" *Research in Higher Education*, vol. 57, no. 6, 2016, pp. 682–713.

Singell Jr., L. D. "Come and stay a while: does financial aid effect retention conditioned on enrollment at a large public university?" *Economics of Education review*, vol. 23 no. 5, 2004, pp. 459–471.

CHAPTER 5

Obscure Beginnings to a National Model

Fitness and Recreational Sports' Role in Student Success

JIM FITZSIMMONS, ED.D, and SHEENA HARVEY, M.S.

Jim Fitzsimmons, Ed.D., is the director of Fitness and Recreational Sports at the University of Nevada, Reno. He has more than twenty eight years of experience in strength and conditioning, clinical exercise, teaching, and coaching as well as facility management, operations, design, and construction. Dr. Fitzsimmons speaks nationally and internationally on the topics of Fitness Facility Design and Programming, Human Work Capacity, and Health, Dose Response of Exercise Intensity, and Volume Density Training. He coauthored the university's Kinesiology program of study and continues to teach in the major on the topics of Chronic Disease and Exercise and Principles of Training and Conditioning. His research on the influence student fitness centers play in the recruitment and success of students was influential in the construction of the $50 million Wiegand Fitness Center on the campus of the University of Nevada, Reno.

Sheena Harvey has been a part of the University of Nevada, Reno (UNR) community for more than a decade. She is currently the associate director for Fitness and Recreational Sports at UNR, where she primarily oversees the intramural sports and group fitness program. She earned her bachelor's degree in Interior Design at the University of Nevada, Reno followed by her master's degree in Equity and Diversity in Educational Settings. She is currently a doctoral student within the College of Education's Equity and Diversity program at UNR. She enjoys researching all components surrounding collegiate fitness and recreational sport programs and their pivotal role in supporting student success in higher education.

Introduction

In this chapter, we will discuss the influence that fitness and recreational sport departments and facilities exert on overall student success. It has been our experience that many universities underestimate the power and influence these facilities and programs exert on potential students, current students, and parents. They often fail to recognize the social and academic importance of these facilities and do not understand how to leverage these factors to enhance the overall success of their students, as well as improve their efforts in creating a diverse, inclusive, and equitable campus.

Recruitment

As recruitment of students has become more vital to an institution's mission-based objectives, and financial bottom line, it has also become highly competitive and expensive (Taylor et al.). Each successfully recruited student represents, on average, a \$400 expenditure for public institutions and \$2,000 for private institutions (Cohen). Many state universities, particularly land-grant institutions, are evaluated on the percentage of recently graduated high school seniors that enroll in that institution. The state where the institution is located has a vested interest in whether or not students in that state and from other states matriculate into their own system of higher education (Lamont). While many in higher education would like to think the decision students make about which school to attend is a thought-out, pragmatic decision based upon parameters such as the availability of a preferred major, the quality of instruction, the degree of access to advising, tutoring, and faculty, this is not often the case (Cohen; Oseguera & Ree). For the majority of students, the decision is based upon emotion, how they feel on campus, and how they like the students they meet on campus (Cohen).

In this context, campus fitness and recreational sports programs and facilities have become major components of the modern university recruitment strategy. These programs and facilities are considered to be major components of the ultimate decision a student makes to attend a certain institution (Gray; Haines; Kasin & Dzakira; Lamont; Zizzi et al.). It is well understood that students give a high ranking to campus recreation programs, facilities for personal fitness, participation in team sports, and unstructured recreation when deciding which institution to attend (NIRSA; Student Poll). Prospective students often rank access to recreational sport and fitness facilities for personal use higher than internships, cultural activities, part-time/

full-time work, student clubs, student organizations, study abroad, Greek life, and watching or participating in NCAA sports (NIRSA; Student Poll). The literature is less clear in the importance of fitness and recreational sport facilities and programs in the student's decision to attend a particular institution. This is a question that requires more data to answer. However, some studies suggest that up to 30 percent of students base a significant portion of their decision to attend a particular institution on the quality and availability of extracurricular facilities and programs (Bryant and Banta; Reynolds).

It is critical for educators to monitor sport value cultivation within collegiate fitness and sport departments and program offerings. Early access and early recognition of recreational sport activity for incoming students correlates with allowing the general student population to create a long-term practice of healthy habits while enrolled in coursework. Structured associated activities allow for safe, informal, and competitive game play opportunities for students. Recreational sport participation exposes students to an active learning environment that produces a diversity outcome through sport play. Physical and sociocultural environments affect physical activity and the association between school fitness and recreational settings promote or hinder the physical activity of students during time spent at their home institution (Nichol, Pickket and Janssen).

Examining the cultural context, perspectives, and perceived barriers of recreational sport participation for students is connected to the influential affect or interpersonal barriers, intrapersonal barriers, and the structural barriers that are present during the initial introduction phase of recreational sport program promotion. First impressions, access to sport program information, individual registration, team formation, and the launch of sports seasons are program areas that must be executed to gain a dedicated and invested participating population. First exposure to sports programs during campus orientation sessions should be connected to basic physical education practices and movements. Presenting students with a chance to participate and potentially succeed, can create a sense of belonging and potential future success for students who participate in sport-related activities.

Retention

Getting students to the campus is only one goal; getting students to stay and then graduate is still another. Most institutions experience their most dramatic loss of students after their first year. Institutions report between 19 percent and 50 percent of students entering college leave before their second year (Kuh; Reason). Interestingly, 23 percent of these drop-outs do not leave due to academic failure. Instead, they voluntarily withdraw from the institution. Furthermore, while it may be counterintuitive, the students who drop out due to both academic failure and for other reasons are, by all measures, more academically able than those who stay. There are a variety of possible reasons for this phenomenon: poor social integration, financial difficulty, familial stress, or matriculation to a school with a more desirable program of study or a more prestigious academic reputation (McCubbins). This first-year dropout rate is even more pronounced in students with the following characteristics: first-generation college students, low high school achievement, poor academic preparation, low socioeconomic status, low levels of social and academic involvement, low interactions with students and faculty both in academic and social settings, and those with a higher sense of isolation and lack of familial support (Oseguera and Rhee). The same characteristics appear to hold true for males and females and for all race and ethnic backgrounds with the exception of American Indians whose drop-out rates remain high even with substantial support (Crozier et al.; Fischer).

One of the critical components of a strategic retention plan is the intentional creation of built environments that act as a catalyst for social integration (Braxton). Commuter institutions, specifically, should make focused efforts to this end and residential institutions should target such efforts to their populations who live off campus (Braxton). Social and academic integration should not be approached as two separate efforts with no potential for collaboration. Academic advisors should aggressively encourage students to take advantage of opportunities to establish membership in social communities affiliated with the campus (Braxton). Interestingly, when retention issues are viewed by race or ethnicity as a predictor of success or failure, these same theories of integration, social belonging, and academic success still function as factors that can mitigate against drop-out (Fischer).

Participation in student fitness and recreational sport facilities and programs is thought to exert considerable effect on first year retention and five-year graduation rates when controlling for financial need, academic preparation, and social fit of the student (Huesman et al.). In both qualitative and quantitative studies the influence of Student Recreation Centers (SRC) on first year retention varies with 37 percent to 75 percent of students stating that participation in campus-based recreational programs played a major role in their decision to stay in school (Haines; Lindsey and Sessoms). Though service learning and mentoring programs remain particularly high on the student retention reputation scale (Bean and Eaton), higher education institution student retention rate data can be contributed to multiple factors and driven initiatives by campus administrators. Traditionally, undergraduate students spend a significant portion of their time on campus and within fitness and recreational sport spaces (Nichol et al.). These areas are then viewed as spaces that are highly communal and interactive in nature (Callender et al.).

Students are readily engaging in recreational sport play in a distinctive manner. In the last five years, distinctive participation (student's participating in more than one sport per semester) averaged out at a rate of 81 percent across the time span within the Nevada Intramural Sports Program at the University of Nevada, Reno. Wade determined that an essential and critical component of retention and persistence of students was their sense of belonging to a community. It has been determined that student retention is greatly improved when college campuses have impressive fitness and sport facilities that provide the campus community with quality programs and services to participate in (Haines and Fortman). The frequency and duration of use is an important factor in the exposure to these shared campus environments. Allowing students to thrive and flourish in their selected atmospheres contributes to their sense of belonging at their home institutes. With the potential and predicted growth of higher education institution enrollments, student populations will not only influence the construction of on-campus housing, but also for fitness and sport facilities dedicated to serve the general student population.

Physical and Mental Health

We know that the transition from high school to college is often marked by increased physical health problems, increased depression, anxiety, loneliness, and lower levels of life satisfaction, all of which put the student at higher risk for dropping out (Bray and Born). In the first year of college, there is often a general increase in the caloric intake of the individual while the nutritional value of calories consumed decreases. This, coupled with a decrease in physical activity, results in weight gain, increases in adipose tissue and decreases in lean body mass, metabolism, and functional work capacities (Whaley and Kaminisky; Dishman et al.). The decrease in physical activity is of particular concern because while only 54 percent of high school students get sufficient physical activity, this number drops to 35 percent of college students (Douglas et al.). Regular physical activity is strongly linked to weight control, decreased rates of heart disease, diabetes, metabolic syndrome, orthopedic disease, acute physical disease, increased life satisfaction, increased functional and cognitive ability, decreased depression and anxiety, increased base line health indicators, improved body image, and resistance to self-destructive behaviors (Belch et al.; Fontaine; Landers; Whaley and Kaminisky; Dishman et al.). These effects impact short- and long-term student success and satisfaction.

College students learn more effectively when instruction incorporates different modes of learning (Haines and Fortman). Physical and mental health support are important factors for student academic performance, especially in higher education. O'Bryan et al. highlight:

> The relationship between athletic involvement and academic performance among students continues to generate a considerable debate, despite the fact that reviewers of the empirical evidence have consistently noted positive association between athletic participation and educational attainment. (402)

For intramural sports participation in particular, supporting the structure to accompany division of participation levels of play fosters thoughtfulness which creates an engagement opportunity for a student to develop and enhance their physical, mental, and emotional capacity (Artinger et al.).

Academic Performance

On a university campus, everything is measured or justified by its contribution to the academic mission. Does it contribute to the student's academic success? For the past century, campus fitness and recreational sport programs have existed without a strong connection to the academic mission. However, in the past two decades, the connection between student recreation participation and academic success has begun to be researched and supported by the literature. It is apparent that participation in campus fitness and recreational sports does play a significant role in the academic success of the student (Smith and Thomas). One of the predictors of poor academic performance, dropping out, and low levels of satisfaction is social isolation. Campus fitness and recreational sport facilities are social focal points for the campus, and the opportunities for social interaction range from quiet discussions, games and participation in informal and structured sports, to working out as a group or individual. Participation numbers in campus fitness and recreational sports programs range from 70 percent to 95 percent of the total student population, making them some of the most highly utilized and communal facilities on a campus (Braxton and Hirschy; Bryant and Banta). It has been suggested and supported by the 20-year Harvard assessment that time spent in recreational sport and co-curricular activities is a better predictor of academic success than academic measures (Light). Students who participate earn higher college GPAs than nonparticipants (Belch et al.; Mass). Students who entered college with lower high school GPA and SAT/ACT scores who participate in campus fitness and recreational sports earn higher college GPAs than their counterparts who do not participate in campus recreation programs and entered college with higher high school GPAs and SAT/ACT scores (Belch et al.; Mass).

Students who participate in campus recreation persist and graduate at higher rates than non-participants (Belch et al.; Mass et al.). Students who typically would be at risk for dropping-out based upon academic performance and GPA persist and graduate at higher rates than students with the same academic predictors and students who are performing academically well, but who do not participate in campus recreation (Belch et al.; Mass).

A resemblance of the co-curricular structure and learning outside of the classroom can be viewed within intramural sport program offerings. Structured sports programming lends itself to educate voluntary student participants in sport specific rules, student behavior expectations, and safe-play protocols. When surveying the relationship between recreational sport involvement and academic success, participation in recreational sport programs have been found to enhance the college experience (Hackett). Though there is a small portion of empirical evidence to indicate that sport involvement influences students to be more academically prepared, sport involvement itself has positive outcomes. Wankel and Berger indicated that sharing intramural sport experiences and working together under conditions of competitive stress drew teammates closer. This supports Barcelona's viewpoint, that the involvement in recreational sports and its potential to yield positive gains in a student's ability to function as a member of a team, could be beneficial whether a student is in a classroom setting or participating in a recreational sports game: "Participation in recreational sports is a key determinant of college satisfaction, success, recruitment, and retention" (Blumenthal 60).

What Is the Program?

In 1994, there was no fitness or recreational sport department or dedicated facilities on the University of Nevada, Reno campus. There was a part-time Intramural (IM) Sport position, and the IM Sport Program was run from the Lombardi Recreation Building in the evenings. Lombardi Recreation Building housed a declining Recreation, Physical Education and Dance (RPED) Major and was open 8 to 5 p.m. Monday through Friday; the facility was closed all weekends, holidays, and University breaks. Part-time Intramural Sport Coordinator, Steve Pomi, convinced the RPED Chair, Olena Plummer, to allow him to install a small amount of fitness equipment on one of the basketball courts for a rental fee of three-percent of the gross profit derived from any membership sales. At the time there was no institutional support for the project, so a $10,000 loan was obtained in order to fund the first installation of equipment. Much of the equipment was purchased from used and surplus sources. In one case, a set of dumbbells were rescued from a high school dumpster. In the first year, 200 memberships were sold at a price of $25 each and the rest, as they say, is history. The enterprise grew to the point where it was generating $1.5 million in annual revenues, ultimately funding $8.5 million in renovations over a fifteen-year period, allowing the Lombardi Recreation Building to keep pace with growing student demand for fitness space.

From those inauspicious and truly entrepreneurial beginnings, in 2017 the Fitness and Recreational Sport Department moved into a $46.5 million "state-of-the-art" facility considered by industry experts a model for fitness facilities and programming. The facility itself recently won the National Intramural Recreational Sport Associations (NIRSA) National Award for Outstanding Sport Facility Design. The conversation and ultimate decision to invest in such a building was largely framed by the previous review of associated literature. Facilities and programs of this nature play a highly influential role in a student's ultimate decision to attend, remain and succeed at a specific institution.

What Is the Program? Intramural Sports

Physical and sociocultural environments affect physical activity, and the association between school fitness and recreational settings may promote or hinder the physical activity of students (Nichol et al.). Developing a standardized solution to accommodate student sport and fitness practices while enrolled in higher education has many supportive components. Whether it be open recreational game play, formal play or informal engagement, building the bridge between education, sport, and fitness will allow for students to have the appropriate space to socially integrate while engaging in these activities. The creation of built environments in which students can occupy to conduct fitness or recreational sport-like activities must be a part of a higher education institution's master plan. Gaining an opportunity to participate in recreational sports continues to be popular amongst collegiate recreation programs across the nation and enhancing the physical and social self of students through recreational activity can be achieved through intramural sport participation (Artinger et al.). While enriching the growth of college students and having the understanding that sport activity is a common campus activity, semester operations are focused on elimination of barriers for students who voluntarily participate.

Pay before you play. This was not always the case for students yearning to participate in intramural sports offered programs at the University of Nevada, Reno. In the early 1990s, and into the late 2000s, intramural sports play and the campus' identifiable sport culture shifted. From the beginning, campus Greek-affiliated organizations led the charge in sport team participation numbers, and these competing teams produced the assembly of great spectating crowds that could compete with home institution intercollegiate athletic fan groups. The intramural sports program has worked exceedingly hard to position itself to truly serve the general student population. Departmental responsibility for maintaining the life of available sport surface programmable spaces and accurate program participation reports have helped develop the unique snapshot of participation in terms of gender, academic class standing, and sport specific participation data for each academic year.

Population We Serve: Campus Community Primary Focus on Students

"Sport has been a part of civilized societies throughout history" (Sidentop 89). Recreational sport participation in higher education allows students to play for fun, competitively, or simply engage in physical activity. Recent student survey feedback indicated that a student's primary motivation for participating in intramural sports were due to: recreation and to have fun

(51 percent), compete (27 percent), social benefits (10 percent), physical fitness, develop sport skills (2 percent) and other (1 percent) (Office of Student Persistence Research). Gaining an opportunity to survey over 500 students on campus allowed the Intramural Sports program to devise program structure plans to help support the needs of the participating population. Diversity and inclusion can be realistically viewed through the lens of recreational sports participation. What branches off of recreational sport participation in higher education is the support for sport, fitness, and physical education. The common idea that everyone has an opportunity to participate supports the notion that sport participation provides a universal framework of values which activate learning (UNESCO).

Impact

Since the opening of the facility, initial targets have exceeded expectations. The reality is that there have been numerous redundant studies going back over 70 years looking at the marriage of engagement in recreational sports, fitness, improved academic performance, and cognitive ability, etc. In the past two decades, repeated studies have revealed the same results that students who participate in recreational sports and fitness on campus are retained at higher rates and earn higher GPAs. The one thing we know for certain is that if students do not use the facility or programs, no effect will be made. That being said, daily average student use has tripled with peak use exceeding five times the use in the previous facility. Seventy-five percent of the users are unique users which is exceptionally high for a largely commuter institution with a heavily saturated local fitness market. More significantly, facility use demographics exactly match enrollment demographics with an over-representation of Native Americans as users compared to their presence on campus. International students make higher use of the facility compared to U.S. students which is also atypical. This data speaks to the successful efforts made in creating culturally competent spaces and programs. Groups who are traditionally difficult to capture, or for whom the standard North American approach to fitness and sport on display at the majority of campuses do not resonate, make up UNR's regular fitness facility user base.

It is still too early to review retention and GPA effect on the users, but this data will be reviewed in the near future. We are able to track individual student use through our facility management software. This can then be merged with student data and we will be able to see the dose effect of GPA, retention, progress towards graduation, and graduation rates. We know from historical data collection in our previous facility that regular users defined as "using the facility twice a week," were retained at an 18 percent higher rate, first to second year, and earned on average a 0.8 higher GPA than their counterparts who did not use the facility.

Conclusion

The presence of high-quality fitness and recreational sport facilities and programs for general student use is an important element of the modern campus. It is crucial to recruitment, retention, and overall student success. Like it or not, the health, quality, power, and prestige of a campus is expressed through these facilities and it will be a major factor in how the campus is evaluated by potential students and their parents.

Fitness and Recreational Sport departments can be used to address issues of diversity, equity, and inclusion in both passive and active modes. Campuses will continue to become more diverse and global in their student make-up. Facilities for these future generations must create spaces that resonate with students and encourage engagement in sport and fitness activities that may be in line with their cultural practices or rituals.

Critical partnerships between campus entities such as Counseling and Student Health Centers can be utilized to provide holistic multidiscipline approaches to the treatment of chronic physical and mental health issues within the student population. At the end of the day, campuses that fail to recognize the influence fitness and recreational sports departments have on student success do so at their own peril.

REFERENCES

Artinger, L., Clapham, L., Hunt, C., Meigs, M., Milord, N., Sampson, B., & Forrester, S. A. "The Social Benefits of Intramural Sports." *Journal of Student Affairs Research and Practice*, vol. 43, no. 1, 2006. doi:10.2202/1949-6605.1572.

Bean, J., & Eaton, S. B. "The Psychology Underlying Successful Retention Practices." *Journal of College Student Retention: Research, Theory & Practice*, vol. 3, no. 1, 2001, pp. 73–89. doi:10.2190/6r55-4b30-28xg-l8uo.

Belch, H., Gebel, M., & Mass, G. "Relationship between student recreation complex use, academic performance, and persistence of first-time freshman." *NASPA Journal*, vol. 38. no. 2, 2001, pp. 254–267.

Blumenthal, K. J. "Collegiate recreational sports: Pivotal players in student success."

Planning for Higher Education, vol. 37, no. 2, 2009, pp. 52–62. http://unr.idm.oclc.org/login?url=https://search.proquest.com/docview/212568746?accountid=452.

Bray, S., & Born, H. "Transition to university and vigorous physical activity: implications for health and psychological well-being." *Journal of American College Health*, vol. 52, no. 4, 2006, pp. 181–188.

Braxton, J. "Using theory and research to improve college student retention." *Journal of College Student Retention*, vol. 3, no. 1, 2002, pp. 91–118.

Braxton, J., & Hirschy, A. "Reconceptualizing antecedents of social integration in student departure," in M. York & B. Longden (Eds.), *Retention and student success in higher education*, pp. 89–102. Berkshire, England: Open University Press, 2004.

Bryant, J., Anderson, B., Dunn, M. "Rational for independent administration of collegiate recreation sports programs." Paper presented at the midyear NIRSA board of directors meeting, Corvalis, OR: October 1994.

Bryant, J., & Banta, T. "Assessment provides insight into the impact of campus recreational programs." *NASPA Journal*, vol. 32, no. 2, 1995, pp. 153–161.

Callender, M., Brown, T., & Haines, D. *Space planning guidelines for campus recreational sport facilities*. Champaign: Human Kinetics, 2009.

Cohen, S. "What colleges don't know about admissions." *National Association for College Admissions*, 2009. http://www.zinch.com/.

Crozier, G., Reay, D., Colliander, L., Grinstead, J. "Different strokes for different folks: diverse students in diverse institutions—experiences in higher education." *Research Papers in Education*, vol. 23, no. 2, 2008, pp. 167–177.

Dishman , R., Washburn, R.& Health, G. *Physical activity epidemiology*. Champaign, IL: Human Kinetics, 2004.

Douglas, K., Collins, J. & Warren, C. "Results from the 1995 national college health risk behavior survey." *Journal of American College Health*, vol. 46, 1997, pp. 55–66.

Fischer, M. "Settling into campus life: differences by race/ethnicity in college involvement and outcomes." *The Journal of Higher Education*, vol. 78, no. 2, 2007, pp. 126–161.

Fontaine, K. "Physical activity improves mental health." *The Physician and Sports Medicine*, vol. 28, no. 10, 2000, pp. 126–130.

Hackett, M. "Exploring the relationship between recreational sports employment and academic success." *Recreational Sports Journal*, vol. 31, 2007, pp. 69–74.

Haines, D. "Undergraduate benefits from university recreation." *NIRSA Journal*, 25, 2001, pp. 125–133.

Haines, D., & Fortman, T. "The college recreational sports learning environment." *Recreational Sports Journal*, vol. 32, 2008, pp. 52–61.

Huesman, R., Brown, A., Lee, G., Kellog, J., Radcliffe, P. "Gym bags and mortarboards: is use of campus recreation facilities related to student success?" *NASPA Journal*, vol. 46, no. 1, 2009, pp. 50–71.

Kasim, A., Dzakiria, H. "Influence of recreation on educational aspiration." *Asian Pacific Journal of Tourism and Research*, vol. 6, no. 2, 2001, pp. 53–64.

Kuh, G. "What we're learning about student engagement." *Change*, 2003, pp. 24–33.

Lamont D. "Undergraduate student recruitment and retention and the centralized on-campus recreational sports facility." *National Intramural Recreational Sport Association Journal*, Fall 1991, pp. 3–26.

Landers, D. *The influence of exercise on mental health. President's council on physical fitness and sports research digest*, vol. 2, no. 12, 1997.

Light, R. *The Harvard assessment seminars: Exploration with students and faculty about teaching, learning and student life*. Cambridge, MA: Harvard University Graduate School of Education and Kennedy School of Government, 1991.

Lindsey, R., & Sessoms E. "Assessment of a campus recreation program on student recruitment, retention and frequency of participation across certain demographic variables." *Recreational Sports Journal*, vol. 30, 2006, pp. 30–39.

Maas, G. "Relationship between campus recreation participation and measures of college success." Presented at the 50th Annual Conference of the National Intramural Recreational Sports Association. Milwaukee, Wisconsin: April 1999.

McCubbin, I. (2003). "An examination of Tinto's 1975 student integration model of attrition." *Journal of Higher Education*, vol. 12, pp. 1–12.

National Intramural-Recreational Sport Association. *The value of recreational sports in higher education impact on student enrollment, success, and buying power*. Champagne IL: Human Kinetics, 2004.

National Intramural-Recreational Sports Association. "NIRSA collegiate recreational sports facilities construction report 2006–2011." Corvallis, OR: NIRSA, 2008.

Nichol, M. E., Pickett, W., & Janssen, I. Associations Between School Recreational Environments and Physical Activity. *Journal of School Health*, vol. 79, no. 6, 2009, pp. 247–254. doi:10.1111/j.1746-1561.2009.00406.x.

O'Bryan, S., Braddock, J., & Dawkins, M. "Bringing parents back in: African American parental involvement, extracurricular participation, and educational policy." *The Journal of Negro Education*, vol. 75, no. 3, 2006, pp. 401–414.

Office of Student Persistence Research, University of Nevada, Reno (2017). *Descriptive Results for the E. L. Wiegand Fitness Center Survey*. Unpublished raw data.

Oseguera, L., & Ree, B. "The influence of institutional retention climates on student persistence to degree completion." *Research in higher education*, vol. 50, 2009, pp. 546–569.

Reason, R. "Student variables that predict retention: research and new developments." *NASPA Journal*, vol. 40, no. 4, 2003, pp. 172–191.

Reynolds, G. "The impact of facilities on recruitment and retention of students." *New Directions for Institutional Research*, vol. 135, 2007, pp. 63–80.

Sidentop, D. *Introduction to physical education, fitness and sport*. Mountain View, CA: Mayfield Publishing Company, 1998.

Smith, M. K., & Thomas, J. *The relationship of college outcomes to post-graduate success. Assessment of student outcome in higher education*. Knoxville: The University of Tennessee, Center for Assessment Research and Development, 1989.

Taylor, H., Canning, W., Brailsford, P., Rokosz, F. "Financial issues in campus recreation." *New Directions for Student Services*, vol. 103, 2003, pp. 73–86.

UNESCO. *The Power of Sport Values*, Paris: UNESCO, 2016.

Whaley, M., Kaminsky, L. "Epidemiology of physical activity, physical fitness and selected chronic diseases," in J. Roitman (editor), *ACSM's resource manual for guidelines for exercise testing and prescription*, pp. 17–34. Philadelphia, 2006.

Zizzi S., & Ayers S. "Assessing the impact of new student campus recreation centers." *NASPA Journal*, vol. 41, 2004, pp. 588–630.

CHAPTER 6

Residence Hall Students Earn Higher GPAs and Have a Higher Graduation Rate

Here's Why

TOBY TOLAND, M.S.ED., PETER GATTO, M.ED., and ANGIE BRADLEY, M.S.

Toby Toland M.S.Ed. is an assistant director for Residential Life, Housing and Food Service at the University of Nevada, Reno where he oversees leadership initiatives and operations of multiple living communities. He is originally from the Midwest, where he received his B.S. degree from Missouri State University and completed graduate work in Counseling at the University of Nebraska, Kearney. For the past 17 years, he has worked in Student Affairs and higher education.

Peter Gatto M.Ed. is an assistant director for Residential Life, Housing and Food Service at the University of Nevada, Reno where he oversees Academic Initiatives, Recruitment and Marketing. He is originally from Cleveland, Ohio, where he received his B.A. from John Carroll University and his M.Ed. from Cleveland State University. He obtained a graduate certificate in Teaching English to Speakers of other languages (TESOL) from California State University, San Bernardino. He has worked in Student Affairs and higher education for the past ten years.

Angie Bradley is the coordinator for Residential Education at the University of Nevada, Reno where she coordinates academic initiatives and recruitment, selection & training for the Department of Residential Life, Housing & Food Service. She earned her bachelor's degree in Biological Sciences from Eastern Illinois University followed by a master's degree in College Student Affairs at the same institution. She is currently working on her Ph.D. in Education at the University of Nevada, Reno.

The Mission

Every policy, practice, and employee in the Department of Residential Life, Housing, and Food Service is dedicated to supporting the education and holistic development of the residents living within the halls. We do this by striving to create safe and comfortable environments where residents are encouraged to reach their highest potential. This does not mean simply graduating with a GPA to be proud of, it means developing life skills and a strong sense of global citizenship.

All of the buildings, especially those built within the last 15 years, were structurally designed to create common spaces where residents can not only connect with their peers socially, but also have convenient and quiet places to study alone or work on group projects.

Living Learning Communities

The department caters to students' various academic and personal interests by providing communities with intentional learning objectives formed around staffing, community development, and educational programming. Nevada Living Learning Community (NLLC) and Great Basin Hall are the two most academically focused halls with communities geared toward specific colleges or individual majors. The Nevada Living Learning Community holds a variety of living learning communities including Honors Residential Scholars, Health Sciences, Business, Journalism, Education, Undeclared, Gender, Sexuality & Identity, and Latinx Cultural Heritage Living Learning Communities. Great Basin Hall is home to the Women in Science and Engineering (WiSE), College of Science, and Engineering Living Learning Communities.

All communities have a required common course component such as BUS 101 or CHS 102. For both fall and spring semesters, students are also offered the opportunity to enroll in math and English classes with other students in living learning communities. Each living learning community is assigned a Resident Assistant (RA) that has either been a resident of that community or shares the same major or interest of the community. The living learning communities are also assigned at least one faculty advisor that collaborates with the Department in establishing expectations, learning objectives, programming, and common courses for residents.

Themed Communities

Great Basin Hall is a STEM-themed community focused on supporting and promoting the academic success of students pursuing a degree in Science, Technology, Engineering, or Mathematics. Programming offered during the academic year supports the development of scholars who are prepared to pursue a STEM graduate education and enter the STEM workforce. Students hear from faculty, staff, and professionals in the STEM disciplines to gain a better understanding of the various types of careers they can pursue. The community also helps students explore opportunities around STEM research and begin developing professional skills needed to succeed in a STEM career. This STEM community is a dynamic, energetic community of scholars who exemplify academic and personal success and are actively engaged in the UNR community. Eligible students for Great Basin Hall must be enrolled in a STEM (Science, Technology, Engineering, and Mathematics) focused academic program.

Argenta Hall focuses on civic engagement, where the residents have ample opportunities to connect with at least seven charitable organizations in the Reno-Sparks area. Civic engagement in Argenta Hall is centers around being actively involved in enhancing the immediate campus community and greater Reno community in a way that makes residents part of something bigger than themselves. It means taking a step back from one's own life and using one's privilege to improve the lives of others in the community through service. While making a direct impact on the community around them, residents have the opportunity to learn more about themselves through self and group reflection. While living in Argenta Hall, residents can become part of a community that gives back and inspire their peers to do the same.

Peavine Hall, the wellness-themed living environment, offers residents an opportunity to explore the seven dimensions of wellness through monthly wellness meetings and regular programming facilitated by the Resident Assistants. This wellness-themed community provides residents with an opportunity to place a priority on health and wellness topics that intersect with the daily lives of college students. Residents develop a personal wellness challenge with goals that fall within the seven dimensions of wellness. Peavine Hall programs and activities focus on these dimensions and provide an opportunity for students to explore how each dimension of wellness has an impact on them.

Housing for Returning Students

The facilities also provide environments dedicated to serving the upperclass population wanting more independence and privacy. The highest demand is Canada Hall; an apartment-style living environment that provides kitchens for food preparation. Students returning after their first year at the University also have the opportunity to live in other residence halls including Great Basin Hall, Sierra Hall, and Juniper Hall.

Staff

Residential Life has a multitude of staff at various levels dedicated to serving residents and communities. The most easily accessible are the student staff. They can be seen at the front desk of every residence hall, providing weekly tutoring hours, or living in a room down the hall.

Each floor or wing is equipped with a Resident Assistant. These staff members are students with a minimum 2.7 GPA who have previous experience living in the residence halls as students. They experience a competitive interview process and weeks of training prior to opening in August. This extensive training prepares them to help students be successful by relaying information about campus resources, responding to emergencies, setting standards for communal living, and assisting with the overall transition to college life.

Over the last seven years, the department of Residential Life has expanded the Academic Mentor program. These student staff members have a minimum 3.0 GPA and focus on provide in-hall tutoring hours as well as programs to help residents develop strategies for academic success. For the 2018–2019 academic year, eleven Academic Mentors provided weekly tutoring hours and in-depth programming for Academic Skills, Stress Management, and Registration/Academic Planning for all residence hall students through in-hall programming as well as outreach programming to Canada Hall, Juniper Hall, and Sierra Hall.

- Partnered with Admissions & Records, and the College of Liberal Arts Academic Advising to provide training for all Academic Mentor staff on MyNEVADA and academic resources to support on-campus residents.
- The Academic Mentor staff was trained on tutoring expectations and creating a tutoring philosophy during their training.
- Academic Mentors are able to tutor all remedial courses (ENG 98, ENG 100J, MATH 95, MATH 96, MATH 120E). Academic Mentors create business cards and other marketing materials to inform students of other courses they can assist with, including higher-level math courses, engineering, biology, chemistry, psychology, and even French.

- During spring 2019, the Academic Mentor staff provided a total of **1,244** study hours serving **1,279** unique residents (43.4 percent of the on-campus population).

Providing direct oversight and supervision to the student staff in each building are the professional and graduate resident directors. These individuals either have a master's degree in a student development field or are in the process of getting one. Each larger building in the system has at least one full-time professional and one graduate-level resident director. They respond to emergencies around the clock, address community concerns, and work with their staff to provide academic and personal support to the members of their communities.

Providing support to the in-hall staff previously mentioned are the various coordinators who specialize in specific areas to created large scale initiatives for all of the residence halls. The coordinator for Student Leadership & Activities, provides direction and advice to the student leader organizations representing the residents. The coordinator for Residential Education provides support to all of the staff recruitment and academic initiatives. These include recognition events for students achieving high GPAs and providing Academic Intervention to those who are struggling with their academic goals. In Fall 2020, a new coordinator will be added who specializes in diversity, social justice, and inclusion initiatives.

Academic Intervention

Students that earned a Fall 2018 GPA of less than 2.0 were placed on the Academic Intervention program, which included:

- Attendance at the Academic Success Conference
- Individual meetings with a Residential Life professional staff member to develop an individualized academic success plan
- Completion of progress reports
- Follow-up meetings throughout the semester

Additional academic success plan requirements may include tutoring, meeting with professors, attending academic success workshops and referral to outside resources.

The conference this past spring 2019 included an overview by faculty from the Advising Center who reviewed the University Academic Standing policies, as well as tips to raise their grade point averages. Breakout sessions included:

- "Thinking About Your Future"
- "College Survival Skills"
- "Managing Stress and Test Anxiety"
- "Benefits of Fitness & Sports Participation While Enrolled in Higher Education"
- "Improving Grades with Classroom Accommodations: Who Qualifies & What Services Are Provided?"

Academic Intervention Results for Spring 2019

- 184 students with GPA between 1.0 and 1.99 completed Regular Academic Intervention
  - **66.8% GPA improved**
    - 14.7% achieved a 3.0 or better
    - 54.3% achieved a 2.0 or better
- 91 students with GPA of 1.0 or below completed Intensive Academic Intervention
  - **81.3% GPA improved**
    - 8.8% achieved a 3.0 or better
    - 40.7% achieved a 2.0 or better

Programming and Community Development

Providing a safe and comfortable environment where students can reach their highest potential is the basis of the Department's goals when it comes to providing social and educational programming through community development efforts.

Safety does not just mean locked doors and RAs doing rounds; people feel safe when they know who is living around them and the community as a whole looks out for each other. All community building efforts should help establish a safe living environment.

Comfort goes beyond the furniture and facilities people live in. Residents should feel comfortable being themselves, expressing their identity, communicating freely and appropriately with roommates and other community members. Communities should be welcoming so residents feel included and connected. Residents should feel like they belong in their community.

To reach the highest potential, we strive to connect residents to the university to improve retention and promote their academic success. We challenge residents to invest in their personal growth and engage in improving their community.

Leadership Opportunities

It is proven that students who are actively involved in campus organizations are more likely to be retained and eventually graduate (Tinto; Astin). Not only do the staff promote involvement on campus, we also provide easy access opportunities within the communities. Each residence hall maintains a Leadership Council (LC). These groups meet weekly and are comprised of students looking to gain leadership experience. They serve as the voice of the students and are allocated a budget to implement large-scale events in their buildings.

Each LC sends representatives to their parent organization, the Residence Hall Association (RHA). This group provides support to each LC by providing structure and training to other student organizations. They also represent the student perspective within various campus committees and administration. Students actively involved with RHA also have to opportunity to represent the University at regional and national levels.

We also offer residents the opportunity to join the National Residence Hall Honorary (NRHH), which is comprised of the top 1 percent of student leaders living in the residence halls. Members of NRHH focus on recognition and service. The Nevada Chapter of NRHH assists with the facilitation of Appreciation Days for all staff members that work for on-campus residents as well as service initiatives for students to participate in throughout the academic year.

Committee Initiatives

The Department assembles other committees to emphasize topics that are crucial to student success. First and foremost is the academic success committee. They recognize high standards of academic achievement, and partner with other campus resources to provide academic guidance within out hall. This committee organizes the Annual 4.0 Luncheon and 3.0 Ice Cream Social which provide recognition to those residents that have been academically successful during the previous fall semester. This committee also organizes the Academic Success Conference, an annual event that provides residents with an opportunity to start their spring semester strong by gaining knowledge and resources from campus partners such as the Financial Aid Office, Disability Resource Center, University Advising Center, and the Fitness Center.

Beyond academics, Residential Life, Housing, and Food Service acknowledge that raising awareness on social justice and inclusion initiatives are pertinent for the students. Therefore, they have a committee that leads education and inclusion initiatives in the department. The committee provides programming and education on a variety of subjects each year with the goal of recognizing and creating an environment where all identities feel appreciated.

Responding to Community Disruption/Issues

As previously mentioned, the Residential Life, Housing, and Food Service department has established guidelines or policies to help ensure safe and comfortable living environments. Student and professional staff are charged with monitoring that these community standards are upheld. Students found responsible for violating those policies are given sanctions intended to be developmental and staff work with the individual to reflect and evaluate their decision-making skills. The basis for this entire system is to provide educational opportunities that will hopefully assist in the student development process.

Students often struggle with the transition to a university and gaining a foundation in autonomy. The staff within the Residential Life, Housing, and Food Service department spend a lot of time assisting students deal with issues causing them distress. These include basic issues as homesickness, relationship issues, conflicts with peers, and overall stress management. Staff are trained to be first-level responders to these issues, but also know that when a student presents serious concerns, we refer to professional campus resources.

Dining Services

One of the most important aspects of the UNR student experience is the ability to find food that is nutritious, affordable, and conveniently located. Students have a variety of food options all over campus for breakfast, lunch, and dinner. The Residential Life, Housing, and Food Service department offers several meal plan options for both on-campus residents and commuters. With the Dine On campus app, students are able to quickly access dining locations, hours, and menus. They are also able to give immediate feedback regarding their experience which goes directly to Dining Management for review.

All of the food offered by Dining Services includes nutritional information. If students have special dietary needs, we offer written guides to help them navigate the appropriate food choices. This can be anything from gluten-free choices to vegan and vegetarian options. The Dining Management staff will even give one-on-one consultation and help the students develop their own personalized dining plan.

Finally, students have the opportunity to join the Food and Dining committee which meets weekly throughout the academic year. This committee is specifically dedicated to support students and their dining experience. They are able to provide regular feedback during the weekly meetings and cover what foods and services they enjoyed, but also share their suggestions to possibly improve the dining experience.

Moving Forward

The Department of Residential Life is constantly evaluating and assessing its procedures and initiatives, and, where necessary, adjusting to meet the growing needs of students. Initially, the Department will be looking at areas where, with the addition of more staff, current programs can continue to grow and thrive. There has been enormous success with the academic commitment as seen through the learning communities, incentives, and intervention. They have nurtured growth in this area over the last six years and will continue to do so as results prove their worth and demand increases.

Diversity and inclusion are already prominent themes in staff training, programming and community building. They will continue to emphasize this more as we update common areas and develop both professional and student staff positions that will implement more forms of education and methods of celebrating the diverse student body.

In the coming years, there are two areas they would like to explore. The first will be incorporating a stronger academic curriculum theme into the community development model. The second will be implementing retention strategies for upper-class students by providing living environments that meet the needs of individuals preparing to graduate and enter the work force.

REFERENCES

Astin, A. W., & Sax L. J. "How undergraduates are affected by service participation." *Journal of College Student Development*, vol. 29, no. 3, 1998, pp. 251–263.

Tinto, V. *Leaving college: Rethinking the causes and cures of student attrition*. 2nd edition. Chicago: University of Chicago Press, 1993.

CHAPTER 7

Dispelling Myths of Studying Abroad

ALYSSA NOTA, PH.D.

Alyssa Nota, Ph.D., is president and CEO of University Studies Abroad Consortium (USAC), a nonprofit organization established in 1982 which includes fifty three programs across twenty seven countries. Alyssa joined USAC in 2000, was named president and CEO in 2017, and was most recently the Regional Resident Director for four USAC Italy programs. Alyssa's study abroad education began at Florida State University's Florence Center and University of Florence, Italy. She completed her master's degree in Italian Language and Literature at the University of Virginia. and continued her studies in foreign language teaching and acquisition at the University of Siena on full scholarship. Alyssa holds a Ph.D. in Education/Curriculum and Instruction with highest honors from Boston College.

Introduction

The field of study abroad is surrounded with many myths. Some people wrongly believe that study abroad is out of reach because of these myths: study abroad costs too much; students need to know a foreign language; certain majors courses aren't offered; it will delay graduation; teaching quality is lower than at a home university; it's too dangerous; potential employers don't value study abroad. On the contrary, an array of study abroad opportunities are available—including USAC options—that dispel these myths and meet the various needs of University of Nevada, Reno (UNR) students.

What Does the Research Say?

Nationally, the number of U.S. students studying abroad for credit during the 2016–2017 academic year grew 2.3 percent from 325,339 students to 332,727 students from the previous year. This represents about 1.6 percent of all U.S. students enrolled at institutions of higher education in the United States and about 10 percent of U.S. graduates—an alarmingly low rate. In Nevada, that percentage is much lower at 0.89 percent. Approximately 320–400 University of Nevada, Reno, students study abroad through University Studies Abroad

Consortium (USAC, UNR's study abroad office) each year, and there is an upward trend. Between 2015 and 2018, there has been a 10 percent increase in the number of UNR students attending USAC programs abroad. However, given the UNR student population of over 22,000 students, there is an enormous potential for growth in the number of students who study abroad during their time at UNR. USAC's mission to prepare students for a global future ties in seamlessly with the University of Nevada, Reno's vision to "educate and graduate the best-prepared, confident leaders for the state, national, and global community; to be a nexus for research and creativity that focuses on vital issues of our time; and to serve as a catalyst for the betterment of our society" (Mission & Core Values).

Contributing to low study abroad enrollments are perceived barriers as noted in a 2017 research article: cost, lost wages, lack of financial support, and safety concerns (Vernon et al.). Concern about cost is a top factor when it comes to students' (and their families') decision to pursue study abroad. USAC was founded on the tenet of affordability. As a nonprofit organization, we offer some of the most affordable, authentic and academically solid programs, even when compared to the University's tuition. In fact, USAC has programs in 13 countries that are comparable in cost to staying at UNR for a semester (USAC).

For reference and planning, students can find USAC program fees and an interactive budget sheet on the USAC website, usac.edu, under Fees and Deadlines. The interactive budget sheet allows students to calculate the full cost of studying abroad, including the program fee, housing, airfare, daily living expenses, etc.

Studying abroad is made affordable through reasonable program fees and access to USAC (and other) scholarships. In recent years, USAC has offered over $2 million in annual scholarships and discounts. Financial aid is also applicable to USAC programs. The global competencies which UNR students can attain from studying abroad are countless and they come with long-lasting value for students' personal and professional futures. More than a simple resume boost, experience abroad provides students with priceless skills and a leg up in the professional world, which some companies say are lacking in today's pool of candidates for open positions or for current staff. A recent survey found that almost 40 percent of companies surveyed report that they missed international business opportunities because of a lack of internationally competent personnel (NAFSA).

As featured in USAC's blog ("Students volunteer in local hospital in Thailand"), a UNR student who wanted to become a reconstructive plastic surgeon used a volunteer opportunity at a local hospital in Khon Kaen, Thailand, to add to her healthcare experience and resume. She stated:

> My ultimate life goal is to become a reconstructive plastic surgeon because I want to help those in need, whether it be burn victims or people with birth deformities. Volunteering ultimately relates to my career goals because I will be working with all different kinds of patients. It's not only something I am passionate about, but also something that will prepare me in my future endeavors.

These career-enhancing stories are engrained in USAC's 35-year history. After graduating in 1995, a USAC Chile alumnus, now Managing Director at Signature Wealth Partners, approached a local Reno office of a large brokerage firm to become a stock broker, referencing his study abroad as knowledge of emerging markets. It worked, and he was hired. Later in his career, he once again parlayed his study abroad experience into a job offer:

> The hiring manager asked me extensively about Chile. He said it 'stuck out.' That hiring manager told me much later that he chose me specifically because living abroad, especially in Chile, demonstrates risk-taking, shows an open mind, and offers insight and life experience that books can't offer. He wanted that type of individual at their rapidly growing firm. (Source: blog.usac.edu)

Additionally, many UNR graduates who are also USAC alumni have remained in the Reno area, bringing their newfound skills back to the community after studying abroad—adding international flair in the form of restaurants and other businesses, and starting careers in journalism, communication, teaching, politics, finance, and law. Many alumni are employed by USAC and have started careers in international education. They report that their own successful study abroad experiences inspired them to help other students to pursue the same. Some have gone on to sponsor generous USAC program scholarships such as a Middle East scholarship for study in Israel, and the Proctor scholarship for study in Italy and Thailand.

Regarding safety concerns, approximately 90 percent of USAC's current program locations are rated as safer than the U.S., according to the Global Peace Index. To help prepare students, USAC holds pre-departure group orientations for UNR students and parents. Students have consistent support (in person, online, in writing, and by text message) from their USAC program advisor, based in the USAC central office on the UNR campus, as well as support from all relevant USAC departments such as accounting, academics, enrollment and program- and region-specific advising. Before departure, students receive extensive, informative documents (including housing and arrival guides) and a "toolkit" with guidelines about studying abroad, including tips on staying healthy, mentally and physically, while abroad. USAC offers many of these documents in both English and Spanish and employs multilingual staff for additional assistance.

Additionally, USAC employs two full-time health and safety managers who work closely with program directors and staff abroad, as well as, stay abreast of international news and related best practices. Once onsite at their program location, students participate in orientations and receive supporting information from the USAC staff and host university.

USAC offers support to students and faculty in need of diverse accommodations for physical or mental health issues. As the number of U.S. university students who report accommodation needs has increased significantly in recent years, USAC has expanded its pre-departure and on-site support. Staff participate in ongoing training, and furthermore, USAC encourages students and faculty to share their own experiences and advice with each other and other potential participants. In keeping with this mission, the USAC blog offers helpful tips. A UNR student, who studied with USAC in Santiago, Chile, wrote:

> Before hearing about USAC, I was under the impression I would never have the chance to study abroad as a STEM major. Fortunately, I was still able to earn the credits I needed, while gaining a whole semester of Spanish and cultural knowledge.

Another student who studied in Palmerston North, New Zealand said:

> I valued my time studying abroad in New Zealand as it gave me the opportunity to experience scientific education in another country. I not only got to learn about the science of New Zealand's ecosystems and environments, but also gained a new perspective on how different countries approach environmental issues with different scientific applications. As a STEM student, I find it incredibly valuable

to not only experience a foreign approach of science, but to see how and why different approaches are needed around the globe.

USAC stays abreast of educational trends, needs, and requests of UNR students, faculty, and administration, and uses this information to develop or adapt program locations and curriculum, particularly in areas where students tend to think they are not able to study abroad and get credits in their area of study. Health, STEM, and engineering are three such fields. For example, USAC opened a new program in Khon Kaen, Thailand in 2018 due to the high demand for health-related courses and internships in a low-cost, accessible, welcoming location. Students of nursing, aging, global and environmental health, and other related disciplines have found it to be a powerful experience to study and intern with local health care professionals in Southeast Asia. Similarly, USAC's STEM-focused program in Valencia, Spain has seen steady growth and support from both UNR students and faculty. Courses are offered at the highly respected Polytechnic University of Valencia in science and math, including chemistry, calculus, physics, and dynamics, often with complementary labs and research opportunities. Supplemental courses in Spanish language, dance, cuisine, and windsurfing round out a high-quality academic and globally immersive experience. Additionally, a business and tourism management program was opened in Verona, Italy, to better serve the needs of the large number of business students and faculty seeking opportunities in a mid-sized, affordable western European city.

Another important example of USAC's commitment to helping all students is the following: In 2018, USAC appointed its first Diversity and Inclusion officer, reflecting the organization's commitment to better serving students of all backgrounds, identities, and needs, providing more informed service, more comprehensive preparation and support, and training for both central office and onsite program staff. USAC recently expanded its website and added a dedicated section to its blog called "My Identity Abroad" where alumni share their stories and advice.

What is the Program?

University Studies Abroad Consortium (USAC) is a nonprofit, university-based organization providing affordable, authentic, accessible study abroad programs at more than 50 locations in 28 countries. Since 1982, USAC has provided over 60,000 students with unique opportunities to live and learn in countries all around the globe. Since its inception, USAC has been based at UNR, and UNR defines USAC as its study abroad office. USAC enthusiastically supports the needs of UNR students and faculty. We strive to provide experiences in which students grow into engaged citizens of the world, not only in the classroom, but also through field trips, integrated living (often with host families or local students), language partners, sports, internships, and volunteer and service-learning opportunities. It is, and always has been, important for us to contribute to the internationalization of universities in the U.S. and abroad. Our mission is to provide students with the opportunity to develop the knowledge, skills, and attitudes to succeed in a global society.

USAC is located on the UNR campus in the Virginia Street Gym and in a new annex at 1317 North Virginia Street. USAC employs approximately 80 staff in its central office, many of whom are USAC alumni.

The student populations USAC serves primarily include:

- Average student age: 21
- Gender: 73.76% female, 25.96% male, 0.28% non-binary
- Class Level: Freshman 8%; sophomore 38%; junior 41%; senior 11%; other 2%.
- Top 5 fields of study: business/management, social sciences, foreign languages/international studies, physical/life sciences, communications/journalism. Additional, quickly growing fields of study include health professions and engineering.

Opportunities also abound for UNR faculty. Faculty global competency is offered through USAC's Visiting Professor (VP) and Faculty International Development Award (FIDA):

- The VP program gives academic faculty the unique opportunity to support the internationalization of UNR departments and colleges by teaching abroad. Visiting Professors establish contacts with foreign colleagues, enhance their own foreign language skills, strengthen and support international education and study abroad on campus, diversify course curriculum, and develop international relationships for research and other purposes.
- The FIDA program is geared toward faculty and staff with limited prior international experience. The goal of this program is to increase awareness of study abroad and familiarity with USAC, which thereby helps UNR internationalize its campus. FIDA recipients participate

> in the program as if they are a student. They are expected to attend class, complete assignments, and fully participate in all aspects of the program.

An art history professor who served as VP in both the Torino, Italy, and Lyon, France programs states:

> The programs in Lyon and Torino were extremely beneficial to my teaching and research. On the teaching front, they inspired me to enhance several aspects of my curriculum and to offer more opportunities for students to connect with local cultural sites and art collections.

An education professor was fortunate to experience four different USAC programs: Heredia, Costa Rica; Reggio Emilia, Italy; Brighton, England; and San Sebastian, Spain:

> Because my field is education, it is useful to learn how teaching takes place in other countries. This includes facilities, equipment, and services available. In Costa Rica, USAC staff arranged for me and my students to visit two elementary classrooms to observe in order to make connections to our course material. The opportunity to get to know students better from various U.S. universities and at levels that extend beyond merely professor-student is based on having a small class size, experiencing cultural difference together, and participating in USAC field trips and tours together.

The international experience is invaluable it helps students to think about problems from different perspectives. Studying abroad does not need to delay graduation. A wide variety of USAC program types, academic focuses, session lengths, and locations are available so that students can choose the best path and place to complete needed credits and graduation requirements. USAC collaborates closely with the University on a macro and micro level (from top administration to departments, on-campus organizations, and student groups) including curriculum integration initiatives. In some circumstances, some students may even graduate early.

USAC strongly believes in creating and maintaining programs known for academic integrity, including intensive language tracks in which students can complete up to two years of language study within one semester in locations such as San Sebastian, Spain, or Viterbo, Italy. Costa Rica and Reggio

Emilia, Italy programs feature language teaching courses for those interested in teaching professions, while the Alicante, Spain program supports heritage speakers of Spanish through specialized courses. Language acquisition is buffeted by regular cultural immersion activities, interaction with local staff and faculty, homestays, language partners, and local "buddies" on campus and in the community. Moreover, USAC programs are traditionally located on a host university campus abroad, meaning there is optimal interaction with local students and learning opportunities for USAC students.

In an ongoing, productive collaboration with UNR, USAC measures impact through UNR student participation and fulfillment of the university's global competencies, core curriculum requirements as well as language skill acquisition.

There has been an increase in the number of UNR students completing their language minor or major requirements on USAC programs. UNR's commitment to the study of world languages and cultures matches well with one of USAC's core strengths: the belief in the value of language study abroad and the high quality of language instruction and immersion at USAC program locations.

Spanish is one of the most studied languages on USAC programs, and is offered at five locations in Spain (including the first USAC program created in San Sebastian), three in Costa Rica, and one each in Uruguay, Chile, and Cuba. Students of UNR's top ranked French program have two excellent locations to practice their skills: Lyon and Pau, France. UNR students have the unique opportunity to pursue a minor in Italian. USAC offers four programs in Italy, all of which offer courses in Italian language, culture, and area studies, which may be applicable to the minor. Two of the top studied languages today, Korean and Japanese, can be studied on USAC Partnership Programs both during the academic year or summer sessions. Less commonly taught languages, such as German, Portuguese, Arabic, Twi, Hindi, and Swedish, among others, can also be studied.

According to a UNR student, who studied with USAC Brazil, studying abroad taught her many things:

> I learned a new language and a new culture. I learned how to travel and live in a country where I didn't know the language. I gained new experiences that can never be replaced. After living in Brazil for four months, I felt like a pro when it came to speaking Portuguese

> because I was surrounded by it 100 percent of the time. I felt very comfortable and at home the whole time I was abroad.

Internships are another way in which students can be significantly immersed into the professional context of the host culture (and usually without local language skills as a requirement). Teaching English to locals is a common internship experience in almost all USAC programs. A wide variety of internship opportunities are available in subject areas such as marketing, communications, journalism, management, entrepreneurship, health, marine biology, art, education, and environmental studies, to name a few.

One UNR student wrote of her internship experience while studying in Chengdu, China:

> I am majoring in biology and minoring in Chinese studies. I was interning in Chengdu, China during Summer Session 2 in 2017. The program that I got involved in is called Maoxi School, where the program selects certain students in the leprosy village to come to Chengdu for a week to experience the city life and provide a chance for them to leave their village. The overall goal was to guide and encourage the students to step out of the village and into the big city. The USAC Resident Director Wentao Song told me and the rest of the students about this program and that's how I got involved. This opportunity was a once in a lifetime experience because it was a mutual learning experience. The kids learned English from the other volunteers and me, and we learned and experienced the history and lifestyle of these leprosy survivors. I was grateful to be a part of their lives and for them to be a part of my life. It will be an unforgettable experience.

Another UNR student who studied abroad with USAC Chiang Mai, Thailand wrote that her pre-departure fears were dispelled by the outstanding support she received from on-site staff:

> Jum, the resident director, and all of her supporting staff, cared very much about my safety and well-being in Thailand and cultivated an engaging and meaningful experience in Chiang Mai. My favorite course was Thai Civilizations. We had many class readings and lectures but most of our time was spent at museums or visiting local temples and nearby cities to attach what we learned in our

> books to Thai history and culture outside of the classroom. From opportunities like volunteering to teach English at the monasteries and refurbishing play equipment at a local orphanage to my internship with visually impaired students, the USAC Chiang Mai Program provided me a foundation of experience and understanding of living and traveling abroad that helped prepare me for my Fulbright program.

USAC originally began in 1982 working directly with UNR, and in particular its Basque Studies leaders and faculty on campus. Over the past thirty seven years, USAC has grown and expanded to offer much more beyond its strong Basque roots and traditions. Students can currently study more than twenty five different world languages. Areas of study vary from health, arts, and sciences to education, journalism, and business. Major and minor courses are often complemented by location-connected courses such as culture, cuisine, dance, photography, travel writing, sailing, surfing, meditation, and yoga, among many more.

All USAC programs are evaluated by students on a per-session basis. Students also evaluate each academic course they take. Program resident directors consistently evaluate and work with faculty and administration to improve the programs. USAC administration, including the CEO/president and academic affairs director, review programs on a regular basis. USAC continuously works to create high-quality academic and cultural experience for all participants. Presently, USAC obtains a 96 percent recommendation rate from evaluations from students who participated on a program, in addition to being named as a Top Study Abroad Organization by GoAbroad.com and GoOverseas.com, two leading industry evaluation sites.

Conclusion

USAC's collaboration with UNR for more than three decades has produced extraordinary results thus far—and shows no signs of slowing. It is estimated that over six thousand UNR graduates have studied abroad with USAC since its inception. USAC and UNR work hard to create and promote opportunities for a wide variety of students and faculty spanning areas of study, diversity, academic, research, personal interests, graduation requirements and financial needs. USAC is known and respected widely as a provider of high quality, authentic, affordable study abroad opportunities. USAC is constantly seeking ways to educate students, faculty, and community members on the value and accessibility of study abroad, despite the myths that exist.

One UNR student's words sum up why study abroad is such a valuable experience and why no student should miss out on—and certainly not due to inaccurate myths:

> Over the past months, living in a different country without the same pressures as the United States, has altered my perspective. Traveling around the world spontaneously, learning a new language, meeting new people in the most random of places—that is the core of the human experience. There is indescribable fear of doing something extraordinary and outside of your comfort zone, but the rewards far surpass your wildest imaginations. We all stand at the precipice of change, and when people fear the world is plummeting into the abyss, do not hesitate to jump and see if you can fly.

REFERENCES

"How do I pay for Study Abroad?" University of Nevada-Reno, 2019. https://www.unr.edu/study-abroad/how-do-i-pay-for-study-abroad.

"Mission & Core Themes." University of Nevada, Reno, 2019. https://www.unr.edu/accreditation/mission-and-core-themes.

"Students volunteer in local hospital in Thailand." USAC blog, June 4, 2019. https://blog.usac.edu/students-volunteer-in-local-hospital-in-thailand/.

"Trends in U.S. Study Abroad." NAFSA: Association of International Educators, 2017. https://www.nafsa.org/Policy_and_Advocacy/Policy_Resources/Policy_Trends_and_Data/Trends_in_U_S__Study_Abroad/.

Vernon, A., Moos, C., & Loncarich, H. "Student Expectancy and Barriers to Study Abroad." *Academy of Educational Leadership Journal, vol 21, no. 1*, 2017. https://www.abacademies.org/articles/student-expectancy-and-barriers-to-study-abroad-6694.html.

"USAC," University Study Abroad Consortium, 2019. www.usac.edu.

"USAC: Your Gateway to the World," USAC blog, 2019. https://blog.usac.edu/.

CHAPTER 8

How to Engage Gen Z?

Reinventing Programs to Maximize Student Participation in Group Advising

ANNA LINCOLN, M.A., and NATALIA MUSGROVE, M.A.

Anna Lincoln is the coordinator of Academic Advising for the College of Liberal Arts Student Center at the University of Nevada, Reno. Anna oversees a variety of advising initiatives contributing to retention, persistence, decreasing time to degree completion, and graduation for nearly four thousand students in the college. Anna is the lead advisor trainer for the College of Liberal Arts and supports faculty and staff programming across the college while managing the CLA Student Center's assessment of Academic Advising. She is also responsible for conducting data analysis using the university's Student Success Collaborative and PowerBI software to make programmatic changes in advising. Anna earned her bachelor's degree in Biology from the University of Nevada, Reno, followed by her master's degree in Counseling and Educational Psychology.

Natalia Musgrove is the former coordinator of Academic Advising for the College of Liberal Arts at the University of Nevada, Reno, where she was responsible for implementing large-scale advising programs and overseeing key projects that involve research, analysis, evaluation, and reporting on student enrollment, persistence, time-to-degree completion, and graduation certification. Currently Natalia serves as the Pioneer Success Coach for the Office of Academic Programs and Services at California State University, East Bay, where she's leading academic advising campaign efforts, conducting trend analysis, and monitoring student progress toward degree as the EAB specialist assigned to the College of Letters, Arts, and Social Sciences. Additionally, Natalia is the Diversity Coordinator for National Academic Advising Association (NACADA) Region 9 that advocates for equity and inclusion in higher education. Natalia earned a bachelor's degree in International Affairs from Moldova State University and a master's degree in Political Science from the University of Nevada, Reno.

Historical Context

Engaging students in learning and advising activities has never been a simple task, notably so in a group setting (Drake et al.; Lowenstein). Alas, for the College of Liberal Arts (CLA) at the University of Nevada, Reno (UNR), there is hardly any alternative to this method. Since professional academic advisors in the CLA Student Center serve nearly four thousand undergraduate students in arts, humanities, and social sciences, they simply do not have enough time in the day to meet with each individual advisee in person. Resorting to group advising in similar circumstances is a viable solution, because it provides an opportunity to share important academic information with a larger audience in a timely fashion, as well as encourage student interaction with their peers (Ryan). In particular, group sessions are desirable when advising is mandatory for specific student populations, such as first-semester freshmen.

In spite of practicing group advising for many years, the College's data analysis from 2012 to 2015 indicated low student attendance and participation rates in second semester mandatory freshman advising workshops. Knowing that these events have been widely advertised using flyers, posters on bulletin boards, student newsletters, and class announcements that prompted students to call or visit the front office to reserve their seat in the workshop, minimal student engagement left college stakeholders puzzled and perplexed. At the same time, it also became apparent that to effectively provide advising services in the largest college on campus, student outreach and advising programs needed to be redesigned. Prior to making any significant changes, academic advisors in the Student Center engaged in scholarly inquiry about the preferences and characteristics of the modern students from the generation often known as 'Gen Z,' particularly in the area of communication. In what follows, the Student Center shares its findings and introduces a new approach to maximizing student participation in group advising and the educational setting as a whole.

Gen Z: Interests, Preferences, and Characteristics

Born after 1995, Gen Z grew up in a time of major economic distress, terror attacks, and social injustice (Beall; Patel; Barr). As a consequence, representatives of this group are concerned with world issues and understand that nothing in life is ever guaranteed. Personal and intellectual development has become one of their most essential goals, transforming them into highly-driven and intelligent individuals who strive to make the world a better place for all. In addition, within the United States, Gen Z is also the most diverse population: nearly 50 percent are members of a minority group and roughly 25 percent have a foreign-born parent (See miller and Grace). Not surprisingly, they embrace and celebrate diversity by promoting such causes as tolerance, fair pay, marriage equality, hate crime prevention, and work permits for childhood immigrants.

In terms of communication, Gen Z students truly are digital natives—they simply don't know and can't imagine life without technological gadgets, internet, and social media. These young adults live in the world of "updates" and stay connected at all times embracing technology that forces them to perceive everything from a global and visual standpoint (Alt; Ravipati; Elmore; Gaines). Gen Z is the most tech-savvy population that communicates across multiple platforms and demonstrates multi-tasking behaviors. In fact, even their learning preferences reflect this tendency, as students crave education that is visually enhanced through media outlets, images, symbols, and videos (Seemiller and Grace). They are active hands-on type of learners who gain knowledge through trial and error, expect services on demand, and prefer smaller groups for collaboration due to their competitive nature. In other words, Gen Z is "leading the change in how learning takes place . . . representing a driving force in the innovation of new learning tools, teaching styles, and unlimited access to resources" (Kozinsky).

Reality Check: Challenges Facing Gen Z

Unfortunately, excessive use of internet and technology also compromise students' psychological and physical well-being. Current research indicates that in an era where people are connected more than ever in the history of mankind, Gen Z appears to be the most socially isolated and loneliest group yet (Alt; Lanquist; Nemko). Interpersonal skills are vanishing today, as individuals turn to social media to engage with the world in search for positive reinforcement and feedback (Macmillan). Stimulated by likes, comments, and followers, Gen Z is constantly flaunting their lives in order to feel important and maintain their image. Yet not too many of them are willing to expose everyday struggles, challenges, and disappointments. Social media has become primarily about vacations, shopping, beauty, and relationship goals—everything that makes them seem happy, while potentially hiding feelings of complete alienation (Manning-Schaffel; Konnikova). Digital spaces have created an artificial reality and set unrealistic expectations that cause feelings of inadequacy and fear of missing out ("FOMO"). As Barr explains:

> ...when it comes to low self-esteem, a lot of young people are putting that down to concerns about...the online world and how its following people around—it's with them 24/7. Every time they switch on their phones they're getting messages about parties they haven't been invited to, or they're seeing photos of their friends doing things, or their whole self-worth is based on how many likes they're getting on Facebook. It absolutely permeates their sense of self-esteem.

The unattainable image of perfection, whether it is their body or birthday celebration, forms 'compare and despair' type of attitude, where young adults are in a constant race with their peers that leads to negative feelings like jealousy and envy, ultimately causing psychological distress (Barker; Barth).

To this effect, recent studies have concluded that individuals who spend more time on social media in general are more likely to report and suffer from mental health concerns (Fuller). Given that Gen Z students spend on average three hours per day online, it is not surprising that they score higher on disability, anxiety, depression, and self-harm. In fact, over 22 percent of students in the US are diagnosed with attention deficit and hyperactivity disorders (Seemiller and Grace), for they simply cannot concentrate due to the digital distractions. Young adults compulsively check their smartphones out of habit and become anxious in the absence of signal or low battery due to the fear of being out of cellular connection—a common syndrome known as *nomophobia* (Elmore). They sleep next to their phones and check for updates first thing upon waking up, thus affecting the overall quality of life and well-being.

Paradoxically, 65 percent of modern-day students reportedly dislike using their phones for the primary purpose of making and receiving calls (Seemiller and Grace; Elmore): instead, they book dinner reservations, maintain personal calendars, complete travel arrangements, shop, ask questions of interest—in other words, multi-task and engage with the world in a way that requires minimal face-to-face interaction. For any formal correspondence, including academic settings, Gen Z prefer e-mail because it does not limit them in terms of space and time (they do not unplug after 5 p.m.). Any attempt at engagement through social media, on the other hand, is perceived as an invasion of privacy. Due to task-switching behaviors and 'get-it-when-you-want-it' mentality, Gen Z students also tend to be less patient and demonstrate a shorter attention span—a mere eight seconds. The reason for this is the more things they are doing at once, the less are they able to meaningfully engage. Put simply, Gen Z students are engaged and bored at the same time. "What causes us to feel bored and, as a result, unhappy? Attention. When our attention is actively engaged, we aren't bored; when we fail to engage, boredom sets in" (Konnikova).

Utilizing Technology for Student Outreach

In an effort to improve student persistence, UNR acquired the Student Success Collaborative (SSC) software and began its implementation in 2016. The platform provides academic advisors with the ability to access historical data analytics for retention efforts, house advising notes and reports for coordinated student care across campus, and offer electronic appointment scheduling to students. Within the scheduling function resides the ability to run appointment campaigns, which allow advisors to conduct targeted outreach to specific student populations. Students included in the campaign receive an email with a link to schedule an advising appointment. They can choose which group session they would like to attend and receive an email confirmation and a reminder email the morning of the appointment. The acquisition of this software coincided with the Student Center's research on the Gen Z student population.

Based on the research, it was determined that the previous scheduling method for mandatory group advising did not align with the preferences of Gen Z students; the Student Center inferred this to be a reason for low attendance rates. Given that over half of modern day students dislike using their phones to make calls, requiring students to schedule their group advising appointment by calling the front office was not an ideal scheduling method. In addition, Gen Z students are plugged in 24 hours a day, 7 days a week, therefore expecting them to make the call between traditional business hours of 8 a.m. to 5 p.m. was not in line with their lifestyle. Evidence of this was seen in the voice messages left after hours in the Student Center, and the phone tag between student and front office during the workday.

The Student Center decided to pilot an SSC appointment campaign in fall 2016 for freshmen needing second semester mandatory advising.

The appointment campaign gave these digitally-inclined students the ability to schedule their advising appointment without having to make a phone call; students were able to use any of their gadgets to view the email, click on a link to select their preferred group workshop, and have their appointment scheduled at any time and immediately upon viewing the email. Not only did this approach cater toward students' connection to technology, but also to their expectation to achieve a result on demand; within seconds, students were able to schedule their appointment without any human interaction.

The content and layout of the initial campaign email was strategically designed to capture the attention of Gen Z students and deliver the most important information before disengagement occurred. The subject of the email addressed the removal of the students' advising holds with the hope that they would open and read without scrolling onto something else in their inbox. The two sentences at the top were intentionally concise, in bold font, and delivered the most important information to the students: why they were contacted and why they needed to attend group advising. The timing of the campaign was also strategic in that it was sent a month after advising holds were placed and two weeks before freshmen registration began, giving students plenty of time to realize that they had a hold and enough time to have it removed before registration the following:

Andrew, Want Your Advising Hold Removed?

N University of Nevada, Reno

Come to College of Liberal Arts 2nd Semester Group Advising and work with CLA advisors to choose your classes!

Registration begins November 15th; come to advising now and have your hold removed in plenty of time!

Hello Andrew:

We are hosting group advising sessions for continuing CLA freshmen. You may choose one of the workshops below. Please sign up as soon as possible because space is limited. All workshops will be held in the CLA computer lab in Ansari Business (AB) 610. Please click on the link below and use the calendar tool to choose the day you'd like to attend. You will be logging in to MyNevada so please make sure to arrive ready to do so, with your NSHE ID and password.

Once you complete this workshop, we will remove your advising hold so you can register for classes in November.

Schedule an Appointment

Group Advising Attendance

The Student Center saw an improvement in workshop attendance, doubling the percentage of students who attended group advising.

In fall 2015, before SSC and when students had to call the front office to schedule their group advising session, only 31 percent of the cohort attended group advising. This resulted in an exhaustion of resources with the Student Center having to see over 200 students for individual appointments within a short window of time before the start of freshmen registration. Using the appointment campaign, student attendance doubled, reaching 60 percent in 2016 and 63 percent in 2017. This reduced the number of scheduled individual advising appointments by more than half and resulted in less students calling the front office and leaving messages, which alleviated the workload on administrative support staff allowing them additional time to focus on other tasks.

Due to this success, the Student Center decided to apply this method to third semester group advising, beginning in fall 2017. Capturing these students was particularly challenging for two reasons: first, they did not receive advising holds and thus were not required to meet with an advisor and second, the cohorts were much larger because all CLA students were invited to workshops ran by the Student Center. For second semester advising, Psychology and Criminal Justice students were advised by faculty and therefore not invited to the Student Center's workshops.

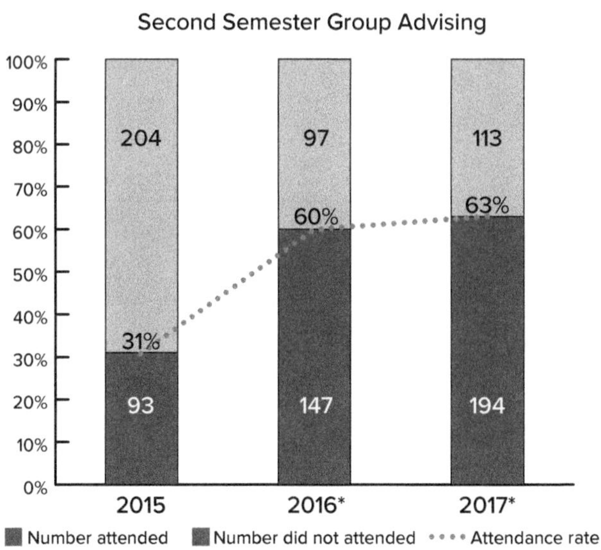

The Student Center implemented third semester group advising for students in fall 2016, with an attendance rate of 6 percent. With the appointment campaign in 2017 and 2018, student attendance rates increased to 19 percent in 2017 and 17 percent in 2018, resulting in almost four times the number of students that attended group advising prior to SSC. Even without the motivation of an advising hold, 100 percent of sessions offered were filled in 2017; 70 percent of sessions offered were filled in 2018.

By using the knowledge gained on the preferences and characteristics of Gen Z students, the Student Center was able to change the method in which they conducted outreach to students and the method in which students were expected to schedule their appointments. By engaging Gen Z through technology and allowing them to schedule when and how they preferred, the Student Center drastically increased the number of students seen at group advising.

Changes to Group Advising

In addition to changing the method in which students were contacted and scheduled their appointments, the Student Center used their research to influence changes in group advising structure to better engage Gen Z students.

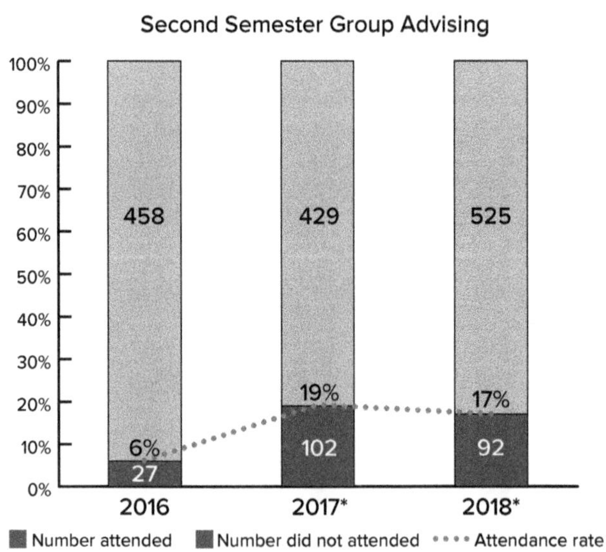

First, the maximum number of students allowed was decreased. Initially, the Student Center allowed 15 students per session but also accommodated walk-ins, which at times resulted in sessions with over 20 students. After learning that Gen Z students prefer to work in smaller groups, the Student Center set the campaign maximum to 12 students and only those who signed up through the campaign were able to attend. Two advisors were present at each session to provide enough individualized attention to each student. This was done with the intention of creating a comfortable atmosphere that fostered collaboration.

The Student Center was cognizant of the fact that Gen Z students conduct business at all times and rarely unplug by 5 p.m. Prior to the research, group advising sessions were only offered during the workday, between the regular business hours of 8 a.m. to 5 p.m. and at times and locations convenient for the advisors. In 2016, the Student Center began offering group advising sessions at a variety of times, including after-hours sessions in the residence halls. The idea was to meet the students in a space and at a time conducive to their lifestyle, in other words, on their terms. More sessions were offered to accommodate as many student schedules as possible.

Given Gen Z's connection to technology, the Student Center incorporated a digital outlet into group advising. All sessions were held in a computer lab with workshop activities flowing between independent work and small group discussion. In order to combat Gen Z's characteristically short attention span, the session moved between small group discussion, PowerPoint presentation, and hands-on exercises in which the students used their computers or smartphones to complete an activity. For example, students were asked to locate their registration date within their student account and put a reminder in their phone. In previous years, advisors would begin the presentation by asking all students to put their phones away. Keeping nomophobia in mind, students were encouraged to be attentive and take notes however, they were allowed to have their phones out and in front of them; advisors incorporated the tool into group advising. The Student Center conducted assessment using Kahoot, an interactive quiz game that allowed students to answer advising questions using their phones. The workshop continued to flow between small group discussion, PowerPoint presentation, and hands-on activities utilizing technology through the first half of the workshop and breaking up the monotony by a constant change in format. The remaining half provided Gen Z students with opportunity to collaborate with their advisor and each other. Students used their computers to build class schedules while advisors walked around, engaged with students individually, answered questions, and reviewed their schedules.

Assessing Group Advising Outcomes

With college retention and graduation in mind, the Student Center established two outcomes for students who attended 2nd semester group advising in 2016. In order to promote college retention, an outcome of students registering in classes for the following term was assessed; in an effort to promote graduation, an outcome of students registering in degree-applicable classes was assessed. After the freshmen registration period, both outcomes were measured by performing schedule checks on 2nd semester group advising attendees.

Results showed that 99 percent of students attending 2nd semester group advising registered in at least 3 credits for the following term.

The Student Center then checked the classes chosen by each student to determine degree-applicability. If at least one class on their schedule was not degree-applicable, the Student Center determined that the student needed schedule changes. All students needing changes were contacted and provided assistance. Results showed that 94 percent of attendees chose the correct classes and did not need to make schedule changes, while only 4 percent of attendees needed to change at least one class on their schedule. Degree applicability of classes chosen by the remaining 2 percent was not assessed as students had declared into a different college by the time the schedule check was performed. It was determined, based on outcomes, that the 2016 2nd semester group advising sessions were successful. Because the Student Center did not have data on the previous year's outcomes, correlation between programmatic changes and outcomes could not be determined.

A Look at Retention

The Student Center looked at CLA fall to fall retention rates of incoming cohorts to determine if correlation between programmatic changes and retention occurred.

Data was acquired from the Vital Statistics application located within the University's PowerBI software. Neuroscience students were removed from the calculation, as those students were not advised by the Student

Class Registration of 2016 2nd Semester Group Advising Attendees

Registered in Classes	% of Attendees
Yes	99%
No	1%

Degree-applicability of classes chosen by 2016 2nd semester Group Advising Attendees

Needed Schedule Changes	% of Attendees
No	94%
Yes	4%
Not Assessed*	2%

*Students changed major into a different college; accuracy of classes was not assessed

College of Liberal Arts Retention Rates

Incoming Cohort	% Retained at University Fall to Fall*
Fall 2015	75%
Fall 2016	80%
Fall 2017	77%

*Data pulled from PowerBI; does not include Neuroscience

Center. Results showed a 5 percent increase in fall to fall retention from 2015 to 2016, when the new scheduling procedure and programmatic changes were implemented. Retention then fell by 3 percent from 2016 to 2017, but still finished at a rate 2 percent higher than 2015, before changes were implemented. Overall, the Student Center saw a positive impact on college retention from 2015 to 2017.

Moving Forward

The Student Center intends to incorporate their research on Gen Z students into their daily practices during individual student advising appointments. Advisors will begin the appointment by asking students what their expectations are and what they would like to accomplish, establishing collaboration between advisor and advisee. Rather than covering the degree audit in its entirety, advisors will ask students what they would like to discuss. Students will be given the option to discuss the full picture or simply the next semester to prevent loss of engagement. All signage asking students to put away their cell phones will be removed from advisor offices and students will be permitted to have their phones out during the appointments.

Overall, institutions of higher education must take the time to learn about the populations they are serving and reinvent their practices to meet the needs of each generation. Specifically for Gen Z, the importance of technology when used effectively, can draw student attention, solve communication barriers, and coordinate advising activities on campus. Academic stakeholders must strive to incorporate technology in ways that appeal to modern-day students, keeping them engaged in learning and advising process. At the same time, technology should be perceived as a tool or an outlet for creativity that supplements vital face-to-face interactions, which are still of critical value to Gen Z. To this effect, academic advisors must serve as guides and facilitators in student academic careers, assisting them across space and time by offering flexible scheduling. Lastly, students shouldn't be expected to conform to the conveniences of academic advisors; as student service professionals, it is the advisors' responsibility to offer practices and techniques that align with the learning styles and characteristics of student populations.

REFERENCES

Alt, D. Students' Wellbeing, Fear of Missing Out, and Social Media Engagement for Leisure in Higher Education Learning Environments. *Current Psychology*, vol. 37, no. 1, 2018, pp. 128–138. http://dx.doi.org/10.1007/s12144-016-9496-1.

Barker, E. "This is the Best Way to Overcome Fear of Missing Out." *Time*, June 7, 2016. http://time.com/4358140/overcome-fomo/.

Barr, C. "Who Are Generation Z? The Latest Data on Today's Teens." *The Guardian*. December 16. 2016. https://www.theguardian.com/lifeandstyle/2016/dec/10/generation-z-latest-data-teens.

Barth, D. "FOMO and the College Student: Tap Your Inner Wisdom." *Psychology Today*. September 22, 2013. https://www.psychologytoday.com/us/blog/the-couch/201309/fomo-and-the-college-student-tap-your-inner-wisdom.

Beall, G. "8 Key Differences Between Gen Z and Millennials." *Huffington Post*.

November 6, 2017. https://www.huffingtonpost.com/george-beall/8-key-differences-between_b_12814200.html.

Drake, J., Jordan, P., & Miller, M. *Academic Advising Approaches: Strategies That Teach Students to Make the Most of College.* San Francisco, CA: Jossey-Bass, 2013.

Drake, J. "The Role of Academic Advising in Student Retention and Persistence." *About Campus*, vol. 16, no. 3, 2011, pp. 8–12.

Eagan, K., Stolzenberg, E. B., Zimmerman, H. B., Aragon, M. C., Sayson, H. W., & Rios-Aguilar, C. 2017. *The American Freshman: National Norms Fall 2016.* https://www.heri.ucla.edu/monographs/TheAmericanFreshman2016.pdf.

Elmore, T. "Curing Students of Nomophobia." *The Huffington Post*, October 26, 2014. http://www.huffingtonpost.com/tim-elmore/curing-students-of-nomoph_b_5710427.html.

Elmore, T. "Nomophobia: A Rising Trend in Students." September 18, 2014. *Psychology Today.* https://www.psychologytoday.com/us/blog/artificial-maturity/201409/nomophobia-rising-trend-in-students.

Fuller, K. "Are We Allowing Social Media to Dictate Our Happiness?" *Psychology Today.* December 7, 2012. https://www.psychologytoday.com/us/blog/happiness-is-state-mind/201712/are-we-allowing-social-media-dictate-our-happiness.

Gaines, T. "Technology and Academic Advising: Student Usage and Preferences." *NACADA Journal*, vol. 34, no. 1, 2014, pp. 43–49.

Karp, M. "Tech Alone Won't Cut It." *Inside Higher Ed.* January 13, 2014. https://www.insidehighered.com/views/2014/01/13/essay-looks-how-early-warning-systems-can-better-boost-retention.

Konnikova, M. "How Facebook Makes Us Unhappy." *The New Yorker*, September 10, 2013. Retrieved from https://www.newyorker.com/tech/annals-of-technology/how-facebook-makes-us-unhappy.

Kozinsky, S. "How Generation Z is Shaping the Change in Education." *Forbes.* July 24, 2017. https://www.forbes.com/sites/sievakozinsky/2017/07/24/how-generation-z-is-shaping-the-change-in-education/#7ae25f0d6520.

Lanquist, L. "6 Potential Mental Health Benefits of Deleting Social Media." *Self.* December 29, 2017. https://www.self.com/story/does-going-on-a-social-media-cleanse-actually-do-anything-for-your-mental-health.

Lowenstein, M. "If Advising is Teaching, What do Advisors Teach?" *NACADA Journal*, vol. 25 no. 2, 2005, pp. 65–73.

Macmillan, A. "Why Instagram Is the Worst Social Media?" *Time*, May 25, 2017. http://time.com/4793331/instagram-social-media-mental-health/.

Manning-Schaffel, V. "Americans are lonelier than ever—but 'Gen Z' May Be the Loneliest." *NBC News.* (May 14, 2018). https://www.nbcnews.com/better/pop-culture/americans-are-lonelier-ever-gen-z-may-be-loneliest-ncna873101.

Patel, D. "David And Jonah Stillman: How Gen Z Will Change Your World Again." *Forbes.* May 24, 2017. https://www.forbes.com/sites/deeppatel/2017/05/24/david-and-jonah-stillman-how-gen-z-will-change-your-world-again/#6fe8d6562b86.

Ravipati, S. "Report: Tech, Creating Defining Characteristics of Gen Z Students." *The*

Journal. November 29, 2016. https://thejournal.com/articles/2016/11/29/report-tech-creating-defining-characteristic-of-gen-z-students.aspx.

Ryan, B. "Integrating Group Advising into a Comprehensive Advising Program." *Academic Advising Today, vol. 33, no. 1*, March 2010. https://www.nacada.ksu.edu/Resources/Academic-Advising-Today/View-Articles/Integrating-Group-Advising-into-a-Comprehensive-Advising-Program.aspx.

Seemiller, C., & Grace, M. *Generation Z Goes to College*. San Francisco, CA: Jossey-Bass, 2016.

PART III

Success Through Outreach

Student success in the university is not only a result of students seeking out programs, but also from programs seeking out students. The research in this section reveals that outreach programs actively seek out students who have exhibited self-help behavior. Students use multiple services to help them achieve their personal and professional goals. Various programs within the University serve the unique group of UNR students with one goal: to retain them and prepare them for graduation and beyond. The programs highlighted in this section include Deans Future Scholars, NevadaFIT, First in the Pack, TRiO Scholars, the Disability Resource Center, GradFIT, and McNair Scholars Program.

CHAPTER 9

Dean's Future Scholars

Mentoring Makes College Possible

MATT SMITH, PH.D., JAMES BEATTIE, PH.D.,
PAT MILTENBERGER, PH.D., and BILL FONG, M.A.

Matt Smith is the director of CASA/MECA at Tacoma Community College (WA) serving students facing societal and institutional barriers to college access through proactive advising, mentoring, and wraparound supports. His research interests include college success for students of color, and the dynamics of ethnicity at HBCUs. Matt holds a Ph.D. in Educational Leadership from the University of Nevada, Reno, and both a bachelor of arts in Music and a master's in Teaching from Hampton University (VA).

James Beattie is the coordinator for First in the Pack, an academic outreach program for first-generation students. The program utilizes a proactive advising approach to work with students to reach their academic, personal, and career goals. He returned to school to pursue a masters in Sociology and a Ph.D. in Educational Leadership after a successful, yet unfulfilling career in the private sector. He found his passion in higher education while developing and implementing a mentoring program for first-generation and low-income college students for the Dean's Future Scholars Program. His research interests include successful characteristics of academic outreach programs, college access, retention, and graduation for underrepresented students, as well as organizational theory.

Pat Miltenberger is the former vice president of Student Services and emeritus professor of Higher Education Leadership at the University of Nevada, Reno. Pat's career spanned over forty years at both the community college and university level. Pat began her career as an Upward Bound director which influenced her commitment and work with first-generation low-income students.

Bill Fong is the interim director of the Dean's Future Scholars program at the University of Nevada, Reno. Bill has served as a school counselor in the Washoe County School District (NV) for more than fifteen years and holds two degrees from the University of Nevada, Reno: a bachelor of arts in General Studies and a master of arts in Counseling and Educational Psychology.

Introduction

College access issues are becoming increasingly important as research indicates that equity and accessibility for first-generation and low-income (FGLI) students has been declining in America (Astin and Oseguera; Long and Riley). FGLI students often lack generalized knowledge about the college system, thus potentially creating significant barriers to college entrance and persistence. As a result, a lack of social and cultural capital can disproportionally impact FGLI student's preparation and understanding of college. Long and Riley argued that a significant barrier for low-income students "is the complexity of the college admissions process and financial aid systems, as well as a lack of accurate information about higher education costs" (41).

In addition, Long and Riley argued, "College attendance is the culmination of a series of steps and benchmarks, and this current landscape is too complex and difficult for many families to decipher and navigate" (41). This systemic challenge can lead to students believing that college is out of reach financially, becoming disenfranchised with the process, and giving up entirely. Tierney and Venegas argued that if students receive support and relevant information about academic preparation and financial aid in timely fashion "then access to a postsecondary education is likely to rise for low-income youth" (384). These findings are important because they support the argument that "existing class-based distributions of cultural capital, economic capital, and other patterns of privilege in our society is apparent in the class-based patterns of participation in our system of postsecondary education" (Paulson & St. John, 201). In other words, social capital and habitus create individual frameworks that influence student perceptions regarding college affordability and directly affect students' decisions on where, if at all, to attend post-secondary education.

Once on campus, students also need to integrate into the institutional social structures in a variety of ways, for example, employment on campus, campus housing, or engagement in campus clubs and organizations (Adelman, 1999, 2006, 2007; Astin & Sax; Bourdieu, 1983, 1988; Coleman, 1988, 1990; Conley; Long & Riley; Riley, 1997; Tinto, 1975, 1993). McSwain and Davis suggested increasing outreach programs and offering support programs that include mentoring for FGLI youth addressing study habits, course taking patterns, and the financial aspects of paying for college.

Among the many components of outreach programs designed to assist young people in their development, mentoring initiatives have proliferated. More than five thousand mentoring programs serve over three million youth across America (DuBois, Portillo, Rhodes, Silverthorn, & Valentine). Although there are at least fifty working definitions of mentoring, Crisp and Cruz's critical literature review of mentoring noted three areas of agreement between mentoring researchers:

> Mentoring relationships are focused on the growth and accomplishment of an individual . . . a mentoring experience may include broad forms of support including assistance with professional and career development . . . role modeling . . . and psychological support . . . Third, there continues to be agreement within the literature that mentoring relationships are personal and reciprocal. (528)

This reciprocity is evident within the experiences of mentors and mentees in the Dean's Future Scholars (DFS) program, as noted in their testimonials, below. As Plaskett, Bali, Nakkula, and Harris noted, "incoming students were most successful when their [peer] mentors didn't just help them meet their immediate needs but also bonded with them personally" (47). Although DFS mentoring is focused on the success of mentees, mentors also experienced growth and development through the bonds of trusting relationships built within the program.

Dean's Future Scholars

Dean's Future Scholars is an academic outreach program focused on increasing the number of first-generation, low-income students graduating from high school, accessing higher education, and entering a career in the field of education. Each year, sixth-grade students are identified from selected Title I schools throughout the Washoe County School District (WCSD) for participation ("Dean's Future Scholars [DFS]"). DFS students (mentees) are recommended for selection into the program by their sixth-grade teachers, counselors, or principals based on their academic ability and potential for success in college (Smith). DFS supports students through six integrated programs throughout middle school, high school, and college, and maintains an open-door policy where program alumni can access guidance and support long after high school or college graduation. This long-term approach fosters a "family feel," which is the secret to the program's longitudinal success. In fact, research indicated, "Student perception of DFS as a family was the cornerstone of the program and led to student growth in both social and cultural capital" (Beattie, 134). Since its inception in 2000, [more than 1100] students in WCSD have participated in the program, and the program has sparked multiple research studies. This chapter is primarily adapted from Smith's single-case study dissertation on the mentoring component of the DFS program and Beattie's dissertation on the six components of the DFS program.

In the nearly two decades since creation, DFS has evolved into six major components based on college outreach research, faculty scholarship, and available funding. These components have integrated to create an extremely successful outreach program. The program components include middle school enrichment (added in 2002); school year mentoring (2004); summer math credits (2004); summer bridge program for college credit (2006); summer internships (2006); and a safe place referred to as "The Lounge" (2007). These components moved the program from simply being a booster program (i.e., 'you can go to college') to a long-term relationship with students to provide the skills and direct assistance needed to graduate from high school, enter college, and graduate (Miltenberger et al.).

Mentoring Cornerstone

In 2002, a director was hired to oversee the program and he felt DFS needed to provide additional support as indicated by his statement:

> I didn't really feel it [conferences and the Summer Middle School Enrichment component] was changing the kids as far as getting them prepared for college. The idea of how to expand the program began with college access and completion research provided by the faculty advisor. The research indicated positive benefits of advanced high school math beyond Algebra 2 and mentoring students on college entrance requirements, financial aid, and academic preparation.

Later the same year, the University of Nevada, Reno, director of the Financial Aid Office made the director of DFS aware of the United Student Aid funds (USA funds). As a result, the Director of DFS applied for and was awarded $50,000 from USA funds. This funding enabled further expansion of the program. In 2004, the USA funds allocation enabled the director of DFS to implement two additional components. One was the School Year Mentoring component. College student employees were trained as mentors and met with program participants at their school site on a weekly basis.

Mentors provided academic advising, college admission and financial aid information, as well as emotional support. These various support systems helped build relationships between mentors and students that may have created an atmosphere and support structure conducive to academic success. Academic goal setting and other support services continued through the high school mentoring process and into college. For example, mentors worked with students to help alleviate anxiety related to often intimidating and hard to navigate college financial aid and entrance requirements. In addition, mentors focused on rigorous course selection. Finally, mentors supported students and discussed various reservations program participants may have had in regard to transitioning and attending college.

In 2010, in response to the observation that students were not persisting into their second year of college at a desired level, the director of DFS decided to provide additional mentor support for college program participants. Initially, the Dean of the College of Education had asked the DFS director to encourage program participants to utilize existing campus resources (e.g. the Center for Cultural Diversity, TRiO Student Support Services, and other related programs). The Director agreed, but also felt that DFS should provide more support, "I think we decided that some kids needed more support, more mentoring, and continued affiliation with DFS even while they are in college," (Beattie, 2013, pp. 87–88). As a result, when program participants entered college, DFS graduate assistants mentored students to help DFS students successfully transition and remain in college. College mentoring began during the summer immediately before students began their first year and persisted through college. College mentoring consisted of core curriculum advising, career planning, emotional and academic support, as well as the provision of general college information. College mentors met with program participants on a bimonthly basis for approximately one half-hour.

Amidst the many services DFS provided, the program's founder and its first two program directors noted that "[M]entoring was the cornerstone of student success through DFS. Successful mentoring relationships were built through genuine care for mentees and investment in their success personally and academically" (Smith, 2012, p. 84). Data from [in-depth, intensive] interviews with three program initiators and nine program mentors were analyzed through a constructivist grounded theory lens (Charmaz, 2006). The program initiators included the dean of the College of Education who founded the program, a white man, and the first two program directors: an Indigenous woman and a white man. Mentors included both former DFS students who completed the program and became mentors, as well as individuals who had no prior involvement in DFS and were recruited by program initiators. Of the nine mentors whose data were included in the study, five were women and four were men. Three mentors identified as Latinx, three mentors identified as Asian, one mentor identified as a Pacific Islander, another mentor identified as multi-racial, and one mentor identified as white. Four of the mentors interviewed were undergraduate students, four were graduate students, and one mentor was a post-master's working professional at the time of the study. The four undergraduates were majoring in elementary education, criminal justice, mathematics, and information systems. All four graduate students were majoring in educational leadership, and the working professional held a master's degree in educational leadership. Five of the mentors had been recruited as sixth graders and completed the entire DFS program as middle and high school students prior to becoming mentors in college. Two of the mentors interviewed joined the DFS program during their junior year of high school, and two mentors were recruited from outside the program: one initially served as a math tutor for DFS students before later becoming a mentor, and another was recruited to manage accounting for DFS and was subsequently offered a mentoring position.

The three program initiators were asked about: (a) the purpose of including a mentoring component within DFS, (b) their role in the design of the mentoring component, (c) their understanding of the influence of mentoring on mentors and mentees, and (d) their perception of whether the mentoring component should be changed. The mentors were asked about: (a) their understanding of the purpose of the mentoring component, (b) their relationships with mentees and other mentors, (c) the influence of the mentoring component on mentees and mentors, and (d) their perception of whether the mentoring component should be changed.

> When we first started there was no mentoring . . . We brought the kids on campus and they found someone who was diverse at the University who would talk to the kids and say, 'Hey, look, I went to college,' and give their life story. We'd feed them a nice lunch, and then send them home and say, 'OK—we'll see you next year.'
>
> —'Tom', former DFS program director

Although the initial consideration for hiring low-income students was a financial one—access to federal work-study funds—the seeds had been planted for what would become a key component of the mentoring program: employing students with ethnic and socioeconomic backgrounds similar to the students served by DFS. Multiple mentors recalled that they did not consider college a realistic possibility before becoming involved in DFS, and mentors also noted that this was a common perception among their mentees. The experiences that helped some participants get to college also shaped their interest in service and helping professions.

> I never would have been in college without DFS . . . Out of all my cousins, I'm one of the few that's in college. Other ones are locked up, or running around, and it's because of the DFS program [that I stayed in school].
>
> —'Tala', DFS mentor

Although far fewer DFS students became teachers than the Dean originally intended, many students altered their majors or career paths to focus on helping professions. Seven of the nine mentors interviewed directly attributed their interest in working in education-related fields to their experiences in DFS.

> I didn't even think I was going to college to be quite honest, I didn't think that I would get the money to do so, but my mentor suggested that I apply, and she said, 'You'll get in, and you'll get financial aid'... and she told me, 'You could become a mentor too!'"
>
> —Sasha', DFS mentor

As multiple mentors stated, [commitment] is a critical element in building trust with a student, and demonstrating an ethic of care:

> In order to build that trust they need to see that you're there for them on a consistent basis. What helps is that the mentors are there every single week, or at least contact the students weekly so the students know that they care, and through time, in talking to them and listening to what they have to say and giving the best advice they can, that's how you build the relationship.
>
> —'Grace', DFS mentor.

In addition to the mentor holding their mentees accountable for their commitments, the reverse is also true: mentees expect their mentors to fulfill their obligations as well, particularly given their status as role models. Multiple mentors identified this dynamic, and one mentor recalled:

> I'll be here on this day, so I expect you to be here... So I'll be checking up on your goals, and contacting them if they aren't at school, or if there are any issues... it's going good. They get motivated, but they also expect a lot. Say I get too busy with school and don't show up at the school twice a week, they'll call you out, like, "how do you expect me to do this, but you're a little behind" [laughter]...
>
> —'Miguel', DFS mentor

The initiators interviewed recalled the development of the DFS program through the constructed theme of "trusting the people". DFS began as a booster program, and expanded its scope and services based on available human and financial resources. The initiators described the program's evolution as both proactive and reactive. Initiators demonstrated proactive practices such as grant writing and aligning program activities with the research literature. Their reactive practices included taking advantage of unplanned opportunities, such as the connection to Nevadaworks grants, and implementing new ideas or techniques suggested by mentees and mentors.

The Dean trusted that the first two program directors would make decisions in the best interest of the program based on their shared vision of college access and success for students through DFS. A fluid philosophy of program development nurtured their creative process to produce the DFS model that appears to meet the needs of FGLI students. As the program developed, the initiators cultivated specific strengths, especially long-term commitments, caring mentor-mentee relationships, and hiring mentors who shared backgrounds and experiences with their mentees. Although the initial goal of producing teachers with diverse backgrounds became a lower priority, an unintended consequence was the large proportion of mentors who pursued helping professions, particularly within higher education student services.

Two major themes were constructed from the mentor interviews: "DFS changed my life", and "I want to help others". The subthemes constructed within "DFS changed my life" were "I can go to college" and "social capital."

Three subthemes were constructed within "I want to help others": "relationship building," "shared background," and "commitment." Seven of the nine mentors reflected on their experiences as both mentees and mentors within DFS. Mentors recalled positive changes in their outlook on life and maturity developed through mentoring, including gratefulness, humility, patience, and empathy. Several mentors who joined the program as mentees stated that they would not have gone to college without the support their DFS mentors provided.

The mentors noted that strong personal relationships with mentees were the key to promoting student success. Academic focus was important, but should be the second priority after consistent, caring interactions with mentees. All of the participants, including both initiators and mentors, agreed that DFS built social capital for its students, and one mentor stated that the relationships built through the program were synonymous with social capital. Mentors emphasized the need to balance the role model aspect of the relationships with the mentees' expectations of friendship, and to maintain mutual respect and accountability. Shared background, especially being a FGLI student or a person of color, were described as helpful in developing mentor-mentee relationships, but not essential. Mentoring experience was seen as more important than knowledge of textbook mentoring practices, particularly for mentors recruited from outside of DFS.

Demonstrated commitment and follow-through were also noted as crucial elements to successful mentoring: mentors indicated that both mentors and mentees held each other to high expectations, through a system of mutual accountability and reciprocity. To that end, DFS mentors demonstrated commitment through support of their students through all manner of struggles, even when students left school.

Implications for Practice

The findings suggest that the initial focus of mentors involved in educational outreach should be on building trusting relationships with their students. Their mentoring relationships should also be intentionally geared towards building their students' college-going capital, academic cultural capital, or both, depending on the program's vision and goals. Educational professionals, particularly teachers and counselors, often focus on immediate academic concerns given the constraints of time and the large number of students for whom they are typically responsible. Mentors were fortunate to work with smaller groups of students through DFS, allowing them the time to build relationships first rather than immediately focusing on academics. Indeed, DFS mentors often found that their students were reluctant to discuss academics before they had built a personal connection. After trust was established, students were more willing to utilize their mentors as resources to achieve their academic and personal goals.

Like many outreach programs, DFS has expanded beyond mentoring to provide other student services. However, participants noted that the *relationships built through mentoring were the foundation on which all other services depended.* In addition, Beattie (2013) found, "The perceived construction of family also appeared to facilitate the necessary social and cultural capital that research has indicated is necessary for college entrance and persistence" (p. 122). Thus, the mentoring relationship should remain the central focus of the program. Initiators and mentors stated that because of their trusting relationships, mentees took advantage of available opportunities and support services as advised by their mentors.

Relationship building was central to the shared vision of access and success for DFS students. Creative tension and flexibility were also hallmarks of the DFS program and are critical to the reinforcement of a shared vision (Senge, 2006). Initiators demonstrated exceptional resourcefulness through this tension, particularly related to acquiring and maximizing financial resources. The program's first mentors were Federal Work-Study (FWS) students, who both reflected the demographics of the mentees, and also provided an efficient return on investment given the federal subsidies supporting their wages and the limited financial resources available to DFS. In an environment that lacked stable state funding, initiators acquired grants through a variety of foundations, built relationships with community leaders to create opportunities, including federally funded internships, and leveraged resources from existing programs that aligned with DFS student demographics. Had the initiators only utilized existing resources and continued to operate the program with only one funded graduate assistantship and whatever volunteers and small, one-time donations could be solicited locally, it appears likely that DFS would have remained a booster program, or perhaps ceased operations.

The findings suggest that program administrators should focus first on the needs of their students, determine what it will take to meet those needs, and look beyond the tools readily available towards what may be possible through creative collaboration, risk-taking, and accessing resources in creative ways. Further, the passion and commitment to the vision demonstrated by initiators resonated with the mentors: If program managers expect to instill a passion for service in their mentors, they themselves must embrace this vision in thought, word, and deed.

The unintended consequence of mentors' interest in helping professions affirmed the original purpose of the program, in part. Although far fewer DFS students became teachers than the Dean envisioned when he created the program, the mentors themselves demonstrated the high value they placed on education, and their commitment to helping younger versions of themselves to access and succeed in college. The initiators made the conscious decision to shift from a focus on supporting future teachers from diverse backgrounds, to a broader focus on helping all eligible students' access college, regardless of their potential majors or career paths. This outcome demonstrates the need for administrators and managers to maintain patience and flexibility as programs develop. Had DFS been assessed based on the number of education majors or teachers it produced, it may not have been deemed successful, despite its positive impact on high school completion and college access for FGLI students. Program managers, and administrators assessing such programs, should prioritize creativity and flexibility. Despite climates of increased accountability and expectations of swift, measurable success in higher education, program managers should consider the best uses of their resources to support students, even if that requires reframing the goals of the program.

Initiators noted that asking for feedback from students was another important element in the program's development. Students who had been through DFS as mentees and had successfully enrolled in college advised the initiators on how the program had helped them to succeed, and how the program could be improved. Practitioners should create feedback loops to get input from program participants, both positive and constructive, to inform the development and enhancement of mentoring initiatives. Without exception, initiators and mentors agreed that the most important element in a successful mentoring relationship was genuine care and empathy for students. Mentors spoke with great passion about students they had helped, and the importance of their work in helping young people to gain access to college. As Tom noted, this intangible quality must be felt, as it cannot be quantified or empirically measured. Program managers must expect their mentors to have great empathy for the students served and should ask questions throughout the interview and selection processes that require prospective mentors to articulate their connection to the students they hope to serve, and their vision for the service their work will provide.

> DFS has changed me as a person entirely. I'm a completely different person, it's the best experience I've ever had in my life. It's been a very emotional experience, to build relationships with these kids . . . they've made me a better person, seeing how they care, and the kind of community they create, it's made me more conscious about things I do.
>
> —'Rick', DFS mentor (Smith, 2012, p. 69).

REFERENCES

Adelman, C. (1999). *Answers in the toolbox: Academic intensity, attendance patterns, and bachelor's degree attainment.* Retrieved Oct 6, 2009, from http://www.ed.go /pubs/Toolbox/index.html.

Adelman, C. (2006). *The toolbox revisited: Paths to degree completion from high school through college.* Washington, DC: U.S. Department of Education.

Adleman, C. (2007). Do we really have a college access problem? *Change, 39*(4), 48–51.

Astin, A. W., & Oseguera. L. (2004). The declining "equity" of American education. *The Review of Higher Education,27* (3), 321–341.

Astin, A. W., & Sax L. J. (1998). How undergraduates are affected by service participation. *Journal of College Student Development, 29*(3), 251–263.

Beattie, J. (2013). *A case study of college persistence for the Dean's Future Scholars program.* (Doctoral Dissertation). Retrieved from ProQuest Dissertations and Theses database. (UMI No. 3595626).

Bourdieu, P. (1983). Forms of capital. In John G. Richardson, *Handbook of theory and research for the sociology of education*, (pp. 241–258). New York: Greenwood Press.

Bourdieu, P. (1988). *Homo Academicus.* Stanford, CA: Stanford University Press.

Coleman, J. S., (1988). Social capital in the creation of human capital. *The American journal of sociology, 94*(1), S95-S120.

Coleman J. S. (1990). *Foundations of Social Theory.* Cambridge, MA: Harvard Univ. Press.

Conley, D. T. (2005). *College knowledge: What it really takes for students to succeed and what we can do to get them ready.* San Francisco, CA: Jossey-Bass.

Charmaz, K. (2006). *Constructing grounded theory: A practical guide through qualitative analysis.* Thousand Oaks, CA: Sage.

Crisp, G., & Cruz, I. (2009). Mentoring college students: A critical review of the literature between 1990 and 2007. *Research in Higher Education, 50*(6), 525–545.

Dean's Future Scholars (n.d.). Retrieved from https://www.unr.edu/education/centers-student-resources/centers/deans-future-scholars.

DuBois, D. L., Portillo, N., Rhodes, J. E., Silverthorn, N., and Valentine, J. C. (2011). How effective are mentoring programs for youth?: A systematic assessment of the evidence. *Psychological Science in the Public Interest,12*(2), 57–91.

Fong, W. (2019). [Retention and completion data for mentors and non-mentors in the Dean's Future Scholars program]. Unpublished raw data.

Long, B. T., & Riley, E. (2007). Financial aid: A broken bridge to college access? *Harvard Educational Review, 77*(1), 39–63.

Mcswain, C., & Davis, R. (2007). *College access for the working poor: overcoming burdens to succeed in higher education.* Retrieved from: http://ryanjdavis.net/control/uploads/College_Access_for_the_Working_Poor_2007_Report.pdf.

Miltenberger, P., Beattie, J., & Smith, M. J. (2019). Dean's Future Scholars: Lessons learned in the evolution of a pre-collegiate outreach program based in an academic college. In M. Choroszy & T. Meek (Eds.), *Hopes and dreams: Access and opportunity services, research, and stories from the University of Nevada, Reno* (pp. 13–22). Reno: University of Nevada Press.

Paulsen, M. B. & ST. John, E. P. (2002) Social class and college costs: examining the nexus between college choice and persistence. *Journal of Higher Education 73*(2)189–236.

Plaskett, S., Bali, D., Nakkula, M. J., & Harris, J. (2018). Peer mentoring to support first generation low-income college students. *Phi Delta Kappan, 99*(7), 47–51. Retrieved from https://doi.org/10.1177/0031721718767861.

Riley, R. W. (1997). In math and college-going, middle school makes all the difference. *Middle School Journal,29*(2), 3–7.

Senge, P. (2006). *The fifth discipline: The art and practice of the learning organization.* New York: Doubleday.

Smith, M. J. (2012). *Mentoring and mental models: Outreach to first-generation, low-income students.* (Doctoral Dissertation). Retrieved from ProQuest Dissertations and Theses database. (UMI No. 3550285).

Tierny, W., Venegas, K., (2009). Finding money on the table: information, financial aid, and access to college. *80*(4), 363–388.

Tinto, V., (1975). Dropout from higher education: a theoretical synthesis of recent research. *Review of educational research* 45(1) 89–125.

Tinto, V. (1993). *Leaving college: Rethinking the causes and cures of student attrition* (2nd ed.). Chicago, IL: University of Chicago Press.

CHAPTER 10

NevadaFIT Academic Bootcamps

A Recipe for Student Success

FELICIA DEWALD, M.A., M.F.A.

Felicia DeWald M.A., M.F.A. is the director of NevadaFIT, Bootcamps for Academic Success for the Office of the Provost at the University of Nevada, Reno. She earned her bachelor's degree in English Literature from the University of Notre Dame followed by a master's degree in Teaching from Santa Clara University, and a master of fine arts degree in Fiction Writing from Saint Mary's College of California. She taught secondary education for six years before transitioning to the University. She applies this experience to NevadaFIT to help students smoothly make the transition from high school to college.

Introduction

What is the perfect picture of student success? Graduation, of course. Monica Vega is the final product. As a graduate of the University of Nevada, Reno (UNR), she is completing her second Master's degree, while working for the NevadaFIT program. Her success story is one we plan for many of our students. However, researchers from Georgetown University's Center on Education and the Workforce estimate that over one-third of top high school students do not complete a college degree. Most of these students will *start* a college degree and assume a significant amount of debt in the process, not to mention the loss in wages by working jobs that do not require university degrees. These statistics are not limited to certain class or race demographics ("Over 500,000 Top-Scoring Students Fail to Complete a Postsecondary Cre," 2018). Many universities offer interventions for students after they experience setbacks but often it is too late. Early challenges students face in their first year of college can lead to diminished confidence, a rash change in major, or, worse, dropping out entirely. The transition from high school to college is difficult for every student in their own, unique way. UNR seeks to prepare all students for this transition

before the semester officially begins with an academic bootcamp program called NevadaFIT. This recipe may be simpler than it first appears.
Prep Time: One Week
Cook Time: 4 Years
Yield: Infinite Possibilities

Description

The transition from high school to college is marked by a brand-new set of obstacles for students. Monica Vega started her studies at UNR in 2011, two years before the NevadaFIT program began on campus. Her transition from high school to college was not an easy one:

> Being a college student is challenging enough but being a first-generation college student is added pressure. I remember coming into college feeling scared, semi-prepared, and nervous. As my first year progressed, I realized the biology major I had chosen was an expectation set by my family. I was a straight-A student in high school and my parents figured college would be just as easy for me. They wanted to have a doctor in the family. There were moments I really struggled and having to manage two jobs, classes, assignments, and familial expectations overwhelmed me. I did not feel prepared enough. I was in remedial courses. If only someone had given me some insight about college expectations, maybe my first year would have been more exciting. I always pictured college to be like the movies. No one in my family had any college experience, so I was left on my own to figure it out.

Monica's perspective is not unlike many others. She persisted despite these challenges, which, unfortunately, is not always the case. College academics are different than high school academics. The pacing and rigor of a college course is accelerated, a semester-long college course equates to a year-long high school course, and some students will struggle in school for the first time. Students who never had to study in high school will realize they need study techniques to grasp the content of their college courses. Many students need to utilize the resources at their disposal and understand that it is not a weakness to seek support. Additional obstacles include social and personal challenges: students may struggle to make new friends, or get enough sleep, or cook for themselves. Students may experience homesickness, or anxiety and depression, or frequent illness while living in close proximity to classmates in the dorms. It is often not enough to tell students how to be successful in college through information sessions, but to allow them to experience these obstacles first-hand so that they know how to overcome them when the school year officially begins. NevadaFIT places students out of their comfort zones and directly into the realities they will face as college students. Though only a week-long program, NevadaFIT has a remarkable impact on participants from their first semester all the way through graduation.

NevadaFIT academic bootcamps are designed to increase student success by exposing them to college prior to the start of the semester. FIT stands for 'Freshman Intensive Transition,' and is open to all incoming freshmen students from every major. Students move into the dorms a week early, attend classes, are assigned homework, and take exams in a low-stakes environment since students are not assigned a letter grade. Students receive feedback on their work and earn one-credit pass/fail. The benefits of doing NevadaFIT can be seen inside and outside the classroom, but our measurable success statistics, GPA and retention, are notably impacted. NevadaFIT participants have a higher average GPA and a 6–8 percent higher fall-to-fall retention rate compared to non-participants. Minority students, Pell students, and first-generation students also show increased retention rates that exceed the institutional average. To put the magnitude of this impact into perspective, if the entire freshman class of 3,600 were to participate in NevadaFIT, about 250 more students would be retained every year if NevadaFIT retention statistics remain the same. Due to its continued success, the program grows every year. In its first year, NevadaFIT 2013 had forty eight participants (less than 2 percent of the freshman class), NevadaFIT 2018 had 1,600 participants (45 percent of the freshman class), and NevadaFIT 2019 expects to have about 2,700 participants (77 percent of the freshman class). By 2020, NevadaFIT may be mandatory for all incoming freshmen.

Ingredients: From Summer Bridge Programs to Biology Camps

A pre-semester classroom experience is not a new concept. Summer bridge programs have been utilized on many campuses across the country, but most serve a specific population, usually at-risk students. Often these programs focus on remediation rather than college-level coursework and can make students feel singled out. Instead, the NevadaFIT bootcamp model stems from the discipline-specific BIOS program at Louisiana State University (LSU), which is exclusively for biology majors. Similar to NevadaFIT, freshmen biology majors attend a week-long pre-semester program. Students attend nine lectures in Introductory Biology and take three examinations over the course of a week. LSU's Introductory Biology course has a high DFW rate (Grade of D, F or Withdrawal) due to a lack of understanding of course expectations. With early exposure to this class through the BIOS program, students are not only more likely to pass their Intro to Biology course, but BIOS students are also more likely to stay in their major and to graduate in four years (Wischusen, Wischusen, & Pomarico, 2011). The University executive vice president and provost brought his experience with BIOS as dean of the College of Science at LSU to UNR, and in 2013, teamed up with the dean and an academic advisor of the College of Science to start the first program at UNR called BioFIT. A group of 48 randomly selected biology students were placed into the program in its first year, which allowed us to compare this cohort with a group of students of equal size that applied and did not get into the program. When the program proved to be successful in its first year at UNR, most colleges rolled out their first version of the program in 2014.

While many universities have replicated the BIOS concept for Science students, the University of Nevada, Reno is the first to translate the academic bootcamp model to every discipline. All eight colleges at the University offer an academic bootcamp for freshmen with its own clever play on the program name: Biz-FIT (College of Business), E-FIT (College of Engineering), LiberalArtsFIT (College of Liberal Arts), FIT2Care (College of Education), HealthFIT (College of Health Science), J-FIT (Reynolds School of Journalism), CABNRFIT (College of Agriculture, Biotechnology and Natural Resources), and ScienceFIT (College of Science). Though the basic components of the bootcamps are the same, the way a college chooses to approach the curriculum is unique to each camp.

Procedure

1. Prepare the Tools: Skill Sessions

Students attend Skill Sessions to learn tools to increase success, such as financial literacy, note-taking skills, fitness classes, mindfulness workshops, and diversity and inclusion discussions. Students are not only introduced to the Tutoring Center, Math Center, Writing Center, and Library but they are given assignments and asked to *use* these resources during NevadaFIT week. Survey feedback from a student who later visited the Math Center during the semester indicates that students are more likely to seek out these resources after having used them during NevadaFIT:

> I love the math center! I have never gone to a tutor for math help before, but I had to during NevadaFIT week and I finally understand how helpful and not embarrassing it is to go and just ask some questions to make sure I really know what's going on in math class. Thank you!

2. Combine Ingredients: "Pack" Groups

NevadaFIT students work in groups of six called "Packs" with an upperclassmen mentor who is an academic and social role model. This mentor attends classes with their mentees, shares personal experiences, offers advice, leads group discussions, and organizes study sessions. Participants often establish close bonds with their Pack groups, and it is no surprise that these relationships persist after NevadaFIT ends. One Pack group meets for dinners periodically throughout the school year. NevadaFIT has now become ingrained in the culture that is the UNR experience. A College of Education student, FIT2Care participant, and three-time mentor who has been involved in the program every year of her undergraduate career highlights her involvement:

> I decided to become a NevadaFIT mentor because I enjoyed NevadaFIT as a mentee and had become friends with a lot of the people involved with the program. I thought it was a great way to spread the knowledge I gained as a freshman and make a few extra dollars for textbooks. The most rewarding part of being a NevadaFIT mentor was seeing how confident my pack was when they presented their end of the week presentations. They had grown so much in just five days' time, and I could not believe that I had been a part of it.

3. Make the "Secret Sauce": Core Classes

The College of Science was the first to roll out the program in 2013 with a series of biology lectures that mimicked BIOS. In 2014, when most of the colleges first started their bootcamp, there were very little guidelines and the programs ultimately ended up being less successful than BioFIT. GPA and retention data for the colleges new to the program was not statistically significant.

Math was discovered to be the "secret sauce" for most colleges, doing what biology classes did for many science majors. Most did not have a class that was both real (lecture, homework and exam format mimics the school year) and relevant (it is a class they will take in their first year). When Institutional Analysis did a study on what class common to all freshmen might meet these parameters, math consistently came up as a class that many students struggle in across disciplines. In 2015 when most camps incorporated math into their daily schedules, retention and GPAs spiked. NevadaFIT 2016 seemed to produce the best data of the program so far, when all colleges except for Science used math as their core class. Not only did adding the math component seem to spike overall GPA and retention, but it also had a remarkable influence on Math GPAs, notably with some of the top students in the highest levels of Math. The average math class GPA increase for NevadaFIT participants across all math courses is +.52. "The session that contributed most to my learning was Calculus because it gave me an idea of the pacing and work associated with a college level math class."—NevadaFIT student

4. Add Flavor as Desired: Major-Specific Sessions

Each college supplements this material with their own discipline-specific content. For example, College of Engineering students attend lectures on aerodynamics and projectile motion and work in their Pack groups to build a trebuchet launching device for a competition at the end of the week. College of Business students attend lectures on professionalism, economics, accounting, and marketing, and develop a product in Pack groups to pitch to a panel of judges in a *Shark Tank* styled competition. Early exposure to their majors helps students get excited about college, discern whether their major is for them earlier on, learn what it takes to do well in their majors' classes, meet higher-level faculty they might not ordinarily get to meet until well into their degree, and hopefully inspire passion for their studies before they embark on their first semester classes, which are quite often core classes outside of their major. For some students, they learn that the major is not for them, which is just as valuable of a revelation so that they don't take classes that won't eventually count towards degree

Cohort	Graduation Rates NevadaFIT	Non-NevadaFIT	NevadaFIT Effect
Fall 13-4yr	42%	32%	10%
Fall 13-"5yr"	67%	55%**	12%
Fall 13-5yr	42%	32%	10%
Fall 13-6yr	71%	58%	13%
Fall 14-4yr	45%	36%	9%
Fall 14-5yr	50%	44%	6%

** 55% is the UNR 6-yr graduation rate. Thus NevadaFIT participants are graduating at a higher rate in 5 years than the average UNR student does in 6 years.

completion. One E-FIT participant wrote about the major specific components in survey:

> I enjoyed meeting other engineers before the start of the school year during E-FIT. I was pleasantly surprised by the lessons provided in finance, engineering principles, and self-awareness. They have helped me monitor my credit and spending, consider time, cost, and quality in production, and gain a deeper understanding of my own morals and decision-making process. I was also thoroughly impressed by the presentation given by the Mechanical Engineer with the 3.97 GPA. It gave me an idea of how seriously to take classes and how to study.

Nutritional Information: Graduation Data

Could a one-week program, four years down the line, really continue to spike student outcomes? The answer is an overwhelming yes. NevadaFIT participants not only have higher GPAs and increased retention in their first year of college, but they are more likely to graduate. Even the Fall 2014 cohort which faced some initial challenges and less impressive first semester data, still experienced an increase in graduation rates.

Why is NevadaFIT so impactful for every type of student? The material in and of itself helps students to plan accordingly for their semester. For example, after experiencing several lectures, homework assignments, and an exam in Math, students are more likely to complete the 'optional' homework assignments to adequately prepare for the midterm when the semester starts. After having used the Tutoring Center during NevadaFIT, students do not hesitate to seek out this support during the school year. However, some of the benefits of NevadaFIT are difficult to measure and contribute just as much to student success as formalized sessions. Even if students arrive to college with friends from high school, after NevadaFIT they now know people in their major that will be in the classroom with them the next week when school starts, and who they can study with and form brand new friendships. They now know upperclassmen mentors they can reach out to for guidance and support. Similarly, students are able to get to know faculty outside the classroom. Ice cream socials, faculty panels, and department meals allow students to interact with professors in a less-intimidating atmosphere and help students to feel comfortable reaching out to their professors during office hours. The social aspects of NevadaFIT increase the likelihood that students will feel part of the Wolf Pack family. Retention and GPAs are indirectly impacted because students are more likely to continue their degree if they feel connections to the people and the place, and students will be able to keep their grades higher because they are more comfortable seeking out student resources and asking for help. NevadaFIT may very well be a recipe for student success.

Monica Vega's experience working for the NevadaFIT program has allowed her to look at her first year of college with a new perspective.

I look back and wish I would have participated in such an extraordinary program. I would have quickly figured out that biology was not my passion instead of wasting an entire year in a major I did not like. I could have received an elective credit that usually takes an entire semester to receive. There is the academic aspect of NevadaFIT, but also the social aspect which is invaluable. I felt so lonely my first year. I was never involved because I had other obligations outside of college, but if I had gone through NevadaFIT, I would have had a pack mentor and group that I could socialize with from day one. NevadaFIT shows students how to be successful college students, which is the greatest benefit of all.

Students are grateful and proud when they complete NevadaFIT, wearing their "I Survived NevadaFIT" swag proudly. They have already accomplished a mini college and now not only know what it takes to succeed, but they know they can do it. Student success often starts with the student's own perception. If they see that they can succeed, they will.

REFERENCES

PRWeb, Georgetown University Center on Education and the Workforce. (2018, January 17). *Over 500,000 Top-Scoring Students Fail to Complete a Postsecondary Credential Every Year, Says Georgetown University Research* [Press release]. Retrieved from http://www.prweb.com/pdfdownload/15094508.pdf.

Wischusen, S. M., Wischusen, E. W., & Pomarico, S. M. (2011). Impact of a Short Pre-Freshman Program on Retention. *Journal of College Student Retention: Research, Theory & Practice,12*(4), 429–441.

CHAPTER 11

Closing the Achievement Gap with Nevada First in the Pack

DESIRAE ACOSTA, M.A.

Desirae Acosta is an alumna-practitioner at the University of Nevada, Reno, working in the Academic Opportunity and Support Programs office, where she works with first-generation students, focusing on their transition to college and assisting them in overcoming challenges they may face.

First in the Pack (FITP) is a first-generation academic outreach support program originally designed in 2014 to supplement existing federally funded first-generation support programs at the University of Nevada, Reno. Since its creation, the program has maintained positive outcomes and increased the number of students and amount of time students are served.

The first-year, first-generation student population enrolled at the University of Nevada, Reno has a range of academic, financial, and social barriers that can result in lower graduation rates compared with their peers whose parents completed a college education (Ishitani, 2003). For the past five years, according to UNR Institutional Analysis and the Office of Student Persistence and Research, one-third of the University's entering freshmen class have been first in their family to attend college. The Office of Student Persistence and Research found that there is a 73 percent fall-to-fall retention of first-year, first-generation students at the University which is consistently positively impacted by the increase of students served through support programs, including First in the Pack.

For over sixty years, TRIO programs has successfully supported of first-generation students through the Student Services division at UNR. With Upward Bound being a pre-college program and McNair Scholars being graduate school and research preparation program, TRIO Student Success Services (TRIO SSS) was the only program in Student Services that supported first-generation students through the day-to-day challenges *while* they were students at the University. TRIO SSS has a limiting capacity of 175 students, so First in the Pack was established in 2014 to serve the expansive population of first-generation freshmen at the University. The program is modeled after TRIO SSS, designed to help first-generation college students succeed in persisting in their college experience. In order to be eligible for the program, students must be first-generation, first-time freshmen, and enrolled full-time. For the purposes of this program, a student is considered first-generation if neither parent obtained a bachelor's degree in the United States. It is important to note that because FITP is not a federally funded program, it is the only first-generation student support program in Student Services that does not require U.S. citizenship.

While the full-time enrollment is considered twelve credits, over the past four years over 75 percent of students in FITP attempted and completed fifteen credits each semester. This aligns with the Complete College America 15-to-Finish initiative, leading students to graduate in four years (Complete College America, 2018). While there is no financial need requirement, the majority of FITP students have financial challenges, as more than 60 percent of participants receive Pell grants.

First in the Pack has a track record of improving student outcomes by helping retain first-generation students through one-on-one coaching that focuses on academic support and professional development. Services provided by First in the Pack include academic advising, career counseling, and peer support.

The program has evolved from a budget of $25,000 to pay a graduate student to assist this population into the very robust program that encompasses a wholistic approach to student success. It is funded by state dollars and received a significant funding boost last year when the Nevada Board of Regent's approved allocation of $500,000 in investment income for mentor programs for targeted student populations. The First in the Pack staff now consists of a full-time coordinator, two graduate students, and three undergraduate students all of whom serve as academic coaches to students in the program. The academic coaches are a key component of the program. They meet with each student every two weeks and cover a wide range of topics that impact student success in and out of the classroom. The training for academic coaches is extensive and geared specifically toward topics and skills that will help first-generation students succeed.

With 90 percent of FITP participants being from Nevada and 80 percent identifying as students of color, the coaching relationship and relatability to students is paramount. With the growth of staff in First in the Pack, freshmen were able to continue to participate in the program their sophomore year, as such, the ongoing relationship with the students and academic coach develops a deep and consistent support.

One-on-one meetings with students follow a curriculum that correlates with the University calendar with a foci in academics, professional development, and personal growth. An increase in students served resulted in a need to shift the way meetings were organized. Not only were paper files taking up a lot of space, it was also more challenging to manage with meetings taking place in areas outside of the FITP office. This led to shift the curriculum and updates to one medium, the University's online learning platform, WebCampus. Connecting with students on WebCampus puts FITP in the same space as their classes, engaging students where they are on a medium they utilize often. Utilizing an online system allows students to constantly access resources, refer back to files used in meetings, and communicate directly with First in the Pack staff. In addition to being convenient for students, it is also a more efficient way for staff to measure student participation and follow up with students who have not been active.

Another effort that allows coaches to follow up with students is progress reports. Coaches use the academic progress reports in the middle of the semester to assess how students are performing in class. The report gives the student and the coach an idea of how they are doing in the class at a point in the semester when there is still time to intervene. Reviewing progress reports with students before the University drop date for classes is crucial in ensuring students maintain financial aid eligibility, and utilize resources they were not inclined to seek before. Progress reports are disseminated using the Student Success Collaborative (SSC), which is a system through the Education Advisory Board that links administrators, faculty, advisors, and staff to support students (EAB, n.d.). SSC has expanded FITP's reach to professors and instructors ensuring that they receive notification and access to progress reports via email, rather than using printed copies. The convenience of filling out an online form increases the amount of completed progress reports received. The candid feedback about performance and attendance allows coaches to have effective conversations with students that revisit time management, study skills, and resources available in campus that they may not have considered using before.

In addition to academic success, career readiness is a major pillar in the FITP curriculum. Student meetings include resume building and revisions, social media professionalism, email etiquette, and the importance of pre-professional experience. Each spring FITP has hosted a Professional Development Day that informs and inspires students to pursue not only their degree, but experience that will prepare them for a career they want. The event includes a presentation on developing an "elevator speech" for networking events, as well as how to network with food. Keynote speakers were invited to encourage students that included the University Dean of Students and the state of Nevada's Lieutenant Governor. Following the presentations, students go into a room designated based on their individual colleges. Each room has a panel of professionals that earned their degree in that specific college. Successful graduates who were first in their family to attend college are powerful role models, so the panelists that take the time to share their experience with students is impactful. After the panel students and professionals enjoy lunch together. This allows students to practice networking with food, as well as ask any follow up questions they may have after the panel. Students indicated that life revelations, shadowing opportunities, and internships have come from this event alone (personal interactions). The clarity and confidence many students receive after the development day created momentum that encouraged them to attend other networking opportunities and career fairs throughout the University and community (personal communication).

Although the program serves students for only the first two years of their college experience, with a wholistic approach to academics, professional development, and personal growth, the support and skills provided to students can equip them to persist and graduate. When the program began, the fall to fall persistence rate of the 2014 cohort was 77 percent. The latest 2018 cohort's fall to fall retention rate was an impressive 99 percent. With improving persistence rates, FITP is a promising program with goals to continue supporting first-generation students at the University.

For more information about University of Nevada, Reno student data:

- University of Nevada Reno (UNR) Institutional Analysis: www.unr.edu/ia
- University of Nevada Reno (UNR) Office of Student Persistence and Research: www.unr.edu/student-services/resources-and-downloads/persistence-research

REFERENCES

Complete College America. (2018). 15 to finish. Retrieved from https://completecollege.org/strategy/15-to-finish/.

EAB. (n.d.). The Student Success Collaborative: Navigate for Four-Year Institutions. Retrieved from https://eab.com/products/navigate-for-four-year-institutions/.

Ishitani, T. T. (2003). A longitudinal approach to assessing attrition behavior among first-generation students: Time-varying effects of pre-college characteristics. *Research in Higher Education, 44*(4), 433–449. doi:http://dx.doi.org.unr.idm.oclc.org/10.1023/A:1024284932709.

University of Nevada Reno (UNR). (n.d.). *Institutional analysis.* Retrieved from https://www.unr.edu/ia.

CHAPTER 12

The Trio Scholars Program

Addressing the Needs of Low-Income, First-Generation College Students Using a Three-Pronged Approach

DANIEL M. VALLE, PH.D., and CHRISTOPHER WESTIN, M.A.

Daniel M Valle, Ph.D. is the current associate director for the TRiO Scholars Program at the University Of Nevada, Reno(UNR). He has spent most of his professional career in secondary education and higher education. He graduated from the University of Oregon with a degree in Ethnic Studies. He then went on to teach in Baltimore City public schools, where he earned a master's degree in Teaching from The Johns Hopkins University. He later earned another master's degree in International Management from Whitworth University in eastern Washington, where he studied organizational behavior and worked for various non-profits. He moved to the Reno area in the winter of 2006 and began teaching in the Washoe County School District for six years. In the fall of 2012 he became the assistant director of the TRiO Scholars Program at UNR, and later was promoted to associate director.

Chris Westin M.A. is the counselor for the TRiO Scholars Program at the University of Nevada, Reno. He has functioned in this capacity for nearly seven years. His professional career has revolved solely around serving first-generation college students and is dedicated to providing support to them. Chris earned his bachelor's degree in Psychology and his master's degree in Counseling at the University of Nevada, Reno.

Introduction

Students who identify as first-generation (FG) college student—and come from low socioeconomic backgrounds (low SES)— are subject to the same stresses that all incoming students deal with on a college campus. However, they also face academic, social, and class barriers based on their background and first-generation status. According to Moschetti et al. (2015)

first-generation students tend to be concentrated in community colleges; are more likely to have a low family income; have lower degree aspirations; report less support and encouragement from family to attend college; and have more difficult adjustment periods. Furthermore, the authors contend that low-income, first-generation college students consistently drop out of postsecondary institutions at higher rates than their middle- and upper-income peers who have college educated parents. As an increased number of low-income, first-generation students (LIFG) enroll in postsecondary institutions, these schools are ill-prepared for creating environments to address the issues of these diverse populations (Unverferth, 2012). Foreshadowing some of these needs, TRiO programs were established.

Nationally, TRiO programs are outreach and student services programs designed to identify and provide services for individuals from disadvantaged backgrounds. Historically, the term "TRiO" comes from the first three education opportunity programs that were created: Educational Talent Search, Upward Bound, and Student Support Services. Born out of President Lyndon Johnson's War on Poverty and the Economic Opportunity Act of 1964, the primary goal of TRiO Programs is to provide equal educational opportunities for all U.S. citizens by increasing college readiness and developing higher education aspirations among students from low-income, first-generation college, and ethnic/racial minority backgrounds (Pitre & Pitre, 2009).

Problem

Many of the problems faced by LIFG students were outlined in Access for All (2018) chapter eleven. Unfortunately, many of these problems start in the home, where parents are expected to lay the foundation for a prosperous academic future for their children. Underserved student populations, especially those who are low income or first generation, have a harder time overcoming some of the obstacles to succeed in higher educatio—some of which is due to the student's family members (Forbus et al., 2011; Martinez, 2003; Yeh, 2010). Yeh (2010), for example, discusses the influence families have on LIFG students. She stated, "students from low-income backgrounds whose parents never attended college are less likely to possess the kinds of cultural and social capital valued in higher education institutions, and thus will encounter greater barriers to academic achievement and success" (p. 52). Unfortunately, this is a result of a family history that is void of any sort of experiences in higher education. Harackiewicz et al. (2014) expanded upon this, suggesting that parental education is considered a proxy for social class or socioeconomic status. The authors contended that the more educated the parents are, the higher the socioeconomic status (Harackiewicz et al., 2014) but too many abandon this goal because they struggle in introductory biology. Interventions have been developed to close achievement gaps for underrepresented minority students and women, but no prior research has attempted to close the gap for 1st-generation students, a population that accounts for nearly a 5th of college students. We report a values affirmation intervention conducted with 798 U.S. students (154 first-generation). According to the authors, the opposite is also true. First-generation students often find themselves in a different social class from their continued-education peers. As LIFG students try to bridge the social gap between themselves and their continued-education peers, they find themselves trying to adjust to college life and are in need of guidance and mentorship that will help them acquire the necessary resources and skills needed to succeed in higher education.

Program

The TRiO Scholars Program at the University Of Nevada, Reno is a federally-funded Student Support Services program housed in the Pennington Student Achievement Center. At any given point throughout the academic year, the program serves over 175 active participants. One of five support programs housed in the Academic and Opportunity Support Programs (AOSP) at UNR, the philosophy of the TRiO Scholars Program (or "TRiO," as it is commonly known around campus) stems from the idea that students from all socioeconomic levels should have equal opportunity to obtain a post-secondary education.

Some of the core values of the program include fierce advocacy for social justice in higher education, creating a safety net for our University's most vulnerable students, as well as respecting our diverse student population, their needs, and their cultural heritage. TRiO is rooted in its mission to assist low-income, first-generation students to overcome the cultural, academic, class, and social barriers to success in higher education. It is with this mission in mind that TRiO provides to its participants a myriad of services and resources. Students meet with a TRiO Coach to discuss academic planning, advising, and progress. Peer mentors are assigned to first and second-year students, ensuring that they have someone who can speak to them at their level and who has most recently experienced some of the same struggles and successes. Help with financial aid documents is provided to program participants—how to interpret them, complete the necessary paperwork, and work on verification forms, for those students who were selected. Workshops are also provided to students, from graduate school preparation to finding ways to study abroad. In addition, there are multiple ways for students to be engaged in the campus and surrounding community, either through volunteer projects or social events. Lastly, TRiO provides three services that will be discussed at length in the following section: soft skills, intrusive advising, and relationship building.

Impact

The purpose of most academic mentor programs is to assist students in acclimating to the academic and social culture of the institution (Smith, 2007). According to Smith (2007) underrepresented students, many of which identify as first-generation students, generally have less access to informal networks with faculty and administrators who tend to be primarily white, middle-class males. What's more, Smith notes that students who experience alienation from faculty and administrators on campus are then less likely to utilize other academic support services (i.e. tutoring centers, writing centers, STEM help centers) that could have a positive impact on their academic careers. It is with this research in mind that the TRiO Scholars Program has invested so much in its three-pronged approach.

Three-Pronged Approach

As the research suggests, the implications of first-generation students goes beyond the financial burdens of pursuing a college degree. The magnitude of these challenges vary from student to student. The TRiO Scholars program at the University of Nevada, Reno uses a three-pronged approach to address these obstacles. This approach is rooted in empirical research that supports best practices within the field. The three core values of this approach are rapport building, pedagogy of non-cognitive skills, and the art of proactive (intrusive) advising (Escher, 2010).

Building rapport with individual students is the initial step. This is the foundation of the process. TRiO staff members work diligently to build a strong rapport with students beginning with the application process and continuing throughout the student's tenure on campus. There is an understanding that the more comfortable the student is with the staff member and the program, the more open the student will be with utilizing available resources. The goal of building a strong and genuine relationships with students is to build a sense of trust and thus allowing students to become more open-minded to new ideas and develop a willingness to challenge past behaviors. Building rapport begins with a sincere curiosity from the staff members. With the use of motivational interviewing, self-disclosure, humor, and demonstrating genuine acceptance, staff members create a non-judgmental environment where students are free to discuss issues ranging from personal struggles to academic achievements. Dr. Christian Conte (2013) states that by genuinely trying to gain a better understanding of an individual without judgement, that person will be more open to sharing about themselves and more likely to contemplate change. In order to provide the type of attention needed to build such rapport, TRiO uses a coaching model that assigns students to a specific academic coach. This TRiO Coach is one of three faculty members working for the program. In addition, as outlined earlier, first and second-year participant are also paired up with a peer mentor.

Once a strong connection is created and the students have a sense of belonging, the next focus is to educate the students on essential non-cognitive skills. The term non-cognitive skills refers to a pattern of thoughts, feelings, behaviors, and attitudes such as motivation, perseverance, and self-control (Borghans et al., 2008). One vehicle in which these non-cognitive skills are delivered to students is through a first-year experience course titled ACE 110. The curriculum of this course revolves around eight essential non-cognitive skills: personal responsibility, self-motivation, self-management, interdependence, self-awareness, lifelong learning, emotional intelligence, and belief in oneself (Downing, 2017). Exploring these skills from a first-generation lens allows students to realize what challenges may lie ahead and give them the tools and confidence to persist in higher education—where others like them may have not. Outside the ACE 110 course the TRiO staff intentionally interweaves these non-cognitive skills with the practical skills of navigating the college system throughout the interactions with the student.

First-generation students are the ones in their families who are breaking the cycle when in regards to higher education. It would not be a stretch to suggest that these students are academic innovators, bucking current trends and data which suggest they may neither choose to pursue or successfully obtain a post-secondary degree. As innovators, it is difficult to know what questions to ask or how to specifically identify academic, social, and financial needs on a college campus. With this in mind, we intentionally approach students using the proactive (intrusive) advising method by engaging students regularly to identify issues before they occur, deliberately intervene when needed, genuinely show an interest in the students, and respect the student's autonomy while providing education on all options available and likely outcomes (Varney, 2012). With the proactive approach, staff members create an environment in which it fosters curiosity and allows students to critically think about their current situation and become more engaged in the coaching process. This approach is supported by research on student engagement and retention. Di Maria (2006) suggests that students learn, persist, and graduate at higher rates when engaged on a college campus. Proactive advising helps student develop the tools to think for themselves and identify strategies to navigate the college system interdependently.

Outcomes

The TRiO Scholars program completes an annual progress report (APR) in order to track the program's progress towards meeting the objectives of the grant. Each year we measure retention, academic standing, and graduation rates of the participants among other measurements. In the 2017–2018 academic year the program attained a 99 percent fall-to-fall persistence rate. This is 33 percent higher compared to colleges and universities in the state of Nevada. The University of Nevada has a 60.7 percent graduation rate. By contrast, the TRiO Scholars Program reported a 72 percent graduation rate in the 2017–2018 academic year. Furthermore, 98 percent of the participants were considered to be in "good academic standing" as defined by the institution. In addition to the APR data collected, the staff continually evaluates the program by gathering qualitative data from participants. Countless participants expressed their appreciation for the program and the services provided. For instance, Adriana (student names have been changed in order to maintain confidentiality) shared her thoughts about her experience this way:

> Without this program, I sincerely believe that I would have

> struggled to find my footing during my first year in university, and this would have ultimately led to my failure. Through TRiO I have had access to various resources that have helped me do as well in school as I have done so far, while maintaining a level head and not succumbing to the stress that comes with having two majors.

Many TRiO scholars have shared similar experiences and self-proclaimed their college experience was enhanced because of the TRiO Scholars program. In the past seven years we have seen an increase in participants studying abroad, engaging in faculty-student conversations, volunteering, and actively searching for and utilizing academic resources. According to Harper & Quaye (2009) activities such as these are highly correlated with academic achievement. Alexander Robinson shared this about his experience meeting with his professors:

> After a couple office hours, I realized that the professors really enjoyed talking to someone else, especially those who don't receive a lot of students at their office hours. It was great being able to get to know these professors because many of them have so many interesting stories, along with amazing advice for school, their class, and life. I learned that even though these professors may come off scary and mean during lecture, at the end of the day they are just as human as us and they should be visited more often at their office hours because it is extremely beneficial.

Participants are required to select three activities to commit to and reflect on at the end of each semester. These activities range from meeting with professors, attend weekly tutoring, participate in routine fitness, etc. This process gives participants the ability to exercise their autonomy, partake in behaviors they would otherwise avoid, and then evaluate the benefits.

The three-pronged approach used by the TRIO Scholars Program has been developed and revamped over the past seven years and will continue to evolve with the ever-changing needs of first-generation students. However, as the approach may change, the values of building genuine relationships, teaching non-cognitive skills, and bring proactive in our engagement will remain the core of our values.

REFERENCES

Borghans, L., A. L. Duckworth, J. J. Heckman, and B. ter Weel (2008, fall). The economics and psychology of personality traits. *Journal of Human Resources 43* (4), 972–1059.

Conte, C. (2013). The Tao of Anger Management: A Yield Theory Approach. Retrieved April 22, 2019, from http://www.psychotherapy.net/article/Anger-Management-Conte#section-yield-theory.

DiMaria, F. (2006, October). Keeping our kids engaged, At-risk kids in college. *Education Digest, 72* (2), 52–57.

Downing, S. (2017). *On course: Strategies for creating success in college and in life-Study Skills Plus* (3rd ed.). Boston, MA: Cengage Learning.

Forbus, P. R., Newbold, J. J., & Mehta, S. S. (2011). First-generation university students: Motivation, academic success, and satisfaction with the university experience. *International Journal of Education Research, 6*(2), 34–55.

Harackiewicz, J. M., Canning, E. A., Tibbetts, Y., Giffen, C. J., Blair, S. S., Rouse, D. I., & Hyde, J. S. (2014). Closing the social class achievement gap for first-generation students in undergraduate biology. *Journal of Educational Psychology, 106*(2), 375–389.

Harper, S. R., & Quaye, S. J. (Eds.). (2009). Student engagement in higher education: Theoretical perspectives and practical approaches for diverse populations. New York: Routledge.

Martinez, M. D. (2003). Missing in action: Reconstructing hope and possibility among Latino students placed at risk. *Journal of Latinos and Education, 2*(1), 13–21.

Moschetti, R. V., & Hudley, C. (2015). Social capital and academic motivation among first-generation community college Students. *Community College Journal of Research and Practice, 39*(3), 235–251.

Pitre, C., & Pitre, P. (2009). Increasing underrepresented high school students' college transitions and achievements—TRIO programs. *NASSP Bulletin, 93*(2), 96–110.

Smith, B. (2007). Accessing social capital through the academic mentoring process. *Equity & Excellence in Education, 40*(1), 36–46.

Unverferth, A., Talbert-Johnson, C., & Bogards, T. (2012). Perceived barriers for FG students. *International Journal of Education Reform, 21*(4), 238–252.

Varney, J. (2012, September). Proactive (Intrusive) Advising! *Academic Advising Today, 35*(3). Retrieved from [https://www.nacada.ksu.edu/Resources/Academic-Advising-Today/View-Articles/Proactive-Intrusive-Advising.aspx].

Yeh, T. L. (2010). Service-learning and persistence of low-income, first-generation college students: An exploratory study. *Michigan Journal of Community Service Learning Spring*, 50–65.

CHAPTER 13

Rising by Lifting Others

Peer Mentorship Among Students with Disabilities

ANDREA JUILLERAT-OLVERA, M.F.A.

Andrea Juillerat-Olvera is the staff sign language interpreter and disability specialist at the Disability Resource Center at the University of Nevada, Reno. She holds a vocational degree in sign language from Seattle Central Community College, a bachelor's degree in Philosophy from the University of Washington, Seattle and a master's of fine art in Performance Art from the University Of Nevada, Reno. Andrea's creative manifestations are informed by her daily exposure to a broad range of learning environments, time spent living abroad in Ljubljana, Slovenia and decades of political activism.

Navigating the transition from high school and home life to college is difficult for all students. For many this transition includes exposure to new environments, a lack of parental boundaries, and distance from familiar settings and friends. College is often the first attempt at maintaining adult levels of responsibility. These challenges also intersect with the loss of older social networks and immersion into new, unfamiliar ones. Student retention in the first year has become a major push at universities around the country. Some students are overwhelmed by the confluence of changing currents and daunting expectations that they drop out. Academic supports may not be enough if the student is struggling in more personal ways. Peer mentoring programs have offered at least one path to success for those who feel lost in a new campus environment. After nearly 30 years of practice, there is ample evidence to indicate a need for peer mentoring work to address retention/graduation rates and increase the overall satisfaction of students who can utilized peer mentors (Yomtov, D., Plunkett, S.W., Efrat, R., & Marin, A.G., 2015).

While almost all major campuses support a form of peer to peer mentoring, only some establish a program for students with disabilities. Students with disabilities have additional barriers compared to the general student population, related to inclusion and social wellness (National Institutes of Health, 2018). For students with visible and invisible disabilities, the specter of judgement and stigma looms large with social engagement being especially anxiety-inducing. Newer generations may be highly adept at navigating social media and digital interactions but can be less so with face to face communication skills. Peer mentoring provides holistic support, rather than focusing on specific academic shortcomings.

In 2012, the Assistant Director of the Disability Resource Center (DRC) decided to implement a peer mentoring program for students with disabilities. It began when one DRC student in a Ph.D. program asked to be "paired" with another student, so that they may support each other. At the end of the year, both students reported a high degree of benefit and satisfaction regarding their relationship. After witnessing their success, the Peer Mentoring Program was born in 2013 and has been supporting student success ever since. The Assistant Director's guiding philosophy since the program launched has been one of *social wellness*. The goal is to build connections between new and more experienced students with disabilities. Mentors and mentees work together to promote academic success and personal growth.

The concept of a "mentor" frequently invokes images of gray-haired, bespectacled elders with vast knowledge and practical wisdom; however, generational difference can open a wide chasm between students and older members of faculty. Age differences between mentors and mentees can easily default into parent-child, or grandparent-grandchild social dynamics. Conversely, peer mentors work well because they feel relatable, likely due to the feeling of interacting with a friend and ally. Dr. Gordon Nakagawa, writing for the earliest mentoring program in the University of California system, delineates what a peer mentor is: "Not. . . a surrogate parent, a professional counselor or therapist, a career counselor, a trained tutor, a flawless, infallible idol, a social worker, a lending institution, a playmate or romantic partner" (United Way of America & One on One, 1991). Indeed, the role of a peer mentor is subtle and for that reason, mentor training is essential to success. All programs, regardless of the population they serve, involve some form of training for mentors.

Training helps students carefully define the role they are expected to take with their mentees. Additionally, many programs incorporate a contract explicating rights and responsibilities for both mentors and mentees. In order to build a suitable training curriculum, the Assistant Director enlisted the help of several other departments within the University. Counseling services, Speech Pathology, and Audiology, Title IX, Student Conduct, The Career Studio, and the University of Nevada School of Medicine are some of the departments who have contributed their expertise to train DRC mentors. Evaluations of the workshops are collected from student mentors each semester and used to improve and inform future trainings.

One of the most important sessions in fall 2018 was the "Implicit Bias" training presented by an associate dean for Diversity and Inclusion at the UNR School of Medicine and her team from Behavioral Sciences. This particular training was quickly deemed essential for all participants; as many students with invisible disabilities initially balked at being paired with someone who had a visible disability. The internalized hierarchy of social status within disability community led some to reject initial matches because of their own implicit bias. Making that unconscious prejudice explicit, unpacking it, and deconstructing it helps students see a way out of their own internalized prejudices.

Each semester there are a variety of presentations that mentors and mentees participate in. Counseling Services gives presentations on mindfulness, suicidality, communication, listening skills and motivational interviewing using the OARS technique (Boyle, C., 2015). Title IX has a representative teach a sexual harassment module. The Career Studio offers a Career/Internship Expo for mentors and mentees to practice interview skills and meet with potential employers. The DRC organizes at least one panel discussion a semester on a topic of interest, such as neurodiversity. One of the most popular workshops is "Sexability", formerly called "Relationships 101", which outlines basic social skills for expressing romantic interest. Another workshop is on preventing burnout, something they can all benefit from.

In addition to the initial mentor training and orientation, the DRC hosts a series of events that facilitate relationship-building between mentors and mentees. At the kick-off event each fall, mentors receive training for a half day and are joined by their mentees at the end of the session. Mentors and mentees support many initiatives on campus, including one home-grown idea to create a graduation tassel to represent accessibility

FIGURE 1. Total student participation in peer mentor program by semester

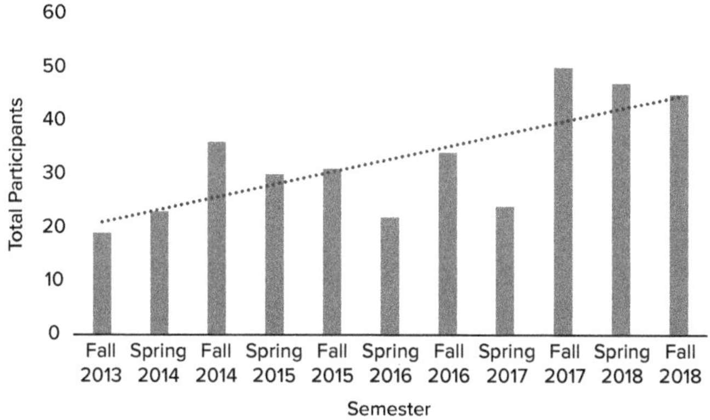

beginning spring 2019. The Associated Students of the University of Nevada (ASUN) passed a resolution approving the new tassel and it will be available to all graduates who support accessibility.

Mentors are obligated to spend at least one hour with their mentee and keep a log of their weekly interactions. As an extension of the DRC, the participants are expected to adhere to University conduct codes. Mentor-mentee pairs have engaged in study sessions, leisure activities, eating out, sporting events, and yoga. The essence of their work is supporting each other's goal through a lens of social wellness. Each semester, both mentors and mentees complete a self-evaluation about their experience and growth. In 2016, the DRC began offering a $100 stipend to mentors. This payment is dispersed at the end of the semester and applies toward next semester fees.

Since 1988, Public/Private Ventures (P/PV) have conducted research on mentoring programs, both in higher education and with the Big Brothers/Big Sisters since 1988 (Sipe, C.L., 1996). The 35-year-old non-profit firm closed in 2012 but leaves behind a trove of high quality data. Additionally, The National Mentoring Partnership has been collating and publishing data on mentoring programs for nearly 25 years.

Evaluations of DRC student success measured by GPA or other academic metrics are confounded by a number of complex variables: additional services a student receives from the DRC, socioeconomic factors and type of disability, quality of the mentor-mentee match, and the appropriateness of the students chosen majors. One simple way to measure mentoring efficacy and value is by looking at program continuity and growth (see fig. 1).

Yet, the most compelling evidence for student success in the DRC's peer mentoring program is found in the voices of students themselves. A qualitative analysis of student comments reveals a highly positive impact on the overall wellness of students who are mentors and mentees. Several current and former program participants were eager to share their experiences.

One mentor has been with the DRC office since fall 2016 and is majoring in philosophy of law and ethics. He first heard about the program from his DRC counselor and decided to sign up. He was initially attracted to the program from his interest in social justice and disability advocacy. "I also wanted to give back, because the DRC services had helped me a great deal." He emphasized how much he appreciated the training program for mentors,

> I'm grateful for the training I received. Workshops on autism and socialization, communication and listening skills, domestic abuse and sexual violence training as well as all the advice and insight from professional therapists really helped. Throughout the process of mentoring I realized that listening makes us vulnerable. When we listen to someone and are receptive to hearing them, we allow our own perspective to potentially be changed. We are allowing their world view to invade our own. That kind of willful vulnerability takes great strength.

The mentor reflects on the measure of his impact,

> Thinking about my mentee, in two years he had made so much progress! The positive impact I'd had on him washed over me. He had developed important friendships, he was in a romantic relationship and he exuded a joy of life that I did not perceive when we first met up.

The student explained that mentoring "catalyzed phases of challenging self-reflection, and forced me to look at some of my own internal pain." In regards to working with others he states,

> I had to always be on guard against thinking that I knew what was best for my mentee. I had to be aware that there isn't one standard for success and that his notion of it (personal, academic, or otherwise) might be very different than my own.

When asked if he would recommend the Peer Mentoring Program to others he answered,

> Absolutely. I've become a more emotionally mature, patient and compassionate human being, and I've come to take great pride in the fact that I have a lot to offer people who might need my help. It's extremely empowering to know that I have a lot to give the world. I came into the program from a place of dependency and need . . . and while that is still there, I realized that those attributes do not deprive me of my capacity to respond to the needs of others.

One student was a mentee for three semesters and now has taken on the mentor role for the first time in spring 2019. When asked why she decided to stay with the program and eventually become a mentor, she references the first time she met with her mentor.

> Just talking with her the first time was an "ah ha" moment for me. We bonded over the fact that we both have anxiety and I realized I'm not the only one. I'm not alone. There's other people on campus like me.

She tells how their relationship developed through time,

> At first we just hung out in the @One (at one) lounge because we are both digital media students. We'd just do homework together, then we'd have some friendly talk . . . to share about life, gossip about roommates, etc. And then, we started problem-solving together. Eventually, we started going to the gym together too. We'd been working so hard on our mental health that we decided to work on our physical health too. Even though our formal mentor-mentee relationship ended, we still work out together and we're still friends.

For spring 2019, she adds,

> Now I'm a mentor and it's a little bit harder. It's a different kind of relationship to navigate. I have to remember to write down my reflections in the log and I think a lot about how to best help the mentee . . . how to really do that. It's not a bad thing . . . to think from the other side now. I'm learning.

Research from P/PV shows commitment of personal time by the

mentor is one of the biggest barriers to running a successful program (Sipe, C.L., 1996). When asked about her time commitment to mentoring, the mentor states,

> I wouldn't say it takes a lot of time. It requires meeting for one hour a week. My mentee and I hang out more than is required. We're both in the College of Liberal Arts and I can show them around. It's more like having a friend... a friend that you also mentor. Actually, I think you can get a lot out of the program for a relatively small time commitment.

She feels that the DRC's mentoring program has made all the difference for her educational journey,

> I learned to reach out when I need help. It sounds simple, but I had a hard time in high school. The people around me didn't have visible symptoms, or even disabilities. That was tough, because it's very obvious when I'm having an anxiety attack. But, I've learned that it's OKAY to ask for help. That's the best lesson I've learned in college so far and having this program as a resource has made me really confident. It's reassuring to hear points of view from people with similar issues. The mentoring program gave me a community I could fall back on when I needed help.

The Assistant Director speaks to some of the big "take-aways" from her mentoring program. Determining a successful match has been challenging. The program application acts as an initial screening tool; collecting standard demographics, but also asks the students to weigh preferences for a match based on disability, major, gender, or additional factors. After the application is submitted, the Assistant Director meets the students and gleans more information from them before attempting to suggest a match. "We've found that we can match by major, or disability condition, or gender, but none of that matters. Some of the unsuccessful matches were made exactly as the students wished, but none of these metrics was predictive of success." Eventually, the Assistant Director noticed that left to their own devices, students will find their own matches.

> At one of the kick-off events some of the students didn't show up, or couldn't make it, so those who did attend simply began talking to someone else. We would provide the safe place and the students

would find each other and pair up naturally forming relationships with other willing participants. In the end, it is the desire to cultivate a relationship and help each other that is the number one predictor of a successful match.

The greatest challenge the Assistant Director has faced within the program was matching people who can "pass" as non-disabled with those who have obvious or visible symptoms. The status anxiety and tension around social issues was laid bare by these difficult matches, one mentee said, "I'm not as disabled as she is. . . . this can't be my match." "These kinds of remarks illustrate the hidden biases within us all," The Assistant Director said, "We clearly needed to talk about implicit bias, equity, values, judgment and stigma." Trainings were enhanced to confront these issues and subsequent processing of that troublesome match forced both participants to self-reflect.

The future of the DRC mentoring program looks bright, as many former mentors and mentees maintain and cultivate relationships with current program participants. All the students interviewed felt that the friendships born of mentoring were built to last and that the lessons learned would equip them for success the rest of their lives.

REFERENCES

[Adapted] from Mentor Training Curriculum, National Mentoring Working Groups convened by United Way of America and One on One, 1991, in One on One "Mentoring 101" Curriculum, The California Mentoring Partnership. Retrieved from https://www.csun.edu/sites/default/files/Student_Resource_Booklet.pdf.

Boyle, C. (2015, March 13). Using OARS in Motivational Interviewing. Retrieved from https://www.veriti.com.au/using-oars-in-motivational-interviewing/.

National Institutes of Health. (2018, December 10). Social Wellness Toolkit. Retrieved from https://www.nih.gov/health-information/social-wellness-toolkit.

Sipe, C. L. (1996). Mentoring: A synthesis of Public/Private Ventures research: 1988–1995. [Information analyses]. Philadelphia, PA: Public/Private Ventures. Retrieved from https://eric.ed.gov/?id=ED404410.

"Social Wellness Toolkit." National Institutes of Health, U.S. Department of Health and Human Services, 10 Dec. 2018, www.nih.gov/health-information/social-wellness-toolkit. (accessed 3/6/2019).

Yomtov, D., Plunkett, S. W., Efrat, R., & Marin, A. G. (2015). Can peer mentors improve first-year experiences of university students? Journal of College Student Retention: Research, Theory & Practice, 19(1), 25–44. doi: 10.1177/1521025115611398.

CHAPTER 14

The Journey to Seamless Transfer

DAVID SINGLETON, M.S., and JANET STAKE, M.A.

David Singleton is the transfer and articulation ombudsperson with the Nevada System of Higher Education (NSHE). He is responsible for helping students, faculty, and staff members learn more about and understand transfer and articulation policies and procedures. He assists with the management of the Common Course Numbering database and has also worked on the 2018 and 2019 transfer and articulation audits. Prior to joining NSHE, David spent over seven years as an academic advisor at the University of Nevada, Las Vegas; Nevada State College; and the College of Southern Nevada. David received his bachelor's degree in Communication from the University of Missouri and his master of science in Education degree from Illinois State University.

Janet Stake is the academic and student affairs officer at the Nevada System of Higher Education (NSHE). She is responsible for the system-wide management of the Common Course Numbering process and database. She also has had oversight of the recent transfer and articulation audits that have been conducted in 2015, 2018 and now again in 2019. In addition, she is the state coordinator for Go to College Nevada and the College Application Month initiative. In this role, Janet is the Nevada liaison with the American College Application Campaign. Janet has been with NSHE since 2015. Prior to that, for seven years she was the catalog and curriculum coordinator for the University of Nevada, Reno. For her bachelor's degree, Janet double majored in Business Administration/Marketing and Human Resource Management. She received her master's in Counseling and Education Psychology with an emphasis in Instructional Design from the University of Nevada, Reno.

When it comes to navigating college life, there are many, many things students need to know and do in order to be successful. One area that may prove to be particularly tricky for students to understand is the transfer of previously earned credits to a new institution. This is an area in which the Nevada System of Higher Education (NSHE) believes strong policies that always bear in mind what is best for students, is key to success for transfer students. This article will discuss some of the concerns transfer students have faced and the various policies, procedures, practices, and remedies that have been written and implemented to help students overcome the typical barriers.

There are two elements to the transfer process which are often used in tandem that need to be defined. The first one is "transfer" which refers to the acceptance of previously completed college credits at one institution that a student hopes to apply at a new institution. Essentially, all college-level credits are transferable with the exception of vocational-type of courses. The second element is "articulation". This refers to the application of those transfer credits to a student's program of study. Both of these impact students by the amount of time it takes to complete a program, and the cost involved with completing that program. Research shows that one of the greatest barriers for students is the loss of credit upon transfer (CCRC, 2015). In these cases, either the credit is not accepted, or it does not fulfill program requirements. When this happens, generally the credits become extraneous elective credit. This loss means that students may need to take additional coursework which extends the time to graduation and results in higher fees. A greater time to completion and rising fees can result in greater attrition leaving students with a lot of credit, possibly a lot of debt, higher risk of student loan default, but no credential. In fact, 90 percent of community college students who have defaulted on their debt left college with no credential (Fain, 2015).

Nevada has a long history of trying to assist students in this area. *Nevada Revised Statutes* (*NRS* 396.568) address the transfer of credits earned at a community college. This statute was originally written and approved in 1997. It was later updated in 2003 and then again in 2005 to its current wording. The statute states:

1. All credits earned by a student in a course at a community college within the System, including, without limitation, all credits earned in a course toward the award of an associates degree must automatically transfer toward the course work required of the student in his or her major or minor, or other course work required of the student, for the award of a baccalaureate degree upon graduation of the student from any university or state college within the System.
2. Pursuant to the policy of the Board of Regents, a student who is awarded an associates degree:

a. Shall be deemed to have completed the course of study required of a sophomore.
b. If the student enrolls in another institution within the System, must be enrolled as a junior.

3. All credits earned toward the completion of a degree of associate of arts, associate of science or associate of business must automatically transfer toward the course work required for the award of a baccalaureate degree upon the graduation of the student from any university or college within the System.

   If the transfer of credit pursuant to this section is denied and the student believes that the credit should be applied to his or her degree, the student may appeal the decision. The appeal process must be made available to all students and may be posted on the website of the System.

In 2005, then NSHE Chancellor, made it clear that he wanted students to be able to "seamlessly" transfer within NSHE. The Board of Regents also subscribed to this goal which is evident in the policies that have been put into place over the years. Although this has clearly been the intent of the Regents, sometimes the actual implementation and practice can come upon actual and perceived hurdles. Based on assorted anecdotal information indicating transfer problems, in March 2015 the Board of Regents requested an audit of the transfer process/system. As a result, the 2015 and 2018 Transfer and Articulation Audits were conducted. The subsequent implementation of audit recommendations show a commitment to reduce barriers and provide the promised seamless transfer experience.

A key provision that has been in NSHE transfer policy for some time is the requirement that the institutions create and post transfer agreements. Transfer agreements are in place between two-year institutions and four-year institutions for all bachelor's programs. These agreements must include a four-year course outline and must show the completion of the associate degree within the first two years. The agreements serve as a roadmap for the student; they inform them of what courses they should/need to take in order to successfully receive their associate degree, and also outlines how those courses from the associate degree apply to the bachelor's degree. In essence, a student should be able to follow a transfer agreement and know exactly what they need to do in order to be able to complete their degree in a timely manner and not lose credits in transfer.

Obviously, the transfer agreement is not a panacea. If a student decides to change their major upon matriculation to their four-year institution, there is a chance that some of the credits they enrolled in to satisfy their previous pathway may not count towards their new degree, and that is something that all students need to be made aware of either through one-on-one academic advising/counseling or via group advising sessions (such as orientation programs). Like any tool, transfer agreements are at their best when used properly and early in their academic career.

Title 4, Chapter 14, Sections 14–18 of the Board of Regents *Handbook* house the policies related to transfer and articulation. The intention of the Board of Regents' policies relating to transfer are directly informed by the *Nevada Revised Statues* previously mentioned. The primary goal of the policies is to make sure that the transfer process for students works in as smooth of a manner as possible. These policies were examined as part of the 2015 Transfer and Articulation Audit performed by the Department of Academic and Student Affairs in the NSHE System Office.

The 2015 audit focused on policy and resulted in three specific recommendations. The first recommendation centered around updating and clarifying the current policy. A correction to a conflict in the policy was noted and clarification of the intent of the policy to preserve the associate degree program intact upon transfer was made. In other words, a student that completed an associate degree will be able to transfer their program credits to the corresponding bachelor's program with minimal or no loss of credit. The changes also preserved the catalog rights upon transfer for students that began their coursework at a community college. The third recommendation addressed the timing, communication of curricular changes, and overall collaboration. It was noted during the audit that sometimes changes are not communicated until the new catalog is released (usually just before the start of the fall term). As a result, the community colleges were often a year or two behind curricular updates by the time changes are moved through their institutional curricular processes. Obviously, this was a concern. This finding highlighted the importance of timeliness, communication, and collaboration between institutions to the successful execution of these policies and use of the transfer agreements.

Collaboration is critical to the continued development of the transfer agreements that serve as the core element of the successful transfer process. In order to maintain the agreements, and to make sure that the agreements are fulfilling their designated role, faculty and staff from the two-year and four-year schools must come together periodically to discuss program requirements and alignment, course requirements and optimal course sequencing. Without that frequent collaboration, it would be easy for the transfer agreements to fall into neglect.

Another policy that assists faculty in this area is the Common Course Numbering policy. This policy states, if the content of a new course is deemed 80 percent or more the same of an existing course by faculty in that discipline, then the course must have the same prefix, number, title, and credits of that existing course. Commonly numbered courses automatically transfer as the same course. This provides an easy and transparent way for students to understand how some of their coursework will transfer, especially in the area of general education. It should be noted, that Nevada is one of only sixteen states in the country that have a Common Course Numbering system in place.

One way that the System office makes sure that the transfer agreements are maintained, and that the collaboration that should be occurring is actually happening, is through the periodic audits. The Transfer and Articulation Phase II audit was conducted in 2018. While the 2015 audit focused on policy, the 2018 audit focused on the intraregional transfer agreements. The System Office completed this audit which was a "deep dive" into the transfer agreements. The System Office received and reviewed 370 transfer agreements out of a possible 551. The remaining 181 agreements were not completed in time for the audit. Of the 370 reviewed transfer agreements, 76 percent resulted in little or no loss of credit (Transfer and Articulation Audit, 2018). While this was a very good result, clearly there was room for improvement. This deep dive intraregional audit revealed that there are some natural difficulties at play with regards to the development and maintenance of these transfer agreements. The sheer volume of agreements is staggering, as there are over 500 individual transfer agreements that need to be created, examined, and refined. Also, some disciplines require extra time and attention because it may be difficult for a student to complete enough appropriate credits at the two-year school before transferring. While this audit has shown that there is still some progress that needs to be made, one of the positive outcomes from it has been the clarification of the policy and a renewed commitment from all of the NSHE institutions.

Another transfer agreement audit will be conducted again during the summer of 2019 in order to review all required agreements with the goal of completing the intraregional phase by the summer of 2020. Once this cycle has been completed and there is strong confidence in the existing agreements, an interregional audit of transfer agreements will take place to examine the agreements for students who desire to transfer from Northern Nevada to Southern Nevada and vice versa.

NSHE policies exist to proactively aid students in transfer to meet the spirit of seamless transfer. However, not every situation or articulation can be captured by those policies. There is a remedy in place though, to assist students who may not have courses that articulate exactly as desired. In early 2018, the Board of Regents approved policies creating the Articulation Coordinating Committee (ACC) (*Handbook*, Title 4, Chapter 14, Section 14). The ACC meets on a monthly basis during the academic year to discuss policies and issues related to transfer and articulation and serve as the oversight panel for the Transfer Credit Request for Review process and the Common Course Numbering System. There are representatives from each institution on the committee, which helps to spur and foster collaboration outside of these meetings.

As mentioned above the ACC assists students who may desire an additional review of their transfer credits. This is called the Transfer Credit Request for Review. Accreditation standards stipulate that the System office cannot mandate that a student's transfer credits be articulated one way or another. That is not the purpose of the Request for Review though. It is not an appeal process. If a student has transferred credits between institutions and is not satisfied with how their credits were articulated, the student has an opportunity to initiate any appeals within the policies that each institution has in place. If a student has exhausted all appeals on their home campus, then they can reach out to the System Office, submit a required form and documentation, and the ACC may recommend that the institution take another look at the articulation decision.

The Transfer Credit Request for Review process is managed by another brand-new resource for students in the System Office—the Transfer and Articulation Ombudsperson. Also in 2018, NSHE hired the very first Ombudsperson whose role is specifically focused on serving as a resource for students who have questions about transfer policies and procedures, as well as for faculty and staff on the campuses if they have questions about transfer and articulation policies as they advise students or try to implement program or degree changes.

In Nevada, students that transfer after achieving their associate degree graduate at a greater rate than students that start at a four-year institution. (Transfer and Articulation Audit, 2015). So it behooves the system as a whole to continuously examine, improve, and refine our policies and procedures to ensure seamless transfer between institutions with no loss of credit. With the recent audits, the formation of the ACC, open lines of communication, and on-going collaboration, these factors have reinforced the importance of transfer agreements. This combination will help transfer student realize the ultimate outcome of seamless transfer which will result in timely graduation and less overall fees. That is the best outcome for all.

REFERENCES

Board of Regents Handbook, Title 4 Chapter 14 retrieved from https://nshe.nevada.edu/wp-content/uploads/file/BoardOfRegents/Handbook/title4//T4-CH14%20NSHE%20Planning%20Program%20Review%20Articulation%20and%20Enrollment%20Policies.pdf on February 12, 2019.

Fain, P. (2015, September 28). Small Loans, Big Problems. Retrieved from http://www.insidehighered.com/news/2015/09/28/four-surprising-findings-debt-and-default-among-community-college-students on March 14, 2019.

Jenkins, D. and Fink, J., (2015). What We Know About Transfer. New Your, NY: Columbia University, Teachers College, Community College Research Center. Retrieved from http://ccrc.tc.columbia.edu/media/k2/attachments/what-we-know-about-transfer.pdf on January 5, 2016.

Nevada Revised Statutes, 396.568 retrieved from https://www.leg.state.nv.us/NRS/NRS-396.html#NRS396Sec568 on February 12, 2019.

Nevada System of Higher Education, Transfer and Articulation Audit, 2015 retrieved from https://nshe.nevada.edu/wp-content/uploads/Academic-Affairs/Transfer-and-Articulation-Audit-2015-FINAL.pdf on February 12, 2019.

Nevada System of Higher Education, Transfer and Articulation Audit, 2018 retrieved from https://nshe.nevada.edu/wp-content/uploads/file/BoardOfRegents/Agendas/2019/03-mar-mtgs/arsa-refs/ARSA-10b.pdf on February 26, 2019.

CHAPTER 15

GradFIT

Fully Inclusive Training for Diverse Graduate Students

VERONICA ZEPEDA, PH.D., MATTHEW AGUIRRE, PH.D., RACHEL ZARNDT, PH.D., and DAVID ZEH, PH.D

Veronica Zepeda is the senior advisor to the Graduate Student Association (GSA) and the director of Graduate Student Services at the University of Nevada, Reno. She works closely with Graduate School staff to offer graduate student services that will ensure the recruitment and retention of both highly qualified and diverse graduate students to the University. As senior advisor to the Graduate Student Association, Veronica is responsible for the training of the GSA Council and Executive Board and oversees all GSA services and events, including the professional development workshop series, graduate student poster symposium, and spring awards program. She earned her bachelor's degree in Biology from the Massachusetts Institute of Technology and her Ph.D. in Molecular and Cell Biology from University of California, Berkeley. She previously served as a Biochemistry lecturer at the University and as a Science Education and Outreach Coordinator at the University of California, San Francisco.

Matthew Aguirre is the director of Postdoctoral Affairs, Graduate Recruitment, and Diversity Initiatives for the Graduate School at the University of Nevada, Reno. He is responsible for designing and implementing Graduate School initiatives such as professional development for postdoctoral scholars and graduate students, graduate student recruitment and diversity. Matthew also supports graduate student recruitment efforts and provides strategic direction to identify, recruit, and support diverse graduate students. He works alongside with the Graduate Student Association to further provide resources and support for graduate students and postdoctoral scholars. Before his position with the Graduate School, he worked in the Office of Diversity Initiatives as a graduate assistant and was a lecturer for the College of Education.

Rachel Zarndt was the director of Postdoctoral Affairs, Graduate Diversity Recruitment at the University of Nevada, Reno, from Fall 2017 to Fall 2019 and lecturer (LOA) in Rangeland and Animal Sciences for the College of Agriculture, Biotechnology and Natural Resources.

In her role with the Graduate School, Rachel implemented sustainable faculty mentorship workshops ("Mentoring Mentors") and supported graduate recruitment and retention efforts. Further, Rachel promoted graduate-level workforce readiness initiatives for careers inside and outside academia and developed lasting partnerships with local industries and start-ups. Rachel earned her bachelor of arts in Neuroscience from Willamette University and her Ph.D. in Biomedical Sciences and Anthropogeny from University of California, San Diego in 2016. Among other careers, she previously worked in San Francisco in a medical communications role, in the documentary film industry, and began her career in research as a Research Biologist studying cardiopulmonary adaptations to high altitude.

David Zeh is the vice provost for Graduate Education and the dean of the Graduate School of the University of Nevada, Reno. He oversees graduate student progress and the rules and regulations governing graduate education. Zeh is an accomplished researcher, professor, and graduate-student advisor with a doctoral degree from the University of Arizona.

Background

A diverse graduate student population enriches the entire academic community. A myriad of success factors can be promoted when inclusive training methods are celebrated and supported by higher education practices. Recent national studies have shown how racial, ethnic, and gender diversity enhances creativity and is essential for sustained innovation, entrepreneurial activity and global competitiveness. Evidence from a variety of sources indicates that racial, ethnic, and gender diversity enhances creativity and improves the way people think and solve problems. A racially, ethnically, and gender-balanced academic and private sector STEM workforce is therefore essential for sustained innovation (Freeman 2014, Levine 2014).

However, diversifying the graduate ranks remains a major challenge for most universities, despite several decades of gradual growth in college attendance by increasingly diverse populations. Historically underrepresented groups (HUGs), for example Native American, LatinX, and African American populations, continue to be poorly represented in many fields, particularly STEM professions and those requiring doctoral degrees. While HUGs comprise 31 percent of the US population, they hold only 11 percent of science and engineering occupations (NSF 2017 Digest).

While incremental progress has been made, the goal of achieving a diverse, graduate-educated workforce representative of the U.S. population remains elusive.

Thompson and Campbell (2013) identify three essential program elements for addressing the challenge of diversity in the graduate ranks:

1. Development of **strategic partnerships with select undergraduate institutions**
2. Educational programs that incorporate **transferable skill-based modules** to augment discipline-specific training
3. Transformational changes to institutional culture through **faculty engagement** in diversity-related practices and goals

Similarly, a more recent study by the Council of Graduate Schools (Sowell 2015) found that three of the top six concerns of underrepresented minority STEM doctoral students complement the program elements identified by Thompson and Campbell (2013) study:

1. Meeting program requirements
2. Having professional and career guidance
3. Having a culture of inclusion at their doctoral institution.

To address both the specific needs of institutions seeking diversified ranks and concerns of minority students considering attendance in graduate schools, the University of Nevada Reno's (UNR) Graduate School spearheaded development of an innovative graduate school preparatory program called "GradFIT." Intensive graduate school preparatory boot camps can be effective in generating enthusiasm for science and technology, building community among participants, and families and providing critical technical and soft skills necessary for the successful pursuit of a range of STEM careers. Since its inception five years ago, GradFIT has received national attention and has contributed to a marked increase in the enrollment of historically underrepresented students in the University of Nevada, Reno's graduate programs.

Program

GradFIT is a 5-day intensive academic program designed to introduce first-generation college students and students from underrepresented backgrounds to the opportunities, challenges and expectations of graduate school.

The aims of the GradFIT program are to: (1) elucidate the world-class scholarship and research opportunities afforded by a graduate education, (2) demystify the graduate school application process, (3) empower students to prepare competitive applications, (4) illustrate how assistantships, fellowships and scholarships can be leveraged to make graduate school a financially viable option, and (5) provide a road map for increasing the

FIGURE 1. GradFIT's 5-day schedOule at a glance.

DAY 1

- Campus Tour
- Why Graduate School? Presentation
- Graduate School Application Workshop
- Motivational Keynote Presentation
- Graduate Assistantships and Fellowships Presentation
- Financial Aid For Graduate Students Presentation
- Professional Development Presentation
- Fitting in Fitness Presentation

DAY 2

- Desert Research Institute Visit
- Preparing for the Graduate Record Exam (GRE) Workshop
- Imposter Syndrome Presentation
- Writing a Personal Statement Workshop

DAY 3

- Lab and Facility Tours
- Mini-Lectures by Faculty and Graduate Students

DAY 4

- Outing at Lake Tahoe
- Impromptu Meetings

DAY 5

- Graduate Student Resource Tabling Fair
- Graduate Student Panel
- Closing Remarks

retention and completion rates of participants who enroll in graduate programs. It is important to note that GradFIT's success is not evaluated on its effectiveness in recruiting graduate students to UNR but rather on its overall effectiveness in promoting successful applications to graduate programs at any regionally accredited university.

GradFIT participants attend academic lectures, tour the campus and labs, meet with faculty and graduate students, attend workshops to develop competitive applications, and learn about career choices afforded by a graduate education. Figure 1 provides an example of the 5-day schedule for students participating in GradFIT.

Strategic Partnerships with Undergraduate Institutions

Recruitment is a fundamental rate-limiting step in diversifying graduate student populations, and institutional resources in support of the program are essential for creating a pipeline for students to enroll in graduate school (fig. 2). To be eligible to participate in the program, students must: (1) be a an undergraduate at the sophomore level or above, or the hold a baccalaureate degree; (2) come from a historically underrepresented background or be a first-generation college student, and (3) have a 3.0 or higher cumulative grade point average. In addition to advertising GradFIT in a number of neighboring Western states (Oregon, Utah, New Mexico, California, Arizona), we have established formal partnerships with three institutions, as described below. These partners provide critical support in identifying

FIGURE 2. Ethnicity of application and matriculation to UNR's graduate programs before the genesis of GradFIT in 2014. The close correspondence between percentages of applications received and admission offers suggest that applications from HUG students are as competitive as white student applications.

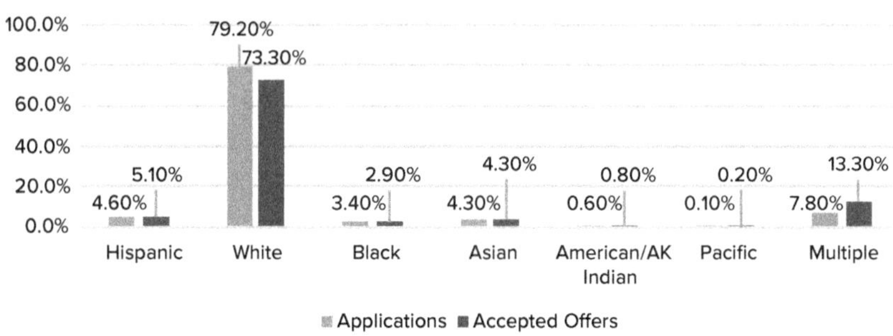

qualified applicants and cover the travel expenses of their participants to and from UNR. We provide free room and board and cover all program costs (food, transportation, materials, etc.) once students arrive on our campus.

Nevada State College (NSC) is a comprehensive 4-year college with a commitment to educating students for success in the real world. NSC is a dynamic, young institution founded in 2002, with more than 4,800 students representing a broad range of cultural and economic backgrounds. The College's main campus is located in Henderson, Nevada (15 minutes from Las Vegas) and boasts an unusually diverse student body. Over 67 percent of the students are of non-Caucasian descent, 55 percent are first-generation and many are also adult learners and career changers. The College has partnered with UNR since the inception of GradFIT and fully supports our efforts to increase diversity in graduate studies.

California State University, Sacramento, better known as Sacramento State, is a vibrant metropolitan university that is among the largest campuses in the California State University system. CSU Sacramento enrolls a multicultural student body of over 30,000, and graduates approximately 6,000 students each year. Sacramento State has a highly diverse student body, with 73 percent of students of non-Caucasian descent and 30 percent identifying as first generation. CSU Sacramento has partnered with UNR for the past 5 years and fully supports our efforts to increase diversity in graduate programs.

California State University, Channel Islands, is the youngest of the California State system universities and has a total enrollment of over 7,000. Located in Southern California, it boasts a highly diverse student population, with 71 percent non-white students and 50 percent self-identifying as Hispanic/Latino. CSU Channel Islands has been a recognized Hispanic Serving Institution since 2010 and a GradFIT partner since 2016.

Outcomes

From 2015–2019, GradFIT Phase I has served 150 students through strategic partnerships and direct recruitment efforts. Participants have consistently been highly diverse. Over 40 percent of participants are Hispanic/Latino, 81 percent are female, and 79 percent are first-generation college students (fig. 3). The success of these formal partnerships has informed the development of new partnerships with American Indian communities to

FIGURE 3. HUG students apply to graduate school at a much lower rate than predicted by their proportional representation in US society.

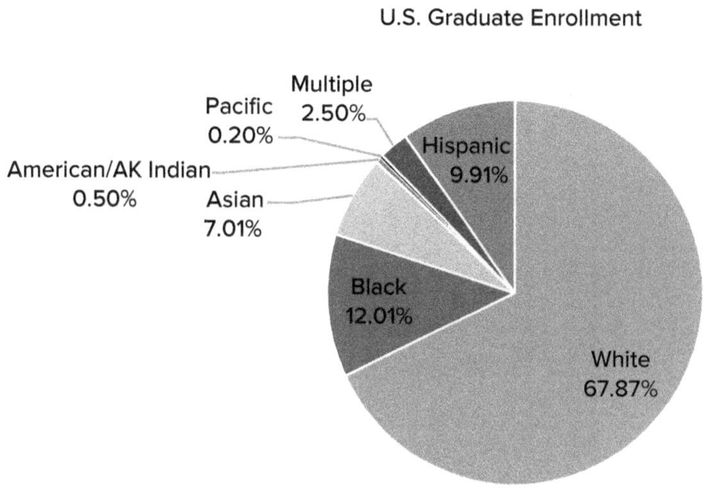

recruit AI/AN students for participation in future UNR Graduate School recruitment and retention programs.

The outcomes for GradFIT participants have been: 1) increased awareness of the opportunities afforded by a graduate education, 2) preparation for graduate studies, and 3) elevated confidence and the ability to develop competitive applications (figs. 3–4). GradFIT has also contributed to the diversifying the UNR graduate student population over the last 6 years (fig. 5). While overall enrollment in degree granting graduate programs increased 27 percent between 2013 and 2018, enrollment of American Indian, Black, and Hispanic students increased by 60 percent, 102 percent and 96 percent, respectively. While the GradFIT program is not solely responsible for these gains in enrollment and diversity, it has certainly played a significant role.

Future Work

Following the success of GradFIT, the UNR Graduate School will soon begin GradFIT Phase II funded by a National Science Foundation Innovations in Graduate Education (NSF-IGE) award. Titled "Enhancing Diversity by Changing Institutional Culture and Scaffolding Student Success," this two-year program that will incorporate a series of summer

FIGURE 4. GradFIT Participant Demographic Data (2015-2019). Self-reported data from the 190 participants in GradFIT shows that 76% are non-white, with a majority (44%) being Hispanic/Latino. The participants are also a majority female and first-generation.

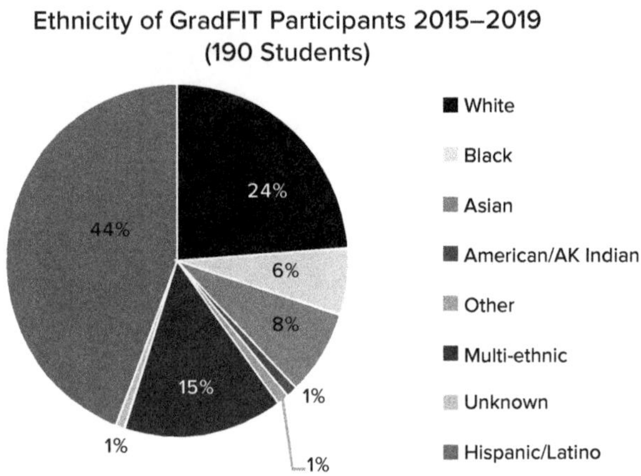

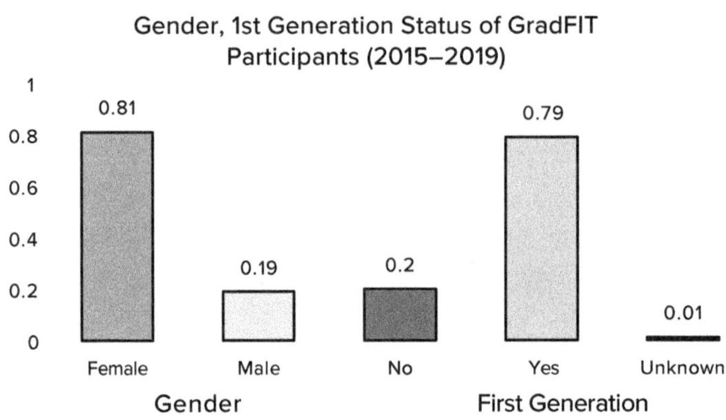

FIGURE 5. Pre and Post-GradFIT participation survey results from GradFIT Cohort 6 (2019) (responses from 42 of 48 participants). (1 = Not at All, 3 = Moderately Well, 5 = Extremely Well)

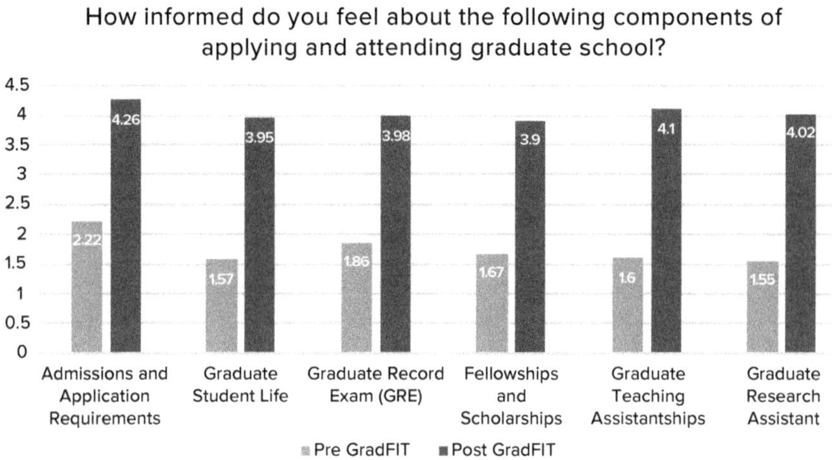

FIGURE 6. Since the implementation of GradFIT, UNR has achieved impressive gains in HUG enrollment, with increases of 60%, 102%, and 96% for American Indian, Black, and Hispanic students, respectively.

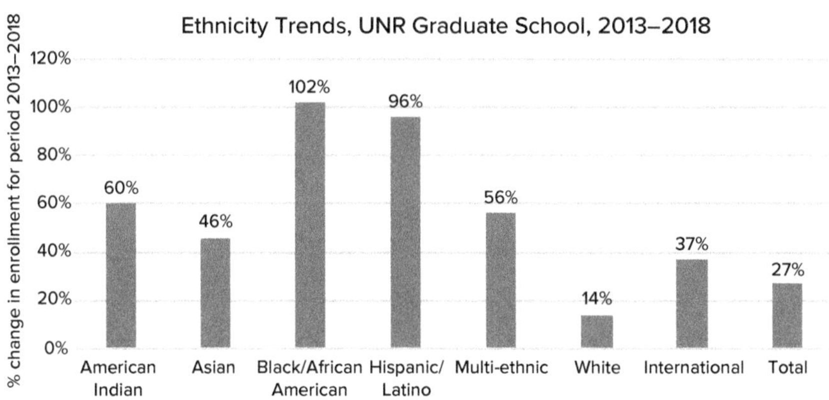

workshops along with academic year professional development to increase the retention and success of historically underrepresented groups in UNR Graduate programs. GradFIT Phase II will have incoming PhD students engage in two 3-week summer boot camps as well as additional professional development, mentoring, and social network support activities during their first year and a half of graduate school (see fig. 5).

Unique elements of this project include (1) intentional development of a recruitment/retention positive feedback loop, (2) family/community involvement to enhance support groups, and (3) training in marketable skills (e.g. communication via virtual reality platforms). Outcomes from this project will generate new knowledge concerning best practices for recruitment and retention of historically underrepresented populations. Specifically, the project will test interventions and compare results across control and test groups to examine potential changes in: (1) academic performance and research quality, (2) non-financial family support, (3) ease of navigation toward degree completion and career placement, (4) recruitment and retention, and (5) student research and communication skills. Interventions include quantitative disciplinary and transferrable skills modules, social support networks, and enhanced mentoring and mentor training. Formative/summative assessment and hypothesis testing procedures will include surveys, academic performance comparisons, course evaluations, focus groups, one-on-one interviews, social network interviews, FIG (Family Involvement in Graduate School) assessment of students/family members, and National Resource Mentoring Network surveys of faculty members. Interventions will be evaluated individually and collectively to determine whether student and faculty participation enhanced graduate education outcomes, improved mentor/mentee relationships, and enhanced recruitment of historically underrepresented groups and first-generation students through positive feedback loops.

The program, which will begin in summer 2020, provides a scalable and sustainable approach for diversifying the graduate ranks and can serve as a model to other institutions for increasing program satisfaction and degree completion rates across all graduate student populations.

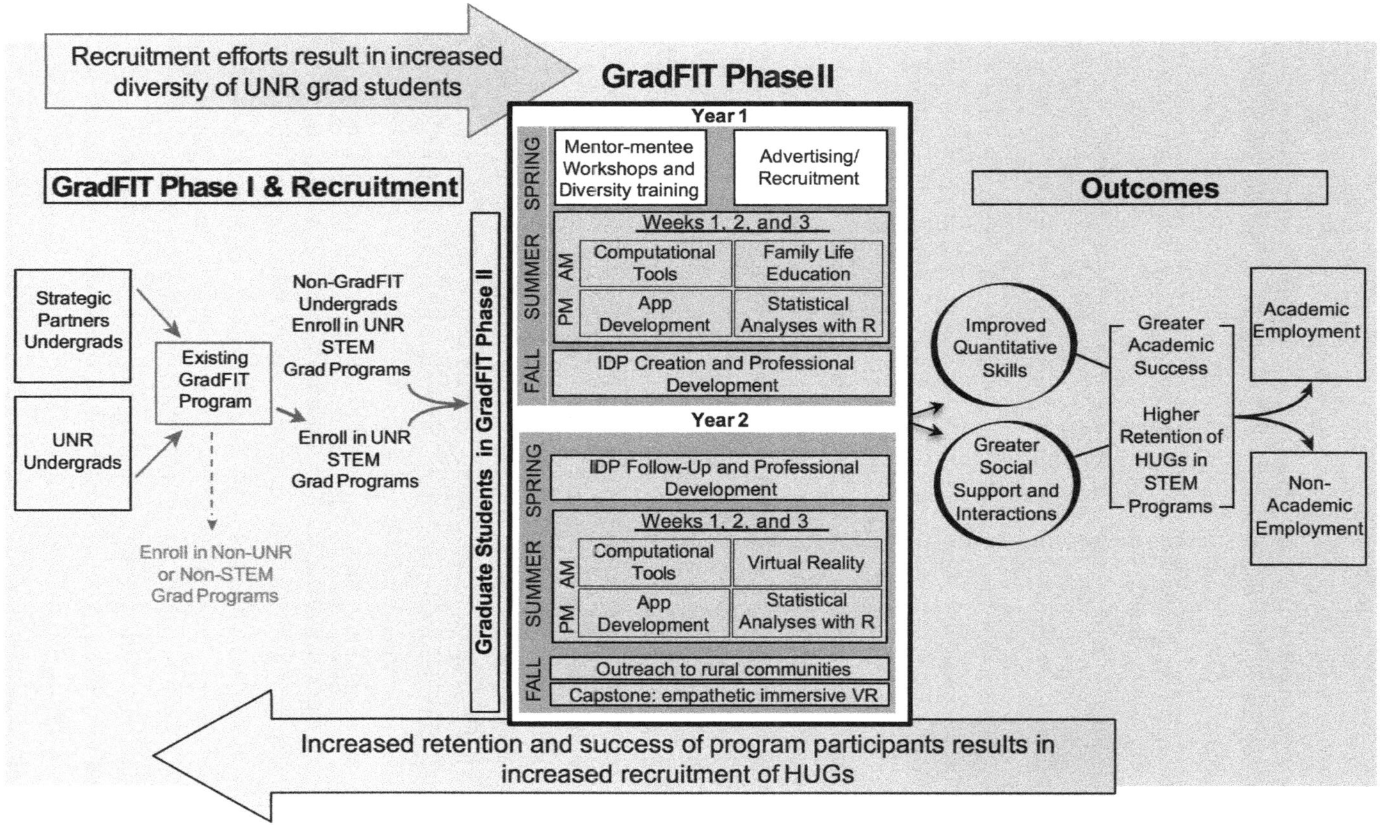

FIGURE 7. The GradFIT Model.

Conclusions and Broader Impacts

There are many challenges in increasing diversity in graduate programs. What is now needed is a comprehensive, scalable, and cost-effective approach that can meet three major challenges facing STEM graduate programs:

1. low ethnic and racial diversity,
2. low degree completion rates, and
3. inadequate student preparation for diverse careers within and beyond academia

Any program that can effectively address these challenges will have major broader impacts on diversifying the ranks of higher education and industry, and we hypothesize that our expanded GradFIT program provides just such a program. At UNR, in coming years (2019–2022) we will quantify and expand our findings on how the GradFIT model (see fig. 7) can increase the HUG pipeline, cultivate a culture of diversity and inclusion, and provide students with transferable technical and soft skills that will enable them to succeed in their courses, research programs, and careers. The GradFIT model has the potential to be adopted widely as a financially sustainable program in which students receive academic credit for their participation and training. GradFIT's modular nature also means that it can be tailored to the specific needs of programs across a range of STEM disciplines in varying academic or industry scenarios.

The work done in GradFIT initiatives benefits not only participants, but also the broader graduate school community of enrolled students, future applicants and academic faculty. Professional development activities designed to cultivate diversity, improved communication, and transferable skills established in programs like GradFIT are used widely across campus for faculty, student and recruitment training events and workshops. By incorporating multi-disciplinary graduate training and experiential learning activities, the GradFIT program and its modules address work force needs and provide transferable skills commonly not developed in graduate students, especially HUGS. The GradFIT model addresses two issues vital to maintaining a strong workforce: 1) training students in technical and quantitative skills and 2) training currently underrepresented populations to be competitive for jobs requiring these skills. By 2020, more than half of the nation's children will be from a minority group, and it is important that programs like GradFIT address the underrepresentation of HUGS in STEM fields in order to promote and increase innovation and reduce threats to global competitiveness and national security.

REFERENCES

National Science Foundation, National Center for Science and Engineering Statistics. (2017) Women, minorities, and persons with disabilities in science and engineering: 2017 digest (NSF 17-310). Available at https://www.nsf.gov/statistics/2017/nsf17310/static/downloads/nsf17310-digest.pdf.

Freeman, R. B., Huang, W. (2014) Strength in diversity. Nature, 513, 305.

Levine, S. S., Apfelbaum, E. P., Bernard, M., Bartelte, V. L., Zajac, E. J., Stark, D. (2014) Ethnic diversity deflates price bubbles. Proceedings of the National Academy of Sciences, USA111: 18524–18529.

Thompson, N. L., Campbell, A. G. (2013) Addressing the challenge of diversity in the graduate ranks: good practices yield good outcomes. *CBE-Life Sciences Education* 12, 19–29.

Sowell, R., Allum, J., & Okahana, H. (2015). Doctoral initiative on minority attrition and completion. Washington, DC: Council of Graduate Schools.

CHAPTER 16

The McNair Scholars Program

Augmenting Undergraduate Research Involvement and Graduate School Preparedness

HEATHER A. WILLIAMS, M.A., and KARLA HERNÁNDEZ, PH.D.

Heather Williams, M.A., is the student success specialist for the McNair Scholars and TRIO Scholars programs, housed under the Academic and Opportunity Support Programs (AOSP) at the University of Nevada, Reno (UNR). Heather has worked for AOSP since 2003 when the McNair Scholars program was implemented on the UNR campus. She acts as an advisor and GRE instructor for students in the program. She completed her bachelor's degree in English and her master's degree in English Literature at University of Nevada, Reno, and worked as a lecturer in the English Department prior to joining the AOSP staff.

Karla Hernández, Ph.D. is the assistant director for the McNair Scholars program, one of the Academic and Opportunity Support Programs at the University of Nevada, Reno. Karla participated in undergraduate research in the materials science and engineering department and in the biochemistry department. She earned a bachelor's and master's dual degree in Biotechnology and subsequently a doctorate in Cellular and Molecular Biology from the Molecular Biosciences Graduate Program at the University of Nevada, Reno. She continued her scientific training at the University of Nevada—School of Medicine as a post-doctoral research fellow in Dr. Cherie Singer's pharmacology laboratory. Afterward, Karla transitioned into the administrative role of program coordinator and community liaison for the Nevada Learn and Earn Advanced-career Pathway (LEAP) program—an NSF funded collaborative effort among the Nevada Governor's Office of Economic Development, Nevada Department of Education, WCSD, TMCC, UNR and various local industry partners.

Introduction

The McNair Scholars Program is a federally funded TRIO program, first introduced at the University of Nevada, Reno (UNR) in 2003. The program's goal is to prepare undergraduate students for graduate school, specifically for entering doctoral programs, through involvement in research and other scholarly activities. McNair participants are either first-generation (neither parent has earned a bachelor's degree) and income-qualified (family's taxable income does not exceed 150 percent of the poverty level) or members of a group that is traditionally underrepresented in graduate education. These groups include American Indian/Alaskan Native, African American, Hispanic, or Native Hawaiian/Pacific Islander. This chapter highlights the successful strategies used by the McNair Scholars Program at UNR to retain, graduate, and ensure enrollment in graduate school for our scholars.

A president of the Associated Students of the University of Nevada (ASUN) described his McNair Scholars participation in this way.

> The McNair Program has provided me with the opportunity to expand my horizons knowing I have created a future for myself after my undergraduate degree. As a McNair Scholar, I gained the first-hand experience of research, career, and personal development. My mentor has provided me with guidance, unlike any other faculty member at the University, for which I am eternally grateful. The program is not only a stepping-stone but a backbone for my undergraduate career at the University to know I am ready for the world and to be a servant leader and provider to many.
>
> —Senior in Political Science and International Affairs

Personal Coaching

Need for Intrusive Advising

Typically, in a counseling setting, the counselee seeks out the services of a counselor. They see a problem they wish to address or have a need that they want resolved, and so counseling is a course of action they *choose*. This typical form of help-seeking is encouraged in the McNair Scholars Program; however, we also realize that a more dynamic and assertive advising style is often needed with our scholars. From the very beginning, McNair Scholars are sought out by our program. Recruitment of students is a must, as the audience we seek to serve—first generation, low-income, and underrepresented students—is often the very population on campus who are unaware of our services. Therefore, the McNair Scholars Program recruits students through a series of campaigns that begin in January and last until October. All eligible students on campus are sent a targeted email with information about the program—its benefits and services as well as a link to apply. Emails are also sent to target groups on campus like the Center for Cultural Diversity, the Advisors' list serve, and multiple clubs and organizations. Additionally, advertising is posted on television monitors throughout campus, tabling occurs at multiple events, specific McNair focused info sessions are scheduled, and staff members visit both faculty meetings and student classes to promote the program. This "intrusive" style of marketing is a must in order to reach students who don't have the cultural capital to seek out services on their own.

This same intrusive format is used in the counseling techniques McNair staff implement as well. In his article, *Intrusive College Counseling*, Robert Glennen offers the statistic that when intrusive counseling was used on his campus, "freshman attrition [. . .] was reduced from 45 to 6 percent during the first 2 years of operation." There was also a "9 percent increase" in the number of students placed on the dean's list (1976, 50). These results can be seen in programs across the country. For example, when University of Southern Indiana implemented their PLUSS Program with intrusive advising for college STEM students, retention rates for underrepresented STEM students was at 32 percent. After participating in PLUSS, retention rose to 53 percent (Rodgers, Blunt, & Trible, 2014, 40.) Currently, intrusive advising takes on the following model in the McNair Scholars Program. When students are brought into the program in the fall semester, they are immediately placed in a one-on-one advising schedule where they meet with a member of the McNair staff on a monthly basis. At their first meeting, students complete a needs assessment where they can identify areas that are concerns for them and discuss these concerns with their advisor. Students also sign a contract, agreeing to meet with their advisor at least once a month (more if needed) for the remainder of their time in the program. These individual meetings are in addition to the monthly group meetings and weekly class sessions which students also participate in. Students renew their contract at the beginning of every semester, reminding them that individual contact meetings are a vital part of the program.

When students meet privately with McNair staff, the main issues of conversation revolve around how the student is doing with their research project, how their relationship with their mentor is developing, their class grades and school projects, etc. As many of our scholars have never completed an outside-of-class individual research project, they are often unsure of the steps they should follow or the proper means for communicating with their research mentor. Step by step guidelines, provided in the research methods class, are reinforced in individual meetings where longer dialogue can take place and individual needs can be met. Furthermore, as each student is assigned an individual coach, rapport is built between students and staff so that students feel comfortable discussing personal matters in addition to research. Frequent topics that occur include imposter syndrome, lack of income, parents' concern about continuing education, and students' concern about moving out of state for the first time. These mandatory meetings, which ensure that students are touching base with a member of the McNair staff at least three times a month for continuing students (individual, group meetings, and senior meetings) and seven times a month for new students (individual, group meetings, junior meetings, and weekly class), may appear excessive at first glance. However, as students become accustomed to the program, they will often schedule to meet with staff on an even more frequent basis, especially at times of high stress, as when they are deciding on which graduate programs to apply to. Students themselves have expressed how the overall program has helped them achieve their goals.

> Undergraduate research at the University of Nevada, Reno has helped me apply the things that I am learning in a classroom setting to work that could potentially save lives. Ever since I joined the University, I have wanted nothing more than to apply my learning to a significant cause. The McNair program has helped me facilitate this experience and has also helped me learn how to take advantage of all the opportunities that our University has to offer.
>
> —Junior in Biomedical and Electrical Engineering

> The McNair Scholars program facilitated the concretization of my abstract goals by providing me with critical information regarding the research process, graduate school, and life with a Ph.D. As a result, I am currently enrolled in the graduate program of my dreams!
>
> —B.A. in Philosophy, UNR class of 2019

Students realize that there is at least one location on campus where they can seek advice on all fronts from financial aid, to housing, to research, to personal life, and everything in between. This increases the student's chance of success as they always have a trusted and knowledgeable staff member to turn to for any crisis or question. The intrusive advising model has been successful for our McNair Scholars; in our 2018 and 2019 cohorts, 91 percent of students enrolled in graduate school. Over the course of our sixteen years on the UNR campus, we have served over 180 students, and in the 2017–2018 academic year alone, six alumni earned doctoral degrees (Ph.D.), 11 alumni earned masters' degrees and one earned a juris doctor (J.D.) Currently, over 50 alumni are enrolled in PhD programs.

While McNair program staff prefer intrusive advising, this is not always the style faculty mentors are accustomed to providing. Because all McNair students must have a faculty mentor with a PhD in their field, we have discovered that it is helpful to discuss expectations of advising schedules with both students and mentors. When students enter the program, one of the first workshops they participate in is, "How to Choose a Mentor." During this workshop, students are encouraged to look at several factors when choosing a mentor including: how much time that mentor has to spend with the student, how well they will communicate (meaning frequency and compatibility), as well as the mentor's ability to prepare them for conferences, discuss graduate school possibilities, write them a letter of recommendation, and help them network both on and off campus. In order to be a strong mentor meeting all of these criteria, it is necessary to know the students very well. In order to know the students well, we support mentors in being "intrusive" in their advising techniques as well. At our first mentor meeting, we discuss with faculty how often we feel they should be meeting with students, typically on a weekly basis throughout the spring when students are preparing their proposal, and even more frequently in summer when students are completing their research. If faculty take a more casual approach to scheduling, we try to empower students to request the number and frequency of meetings they feel is necessary to have their questions answered and for them to be successful. Students often acknowledge that it is the strong mentor relationship which bolsters their esteem and capabilities.

> My mentor has done a great job of preparing me for graduate school within the field of psychology, and it is clear that she has

> my academic development in mind. She has helped me develop my research experience, helped me improve my writing skills, provided me with exposure to the Clinical Psychology program, and she has given me valuable advice on how to better myself as a future graduate student.
>
> —Senior in Psychology

> My favorite part about working with Dr. Yong Zhang was his eagerness to train me on several aspects of a scientific career. Yong trained me to be as well rounded a scientist as possible, from the conception of a projection, to the preparation of a manuscript, to taking me to meet with invited speakers. The most valuable lesson I learned from Yong was his ability to share his time, insights, and resources with his students. Since my time in the lab, I've sought out mentors like him and I find myself acting the same to my mentees.
>
> —Neuroscience Ph.D. candidate
> B.S. in Neuroscience UNR class of 2017

Building a Cohort Model

In addition to developing strong ties between staff and students, a cohort model is used in the McNair Scholars Program so that student to student relationships can be built and a large support network of peers is always available. In her paper, *The Doctoral Cohort Model: Increasing Opportunities for Success*, Mary Nimer claims, "Participation in a doctoral program cohort significantly increases the chances for the successful completion of the course of studies for all members of the cohort" (2009, p. 1373). This is because "the cohort model offers its members a feeling of an extended family or community to witness one's personal struggles, educational challenges, and accomplishments" (2009, p. 1377). While our students are still undergraduates, we are preparing them to go into doctoral programs, and a cohort model similar to Nimer's is purposefully developed so that students may have yet another avenue of support in addition to McNair staff and their research mentor/research group.

Upon entry into the McNair Scholars Program during the late fall semester of their junior year, students attend one group activity whose intention is to allow the students to casually get to know one another in an informal setting. During the 2018 group meeting, students created dream boards over the course of 2 hours with both students and staff sharing their boards at the end of the session. This allowed time for students to ask about each other's families, friends, living arrangements, personal aspirations, and both short- and long-term goals. Once students become more familiar with their cohort, they begin to see similarities that they share which allows them to feel connected to a group. During the spring semester, students meet together in the research methods class on a weekly basis where they are encouraged to share how their research is proceeding. They have the opportunity to discuss development of projects and relationships with faculty mentors so that they can learn from each other's differing approaches, successes, and failures. As students see their peers' progress, they are inspired, working amongst a group of like-minded individuals. They have a group of peers they can turn to if they have questions about performing research or how they handled problems. A McNair Scholar and commencement speaker at the 2019 AOSP graduation ceremony, said in his address,

> We are offered a special opportunity to share truths with those who have had similar and unique experiences. We learn about the unique struggles of others, and the various means of resilience that our fellow humans are using to ease their struggles. A space is established where individuals from diverse backgrounds can find unity and support in their efforts to create knowledge. These communities force us to realize that we are not alone in the world and that others are there to help when we are struggling. These communities that we have established are not constrained by the academic sphere, however. The relationships that we build with others remain with us so long as we care to keep them alive. I deeply hope that each of my friends in my beloved cohort find fundamental happiness and become who they hope to be, and I can definitively state that this desire is not going to dissipate when I graduate.
>
> —B.A. in Philosophy, UNR class of 2019

Such strong student bonds are encouraged throughout the McNair experience. During monthly meetings, program updates are provided not only by McNair staff but also from McNair students, and students are informed about opportunities on campus that range far and wide from the possibility of applying for research funding, to free socials for first-generation students, group counseling, intramural sports, or updates on ways to be involved on campus such as voting in student elections or joining clubs. This cultural capitol allows students to feel "in the know" and connected to the University. For first generation students, trying new social activities can be challenging; however, McNair Scholars have a group of peers with whom they may experience these events and who encourage them to attend and try new activities.

During the summer program, the McNair Scholars cohort has its most intensive opportunity for building the cohort dynamic. During this 10-week time period students meet daily from 8 a.m. to 10:30 a.m. for workshops, and for a briefer part of the summer from 8 a.m. to 12:30 p.m. for their GRE (Graduate Record Exam) course. They see the same faces every day at a time when their research activity reaches its peak. The first week of the summer session is devoted to team building and group bonding activities. On day one, students are taken to an all-day ropes course that emphasizes not only relying on each other for physical activities and trust exercises, but also discussion of problem solving tactics after each activity that delve deeply into ingrained personal beliefs, communication strategies, and how to build on strengths in both the personal and academic life as well as how to acknowledge areas for growth. In past sessions, students have shared about their childhood and family life, personal heroes who inspire them, and their fears of failure or change. Several workshops during the first week of summer focus on fears and myths related to graduate study with the introduction of practical information used to alleviate those fears. Week one is ended with a trip to a local "escape room" experience where the group is divided into teams that are locked in a room for an hour with clues provided on how to "escape." After a week of getting to know each other well through much self-exposure and sharing, this fun activity gives students a chance to unwind, use their skills, and meet a challenge together. It is a small-scale version of the summer as a whole, where students will face multiple obstacles, have their knowledge and resiliency tested, learn to lean on each other for support, and hopefully celebrate victory together in the end.

While some cohorts bond better than others, overall McNair Scholars has had great success in developing a peer support network for our students. During the summer, students have been known to create their own "Group Me" forum in which they all participate in a group phone messaging system so that they can share information more easily. On this platform, they can contribute to discussion on both school and social events. Students also frequently meet outside of their summer research schedule to get dinner, hang out at the end of the week, and even plan trips together. True success of a strong cohort is measured by how much students remain in contact even after they have graduated with their bachelor's degree and have moved on to graduate school. The transition from an undergraduate to a graduate degree program can be daunting, and it is here that students often encounter their worst feelings of imposter syndrome. If those students can reach out to others from their McNair cohort and hear that almost everyone is being challenged, has fears and doubts, may be experiencing home sickness and fatigue—then they are more likely to stay in school. They realize that all of those feelings are normal, and it becomes easier to combat them. This is a lasting benefit of building a strong cohort of peers whom you can trust.

Academic Coaching

Graduate School Preparation

Building strong cohort bonds and establishing a foundation for resilient behavior and mindset has already been discussed. However, there are, of course, several practical components to the McNair Program that set a student up to have the tools to be a successful applicant to graduate school. The ten-week McNair Scholars Summer Research Program is the largest component of our program that aids students' success in this area.

> Participating in undergraduate research allows me to learn advanced knowledge and research techniques in my field of study that are never taught in the traditional classroom environment. The workshops provided by the UNR McNair Program (i.e. Ph.D. panels, GRE preparation course, graduate program application) and the academic resources provided by Richard Kelley (my research mentor) guide me through the research process and direct my path toward a successful graduate program experience. Without the UNR McNair Program and my research mentor, my chance of succeeding in the graduate program would be very slim.
>
> —Junior in Computer Science and Engineering

During the second week of the summer program, students are provided with several workshops that introduce them to what they will encounter when applying to graduate school. The first workshop entails *how* to research graduate schools they are interested in attending. For many first-generation students, even this preliminary step is mysterious. They have often applied to their undergraduate institution because it is in-state, close to home, and less expensive. This approach will not work for graduate education, and many students simply don't know how to locate a graduate program where they will achieve the most benefit and best fit. McNair staff outline for students the items they should be looking for in a graduate program, namely research and advisor compatibility as well as funding opportunities. Students spend time this week performing their first online search for professors at other universities who are engaged in research that the student wishes to pursue. This workshop is followed by another in which students are taught how to write to faculty at other universities in order to introduce themselves, discuss that faculty's research, and address the possibility of attending their university. Throughout the summer program, students must complete three graduate survey assignments showing that they have researched a minimum of nine schools they are interested in attending. Once appropriate graduate schools have been identified, students receive training on how to complete the application process. There are separate workshops centered around completing a personal statement, writing a diversity statement, creating a CV, and obtaining strong letters of recommendation. McNair staff, as well as experts on campus recruited from The Writing and Speaking Center and the Career Studio, teach students step by step components to drafting application materials that will showcase their strengths as a potential graduate student. While generating these materials may seem self-explanatory to some, there is a large degree of social capital needed to understand the societal nuances of something like asking for a letter of recommendation. Therefore, our workshop on obtaining letters of recommendation contains items such as the length of time you should give a professor to complete a letter, the fact that you should ask in person at a scheduled appointment, the documents with which you should provide the professor, how to assess their demeanor in agreeing to write your letter, and how to proceed if your professor does not complete the letter in a timely manner. These can be delicate topics that students have not considered or encountered in the past.

Because at least two-thirds of students in the McNair Scholars program come from low-income backgrounds, funding their graduate education is a topic of strong concern. A workshop is offered during the second week of the summer program to introduce ways in which students can not only make themselves more eligible for funding, but also teaches them resources for locating fellowships and assistantships. Our students often share several reasons why low-income students are hesitant about graduate school: the perceived notion that extending their time in school will increase their student debt or delay their entry into the workforce thereby delaying their ability to begin earning an income, paying off debt, or financially helping their family. In marketing the McNair Scholars Program and recruiting new students, McNair staff assure applicants that highly qualified and strong graduate candidates should have their graduate education paid for through multiple means. Once the hurdle of convincing students that pursuing further education will not bankrupt them or their parents, we deliver on teaching the students the best methods for securing funding for graduate school. The McNair Scholars staff introduces students to fellowship databases and help them with the application process. The staff teaches students how to research the availability of graduate, research, or teaching assistantships and walks them through the process of how to apply for these opportunities. Additionally, workshops are provided on grant funding opportunities—how to find them, how to apply for them, and what committees are looking for in a strong application. In this instance, we often invite experts who have received grant funding (such as NSF or NIH recipients) or who have served on the committees evaluating applicants for grant funding, to speak with our students and share their insight. In past years, our scholars have been very successful in securing funding for graduate school. In the 2019 graduating class alone, scholars were offered a combined total of nearly $300,000 in funding just to complete their first year of graduate school.

> Participation in undergraduate research has provided me the opportunity to do real physics and gain valuable skills not taught within the normal curriculum. My research, and participation in the McNair Scholars Program, have cemented my commitment to pursuing a doctoral degree in physics and provided all the tools necessary to reach that goal. McNair helped me understand how to write the statement of purpose and format the CV all while explaining the overarching application process and how to secure external funding.
>
> —Senior in Physics

The summer program curriculum and activities are updated on a yearly basis. The McNair Program staff regularly work on improving the workshops and trainings to ensure their relevance. In constructing the most recent curriculum, staff added a self-care workshop in conjunction with UNR counseling services. Another recent addition to the program has been a cultural competency training. The McNair Program staff worked closely with the professor of multicultural education in the UNR College of Education to develop a customized one-day training for the summer 2019 cohort of McNair Scholars.

An important piece of the graduate application is GRE scores. While not all schools require students take this standardized test, many do, thus the McNair Scholars Program devotes four weeks of the ten-week summer program to GRE training. As with the SAT or ACT tests, students take the GRE prior to applying to school and submit their scores with the rest of their application materials. Some schools set minimum score levels to be considered a strong applicant, and it can become a source of stress and anxiety for students. Students in our program attend GRE class for four hours of the day; two hours are devoted to verbal preparation and two hours are devoted to quantitative preparation. Not only are students taught verbal and math skills, they are shown best methods for approaching standardized test questions. They are given information about the exam itself including when they should take the exam, how to register, how to pay, how their scores will be interpreted, and what procedures to expect at the testing facilities. Moreover, students who feel overwhelmed with pressure surrounding the exam can seek out their coach's counseling, and students often form their own study groups and register to take the exam together so they can have the support of their cohort as well.

During the fall semester, senior McNair Scholars put to use the skills they have learned during the summer research program. Students are encouraged to apply to a minimum of nine graduate schools and are aided in the process of applying through one on one tutoring and coaching sessions where graduate school application materials are discussed. Additionally, seniors have a group meeting with McNair staff on a weekly basis where time is dedicated to applying for graduate school. In the spring, when students are receiving acceptance notices for graduate school, McNair staff discuss each acceptance and offer letter with students, so they have guidance on how to understand their offer letters and advice on which schools to attend. In the end, the choice of final school lies solely with the student and their decision is recognized in a signing day celebration held in April. Much like the athletic signing days when student athletes reveal the college team with which they have chosen to play, McNair Scholars reveal the graduate program they have chosen to attend and why. Students invite friends, family, mentors, their lab group, and anyone else who is close to them in order to celebrate the achievement of being accepted into a graduate program. The McNair Scholars Program requires much hard work and dedication and just the process of applying to multiple graduate schools is no small feat. This final celebration recognizes each student's effort, hard work, and dedication to remaining on a path of success even when times grow difficult.

Increasing Awareness

It is imperative that McNair eligible students, and all UNR students, are better prepared for the possibility of graduate education. Certainly, not all students will need or want a graduate degree, but students must be given the information and ability for advancement, so they are on an equal playing field with the rest of the nation. To meet this need, the McNair Scholars Program has paired with the department of Undergraduate Research to develop PREP (Pack Research Experience Program). The Director for the Office of Undergraduate Research along with the McNair Scholars Program staff have collaborated to strategically design and provide undergraduate students (freshman and sophomore academic standing) opportunities to work in well-defined research projects. The program was created in 2018 and implemented in 2019 for a group of 11 students. Characteristic elements of PREP include a thorough application on behalf of the potential faculty research mentors and the candidate undergraduate participants. The mentor and mentee are matched based on the student's field of study, the specific research project and the student's interest in the topic. Additionally, the undergraduate research office and McNair Program staff facilitate guidance by providing an individualized orientation meeting, documentation to assess research progress and learning outcomes. This specific approach ensures mentor-mentee commitment. If students are able to experience research at an earlier point in their academic career, they will be able to make decisions about whether or not graduate school should be in their future. It is our hope that the PREP program can serve as a pipeline for McNair Scholars and an additional resource so that more students will be introduced to graduate school possibilities. McNair Scholars is also working with the graduate school to market our services during GradFIT in the hopes of discovering potential candidates and offering assistance to students.

REFERENCES

Glennen, R. (1976). Intrusive College Counseling. *The School Counselor*, 24, 48–50.

Nimer, M. (2009). The Doctoral Cohort Model: Increasing Opportunities for Success. *College Student Journal*. 43, 1373–1379.

Rodgers, K., Blunt, S., & Trible, L. (2014). A Real PLUSS: An Intrusive Advising Program for Underprepared STEM Students. *NACADA Journal*. 35–42. doi:10.12930/NACADA-13-002.

PART IV

Success Through Tutoring

Tutoring programs help students succeed by allowing their peers to tutor and support them with enhanced academic support. The benefits of tutoring go beyond the classroom as it provides a personalized learning experience. The training that peer tutors require within the respected subject not only allow them to help others, but also help themselves become experts in the subject matter. The customized learning experience helps overall academic performance by improving student study habits, study skills, social skills, and self-esteem. By providing personalized and direct feedback, tutors help their students develop critical thinking skills necessary for them to become intellectually independent and confident in the work that they produce. The University of Nevada, Reno, offers a multitude of tutoring programs that provide both group and one-on-one sessions for students who need the extra assistance or students who want to become more experienced in core curricular classes. This section highlights the Tutoring Center, the Writing and Speaking Center, the Math Center, and the accuplacer tutoring program from the Tutoring Center, and the MATH 19 program from the Disability Resource Center.

CHAPTER 17

The Changing Face of Tutoring

CHRISTOPHER CHADWICK, M.A., and
MARSHA URBAN, PH.D.

Christopher R. Chadwick is the program manager of Nevada PASS at the University of Nevada, Reno. In his role, he provides academic support for traditionally difficult courses and works to increase student retention. His professional and research interest include student development and higher education policy. He earned a bachelor of arts in English Literature and a master of arts in Educational Leadership from the University of Nevada, Reno.

Marsha Urban, Ph.D. is the director of the University Tutoring Center. She earned her bachelor's degree in English and Secondary Education from King's College (Wilkes-Barre, PA) followed by the master's degree in English Literature at the University of Nevada, Reno. She earned her Ph.D. in Seventeenth-Century British Literature at the University of Nevada, Reno and she published her dissertation: Seventeenth-Century Mother's Advice Books in 2006.

Introduction

The University Tutoring Center (UTC) has contributed to the academic success of students at the University of Nevada, Reno for nearly 30 years. When undergraduate students saw Student Support Services (SSS) and TRiO students being tutored they asked, "Why not us?" Student Services responded and financed the first free, general tutoring center for all University undergraduate students. Initially, tutoring focused on the core curriculum through bi-weekly group-tutoring sessions covering many of the general education courses. If students needed additional help, up to three one-on-one appointments were available per semester. From this narrow beginning, the UTC has grown to include appointments, small group tutoring, walk-in labs, and Supplemental Instruction (SI) in our core, academic support services.

Appointments

Traditional, one-on-one appointments have been a core demand of many undergraduate students over the years. Students want to meet with a knowledgeable tutor who can answer questions, provide useful insights into course material, and assist in mapping a route for the students' academic success. The availability of these appointments evolved throughout the years. Student demand for appointments resulted in expanding beyond the initial offering of three appointments per semester. As student demand for tutoring grew, so did the UTC services. One-on-one appointments grew until the 2008 global recession.

In fall 2008, the economic downturn forced the UTC to shift from a free model to a fee-based model. This model meant students who wanted tutoring would be required to pay to use the UTC. Charging forced changes to the UTC tutoring model. We sold packages of five appointments and access to a math or science walk-in lab. The income generated from these fees financed the tutors and limited small group tutoring for students who could not afford to pay for tutoring services. During the 2008–2009 academic year, the state funded the UTC coordinator. No other state funds were available to the Center. The coordinator hired an unpaid graduate intern to assist with the SI program.

Charging for tutoring was an ethical and financial problem. Need and affordability were primary concerns. Some of the most at-risk students simply could not afford the new financial burden. As a result, we saw a sharp decline in the number students seeking tutoring services. This also meant a reduction of tutors hired. The decrease in usage also resulted in moving the UTC to a much smaller physical area. The continued financial support of the Student Services enabled SI to continue as a free service to students, but the SI program provided supports for a small number of courses unlike the expansive one-on-one appointment offerings.

Due to these changes, the Associated Students of the University of Nevada (ASUN), the undergraduate student government, proposed the "Joint Vision 2017: A Student Vision for the University of Nevada." This strategic plan included a proposal for increased support and expansion of tutoring services. University undergraduates voted to support the proposal in spring 2009. Beginning in fall 2009, appointment tutoring was once again an undergraduate staple available to all students.

Students were happy to have these "free" services even if they were

FIGURE 1. Appointments Spring 2014–Fall 2017.

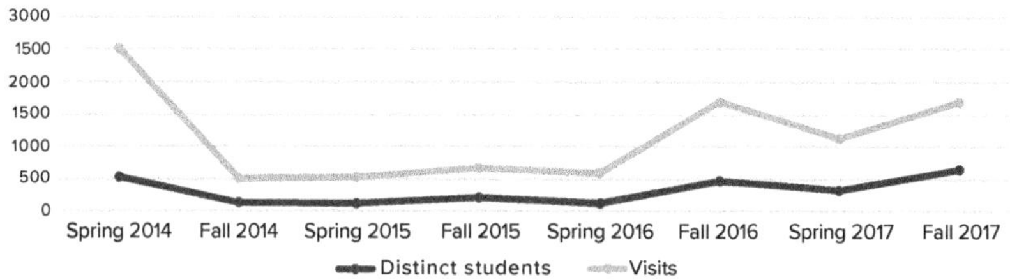

actually paying a $25 a semester fee. This was far better than the five appointments for $60 or walk-in lab access for $150. Tutoring numbers, especially appointment tutoring, increased as students perceived tutoring as free. However, this created an unintended consequence: students were scheduling appointments and not attending. A policy to restrict appointments to one per day created some accountability and reduced the impact on the UTC budget. Additionally, students who were absent twice in a semester were blocked from making further appointments for the remainder of the semester. We established a "No Excuse" policy to remove the daily appeals and to encourage personal responsibility in students. Even with these new policies, appointments grew beyond our budget. We sought additional funds from the Provost's Office. While high use is admirable, exceeding the budget was not. This meant changes needed to be implemented. Again, we charged for appointments for two years. Appointment visits went from 2,516 in spring 2014 to 530 in fall 2014. Finally, in fall 2016, we were provided a small amount for free appointments to resume. Our visits rose to 1,675 that semester. Appointment tutoring never truly recovered from the two years of charging as indicated in the chart below. Although vacillating between free and fee-based appointments impacted usage, the attitudinal change of incoming students may also influence the appointment numbers. Many students expect an immediate response to requests instead of planning ahead by creating dedicated appointment times. We are seeing more instances of immediacy rather than planning. We are also seeing an increase in students looking for answers rather than strategies for learning.

Walk-in Labs

Walk-in tutoring labs have changed both in locations and supported subjects. Due to the size reduction in 2008, we chose to move the walk-in labs instead of discontinuing them. We created walk-in labs at the Joe Crowley

Student Union and eventually moved to the two main campus libraries. While these partnerships worked, the University was growing, and space continued to be an issue. The President of the University proposed a new building to centralize many of the student success services. His vision was a one-stop shop where students could receive support through tutoring, advising, and accommodations. The Pennington Student Achievement Center opened in February 2016. The building brought vast changes to the campus and to tutoring. Now the University Tutoring, Writing, and Math Centers are co-located on the Clarence and Martha Jones Family Foundation Learning Commons third floor. The pattern of student use changed with the opening of the new building. The focus of the building was to be a collaborative hub for students, providing services and space for students to study. The building is similar to a student union, but with the emphasis on the academic component of student life. The focus succeeded and the building has drawn traffic from the library walk-in labs. The UTC saw a drop-in attendance at the two library walk-in labs. To address the shift, the walk-in labs were brought into the Pennington Student Achievement Center. The present UTC design does not meet the needs of a walk-in lab. Presently, we dedicate three large rooms to the walk-in labs with plans to redesign an open space for a better fitting environment. To bring more students into the space, we invited the Chemistry Help Center to join the UTC walk-in lab. This collaboration continues the vision of centralized support services. Additionally, the number of students using our services is growing, thus forming a cogent argument for the needed construction.

Supported subjects in the walk-in labs changes on a semester basis depending on course offerings, demands of the students, tutors hired, and use. Mathematics, chemistry, and physics are core subjects; however, business, engineering, and foreign languages receive varying levels of requests. Walk-in labs require constant assessment to respond to student need.

Group Tutoring

Group tutoring was a central program with the past UTC model. The UTC coordinated small groups of two to five students who met biweekly primarily in introductory and general education courses. The emphasis on collaborative tutoring is still a core philosophy yet is more challenging to implement now. With the demand of one-on-one tutoring and walk-in labs, groups make up a much smaller portion of the UTC services. Students often want to form small study groups directly before an upcoming exam. Forming the group for the last review before an exam often promotes procrastination and other poor planning skills. To combat this mentality, small groups with a peer tutor form only if the group meets weekly throughout the semester. This method emphasizes preparation and allows tutors to facilitate more productive sessions by including study skills specific to the class. In the group sessions, tutors build a relationship with the students which enable the tutors focus on basic skills and concepts. The weekly group sessions solidify academic strategies.

Supplemental Instruction

The UTC began a small, pilot SI program during the 2007 summer semester focusing exclusively on one remedial, noncredit-bearing math course. This new SI program showed promising results and expanded during the 2007 fall semester to include accounting, anthropology, biology, chemistry, math, philosophy, physics, psychology, and sociology. This pilot program with financial support from Student Services gave us the opportunity to work with a small number of courses to build an understanding of which courses would work best for students. Since then, a variety of subjects have received SI support. These subjects include art, history, criminal justice, economics, accounting, and finance. Even though we worked with the initial subjects for multiple semesters, we found low attendance at weekly sessions for some courses. Students in these classes only attended review sessions regardless of marketing efforts. For this reason, we focus on the courses with the best participation: core sciences, engineering, and accounting courses. From this limited launch, the SI program at the University of Nevada, Reno supported sixteen different courses with twenty-seven sections during the 2018 fall semester.

The SI program became so successful that some faculty referred to their own in-class student assistances as "supplemental." We wanted to brand our SI leaders as official UTC employees who are mentored by an internationally certified SI trained supervisors, the SI program changed its name to Nevada Peer-Assisted Study Sessions (PASS) in fall 2016. The transition has been very successful, and the new name brings home our goal of helping students pass their classes the first time.

One staff person directly supervises the Nevada PASS, the UTC

TABLE 1. Total withdrawal rate of students for SI-supported courses

	Total DFW Rates for SI-Supported Courses	
	Non-SI student DFW rate	SI student DFW rate
Fall 2017	39.43%	21.67%
Spring 2018	35.95%	15.93%
Fall 2018	45.22%	18.92%

Tutoring Specialist, who receives as-needed additional support from the UTC Director. The Nevada PASS program also employs Senior PASS Leaders who serve as peer mentors for the current Nevada PASS Leader cohort. These mentors meet weekly to assist with planning, assess current study sessions, and implement ongoing training. These Senior PASS leaders meet with the Tutoring Specialist to develop training topics, identify needed interventions, and assist with the Nevada PASS program growth.

While the name of the program changed to better reflect the goals and expectations of the sessions, the structure matches with the International Center for Supplemental Instruction guidelines. Additionally, a consistently lower D, F, and withdrawal (DFW) rate of students who attend SI versus non-SI students resulted in the Nevada PASS program receiving official certification in spring 2019.

Conclusion

From its inception, the University Tutoring Center focused on assisting students in their academic studies. Over the years, our program changed and shifted to meet the demands of the current student body, but our core tenet is to always support students rising to the academic challenge of their undergraduate degrees. Resources ebb and flow, yet we are here for the current generation of students and will be, in some form or another, for many future generations.

REFERENCE

Associated Student of the University of Nevada (2009). *Joint Vision 2017: A Student Vision for the University of Nevada.* Retrieved from http://de5uoyfu98nbk.cloudfront.net/wp-content/uploads/2015/01/02140926/ASUN-Joint-Vision2017.pdf.

CHAPTER 18

Using Inclusion as a Lens to Support Student Success at Our Writing & Speaking Center

MAUREEN MCBRIDE, PH.D.

Maureen McBride is the director of the University of Nevada Writing & Speaking Center. She has a Ph.D. in Composition and Rhetoric and is currently pursuing a second master's degree in Equity & Diversity. Maureen's areas of research interest and publications include writing centers, reading-writing connections, first-year writing, writing assessment, peer response, and international student education.

Introduction

Although writing instruction can be traced back millennia to the Greek rhetorical traditions, writing is a fairly new college subject, only a little over a century old (Connors, 1997). In 1862 the Morrill Act helped to create state universities like the University of Nevada and contributed to an increase in students attending college, being taught writing, and needing writing support. As the inclusion of writing has increased with writing-across-the curriculum and even reflective writing for service-learning courses, the need for more student support for writing has also increased. Additionally, the types of writing projects, myriad purposes, and even forms of "writing" have diversified, as has the diversity of our student body.

Writing is one of the primary means by which students are asked to make sense of information and their experiences. In *Making the Most of College*, Richard Light (2004) describes the ways students' writing is a key contributor to their sense of engagement with course material and with peers and faculty. In fact, the word composition means to put together or to synthesize (Crowley & Redman, 1975). Through writing, students are asked to take their ideas and create a new structure with which to communicate their understanding, perspectives, and thoughts to other people (Crowley & Redman, 1975). Using the process involved in writing, then, means that students examine their own perspectives more closely and develop a stronger sense of the communities, such as disciplinary and professional, that they interact with. For specific disciplinary acculturation, writing has been shown to help students develop their disciplinary identities (Eodice et al., 2017). The work of synthesizing ideas and information and putting that into writing to communicate with other people, however, is not an easy task—writing is hard work (Crowley & Redman, 1975). Helping students through the process is where a writing center comes into play by helping students to sort through their ideas and then providing them with reader feedback to allow them to revise and clarify their thinking and writing.

Broadly, writing centers contribute to effective practices within undergraduate education. More specifically, Chickering and Gamson (1987) outlined seven practices of effective undergraduate education. Writing centers are able to address five of the seven principles due to the nature of our work and pedagogies: "reciprocity and cooperation among students," "active learning," "prompt feedback," "time on task," and "respects diverse talents and ways of learning." In addition, writing centers help to support three of the ten high-impact educational practices named by the AAC&U (Kilgo, Sheets, & Pascarella, 2015): first-year experiences, learning communities, and writing-intensive courses. Collaborative learning was identified by Kilgo, Sheets, and Pascarella (2015) as having significant impact on positive educational outcomes for undergraduate students. Collaborative learning is the approach of our Writing and Speaking Center. We call our student employees "consultants" and not "tutors" to contribute to expectations from students that the process of support at our Center is one in which the student is an active participant who engages in intellectual conversations, planning, and drafting with an educated and invested peer. Additionally, the structure of a writing and speaking center allows students to get immediate and individualized feedback, which has been determined to be a distinguishing factor for student learning (Kilgo, Sheets, & Pascarella, 2015). As Grimm (1999) explained, writing centers help students develop mental agility—to understand multiple perspectives, to respond to changes in information and technology, to handle complex concepts of authorship, audience, and agency. In the past, there has been some tendency of researchers to separate cognitive and affective aspects, examining cognitive aspects in academic programs and affective aspects in student services; however, an academic support center often merges these two (Griswold, 2003). Ultimately, it is important to recognize both cognitive and affective aspects to understand how our students are navigating their success within our Institution.

Retention research suggests that there are several key factors even if there is not one model for increasing student retention (Griswold, 2003). One factor is that students need to have out-of-class learning opportunities that are academic and non-academic, especially in the first few semesters (Griswold, 2003; Tinto, 1993). Other factors include helping students develop relationships with campus representatives, focusing on academic support, and creating alternatives to passive large lecture situations (Griswold, 2003)—all of these factors are present in an academic support unit like our Writing & Speaking Center. In fact, peer-to-peer academic support has been reported as a key factor in student persistence (Beal and Noel, 1980).

Students who are at higher risk of attrition because of developmental placements gain important support from academic support centers, especially beyond their at-risk semesters (Griswold, 2003). At our Center, students are encouraged in examining their thinking, their writing, and their speaking, which leads them to examine their learning processes, leading to better students and thus retention (Jackson, 2013).

While writing centers "are not a magic bullet that will change student behavior. [They] can serve as one piece of a comprehensive [educational] program—a linchpin of sorts to give coherence to the curriculum and co-curriculum" (Lerner, 2003, p. 64). Providing coherence and curricular support can help to improve retention rates and specifically degree completion averages, which nationally hover around 50 percent. In fact, in ACT's most recent survey of *What Works for Student Retention* (2010), tutoring services rate as one of the most influential services to increase retention and improve graduation rates.

Part of helping retain students is understanding the types of connections they need, including support that can be kept private. Jeanne Simpson (1991) is a writing center studies scholar who also worked specifically on retention. Simpson (1991) explains that writing centers may be a place where students can get information not just about writing but about college life from peers. Part of this, however, requires trust that information has the option to remain between the student and the center. We are a space that does not hand out grades, so we are a low-risk space in which to make inquiries. At our Writing and Speaking Center, we give students the option of sharing their participation at the writing center with advisors and instructors or keeping this information private. This gives the students more control over their experiences and allows them to engage in academic support without the worry that they will be judged for it.

One of the unique problems that writing and communication centers face is that students are asked to read, write, and present for a variety of disciplines, each with its own sets of genres, values, and expectations. Navigating this is difficult. A student may feel confident in one context and may struggle in another. The complexity of the identities they must navigate is situational and contextually bound, which means that having a single approach to providing support for students will not be very effective. So, we use an approach that encourages students to assume agency to make decisions about their texts that reflect their identities and investments. This requires that our Center sees each student as a unique individual in that moment, meaning that even if the same student visits our Center for support multiple times, we must understand that their identities are dynamic and socially constructed, their communication projects may vary assignment to assignment and class to class, and they may be moving through a process of development and be at a different stage each time we see them.

A Little History

The University of Nevada has one of the longest histories of a writing center. Our first Writing Center was established by Dr. Mark Waldo in the 1980s and remained open until the economic decline in the mid-2000s. In 2009, Waldo's Writing Center was closed. However, during that year, the students wrote the 2017 Vision Proposal in which they explained the importance of tutoring services, such as writing centers, math centers, and tutoring centers. In fact, that year the Associated Student Union of Nevada (ASUN) voted to approve a student fee to support these academic centers. This student support, political and financial, helped to reestablish a writing center in 2010.

The Writing Center established in 2010 lived in the basement of the oldest science building on campus. We existed, but we were difficult to find and had to rewrite our campus's narrative that said the writing center had closed. We started with twelve consultants and an 8 a.m.–5 p.m. schedule. It's been eight years, which seems like no time at all in so many ways. Our Writing Center is now a Writing and Speaking Center. We now have a purpose-built space in one of the newest buildings, a building that is intended for student use and sits prominently in the center of our campus. We now have between 45–50 consultants, representing every college and all major programs on campus. Our services have been extended to include support four days a week from 8am to 8pm and offerings on Sundays. We now have four types of writing support that include a) supported lab space; b) face-to-face consultations; c) online asynchronous consultations; and d) online synchronous chat sessions. Additionally, we offer support for students who are developing presentation materials and practicing delivery through our newly added speaking consultations.

Many students who think they would benefit from but do not use our academic support services say they are afraid of being criticized. This fear of asking for help and of assuming an identity that is not confident with communication skills puts many students in a vulnerable position. Understanding the perceived risks students are taking by asking for assistance is an important part of the work that we do. Repeat clients and those making appointments represent students who are making intentional choices about their academic progress, which contributes to retention (Jackson, 2013). Unlike other academic support centers, the Writing & Speaking Center responds to the entire range of the curriculum, including all disciplines and students working at all levels. This means that our Center might see international students working on dissertations in physics as well as first-year students navigating a Core Writing or a Core Humanities assignment. The diversity of writing and speaking projects that we support requires that we mimic that diversity in our staffing and training—a huge undertaking.

Using a Lens of Inclusion

To address the unique concerns of individual students' writing and communication projects as well as to support the mission of the University—"The University recognizes and embraces the critical importance of diversity in preparing students for global citizenship and is committed to a culture of excellence, inclusion, and accessibility"—our center uses a lens of inclusion to shape our work (University of Nevada, Reno, 2014).

Part of our commitment to diversity and inclusion is specifically hiring students from a range of disciplinary, cultural, and language backgrounds. For example, we intentionally recruit students who started in developmental writing courses because they understand the perspective of students in similar academic positions. We try to hire multilingual learners whose primary language(s) does not include English so they can better support our multilingual learners. While the primary language spoken by our staff is English, we also have nine other languages that are spoken. We recruit students pursuing majors that are typically not associated with writing, such as engineering majors and biochemistry majors, because students working in these majors may need a unique understanding of what is valued and what is not in written projects. Currently 36 percent of our consultants are STEM majors. We also understand that our consultants must represent a range of affiliations and beliefs. For example, our consultants have identified seven different sexual orientations, eleven different religious affiliations, nine different political affiliations, and six different (dis) ability concerns. Our consultants represent twelve different ethnic and racial identities. The importance of the diversity of our staff is essential to students seeking help and receiving support within our Center.

Much of what we are currently focusing on has to do with seeing each student as a unique individual, a person who is navigating many identities, including student, sometimes-writer, reluctant reader, as well as the other cultural, gender, familial, political, language, and social identities that students must balance, move in and out of, and weave together. Nancy Grimm (1999), a writing center studies scholar, says that "diversity in programming and responsiveness to local contexts are essential to the vitality of writing centers" (p. xv).

As a starting point, we want students to feel comfortable in our space and confident to assert their agency within this space. As such, our staff developed a pledge that demonstrates our ongoing commitment to inclusion:

University Writing Center Pledge

We are committed to providing a space free from emotional or physical discrimination and harassment.

We commit ourselves to the safety, comfort, and well-being of students and employees.

We support free and open discussion among those with different perspectives, but we do not condone hate speech.
We strive to welcome writers with diverse backgrounds and expertise.
We work to accommodate students' learning and physical abilities.
We strive to respect students' personal pronouns.
We strive to employ a more diverse group of students.
We strive to recognize marginalized communities, collaborate with associated clubs and groups, and engage in expert-led sensitivity training to facilitate this.
We immediately report any discrimination towards protected groups of students to the administration and/or Title IX office.
We are in process of adding to this pledge so that is a dynamic document that can adjust and respond to the needs of our campus community and to specific student groups.

Our pledge is one way we attempt to demonstrate our commitment to students. The diversity of our staff and the variety of ways to use our academic support services and our space are others. Small things like asking students their preferred pronouns when they make appointments is one small demonstration that we understand some of the difficulties of moving through a binary world that does not allow the complexity of identity to be acknowledged. We also try to highlight this commitment through events such as our Human Library. Through the lens of diversity and inclusion, we believe that every student has many stories regarding how they are navigating individual classes and broader identities of "student."

In response to our electronic survey of students who have used our services, students have made statements such as the following:

- *The consultant was calm in the face of my anxiety and helped me accomplish more than what I intended.*
- *I can't say enough how helpful and encouraging and enlightening my first session with a writing tutor was. I feel like I can see a path out of the hellish life-long writer's block mostly caused by my ADHD. I appreciate this service so much.*
- *Very good job in general on behalf of every person this week. The work of my consultant was amazing because provided me very good comments about grammar and other English stuff very useful for me*

since I am not a native English speaker. Thank you so much for every comment.

- *It really helped that my consultant had a good understanding of scientific writing and how an introduction is supposed to be formatted.*
- *Even though I took a long time to gather my thoughts, my consultant didn't put pressure on me, and was willing to wait. My consultant also gave me control over the session, and over the content of the paper.*
- *My tutor was skilled and knowledgeable about my topic so that helped the most overall.*
- *This session was very helpful and made me want to come back when working on future assignments.*
- *The convenience of the asynchronous e-appointment and the comments that my consultant left on my paper.*
- *My consultant was very willing to hear the things that I wanted to work on and then went through my paper with me and helped me address the things that I was worried about.*
- *My consultant provided positive feedback and made me more confident about the rest of my paper because of the things that we went over in the appointment.*
- *My consultant was great at making me feel encouraged and especially at keeping me grounded, because I struggle with seeing my ideas in an organized way. I mean to say my consultant was awesome nonstop the whole hour. Thanks so much!"*

This may all seem "nice," but the question of how this relates to writing and speaking support may still be lingering in many of your minds. What impact really does this make? Well, our use of language, both written and oral, is inherently linked to our sense of identity. When we invite someone to critique our use of writing or our plan for a presentation, there may be an undercurrent that we are inviting a critique of ourselves, of who we are as students and as people. This is a very vulnerable position to be in. Since academic preparation is a key factor in student success and retention (Habley, Bloom, Robbins, & Gore, 2012), it is important that students seek out and receive academic support when needed. If students can see our Center as a place that responds to their academic concerns, we can provide the support that may make the difference in their persistence at our University.

Our impact is about seeing students as individuals with unique identities and accepting that "identity" is a dynamic concept that is adaptable in different contexts and situations. Our academic support starts to encourage students not just to adhere to a standardized English, but to understand how to use their language(s) and identity(ies) to explain, to challenge, to converse, to complicate their thinking and the learning they are doing.

Impact is a complicated concept for an academic support unit, or really for any part of a whole. So, I can provide some numbers that we think imply certain types of impact, but it is probably the total of students' experiences—their relationships with faculty, staff, and peers; feeling like they belong; achieving academic success; matriculating at a steady pace—that leads to graduation and retention. However, the University Writing & Speaking Center is one of those pieces of a student's puzzle.

Data from our survey of students indicates that students perceive value to the services we offer, even when they did not seek out the support on their own (i.e. were required or incentivized with extra credit). Once a student has used our Center, they are also more likely to return in the future. Below is a graphic that illustrates some of the data collected in our student survey.

I sought the center on my own	I will return to the center	I would recommend the tutor I worked with	I would rate this session
• 65% Yes • 35% No	• 94% Yes	• 96% Agree	• 93% Excellent/Very Good

We use observations of our consultations to help us assess our services and impact. Observations are completed by the director, peer consultants, outside graduate students, and outside undergraduate students. This gives us a wealth of information about the ways in which our consultations work and how students respond to different strategies. This also provides us with data on the obstacles we may face to provide support and/or the obstacles students may face as they try to navigate their academic assignments and other writing and speaking tasks. We use observations as opportunities to refine our practices, provide employee feedback, and assess the writing and speaking needs that students on our campus encounter.

Our Center is in the process of linking to other University data systems to improve the comparison of our usage data with institutional statistics.

Additionally, we are embarking on several course-specific services that will allow us to understand some of our Center's unique contributions to student success and retention for the students in those courses. However, it is the view of writing center studies to be cautious about claims of direct impact and to focus more on the qualitative aspects of how we contribute to students' academic success.

Impact on Student Employees

One of the student populations we have consistent and intimate contact with is our group of student employees who work for the Writing & Speaking Center. We typically employ between 45 and 50 students during a semester. These students are constantly interacting with writing and speaking in diverse ways. Our student employees explain the impact of their experiences working in our Center by identifying the impact on their university education as well as on their professional opportunities after graduation. In terms of impact on their education, our student wrote the following responses:

- *During my time as a consultant, I have learned a plethora of new writing strategies. This has translated to my classes and allowed me to become a better writer.*
- *I found that the organization of my own papers improved dramatically, as well as things such as sentence structure and grammar principles. I also developed the type of outlines I help clients with for myself after a while.*
- *Well, I got two interviews at academic research centers because of this job. Also, my English grades exploded positively after being hired.*
- *I think that the experience helped me become a more complex thinker. The exposure to articles, students from diverse backgrounds and the research apprenticeship helped me develop a more nuanced perspective in my own papers.*
- *The Writing Center helped me stay committed to completing tasks and by learning citation styles, and my paper grades improved.*

Student employees also made the following statements about how their experiences have impacted their professional preparedness and opportunities:

- *The ability to communicate complex ideas simply is something I will use in every job after this one. Reducing already complex information to base ideas is something that will serve me well if I return for a masters or doctoral program.*

- *It already landed me a job at the state! They knew I had the ability to deal with a diverse clientele.*
- *Over the last couple of months, I have been thinking about the career path that I want to take. I realized how much I love being a writing consultant, and now I want to become a teacher.*
- *I can communicate effectively verbally, nonverbally, and through writing.*
- *I've become a much more confident person because of this job. I am also more comfortable in a conversation with a wide variety of people.*

Conclusion

Ultimately, the Writing & Speaking Center is an integral part of the University's mission and aligns our goals with the three Core Themes of the University: learning, discovery, and engagement. As an academic support center, we are particularly situated to support the Core Theme: Learning. Our goals include to help students develop their writing and speaking skills to better support their learning during their degree programs and into their professional careers. In this Core Theme, the University explicitly names liberal arts, sciences, and professional programs. To support this range of learning, we must develop the diversity of staff and the adaptability of our strategies to meet this range of learning. While our ability to support the Core Theme: Discovery may not seem apparent, the Writing & Speaking Center is an active research site and a regular contributor to published scholarship and to national writing and speaking organizations. Since we are primarily funded through student fees, our focus is the support of University of Nevada students' learning while they are enrolled in their degree programs. However, we also understand the importance of contributing to engagement opportunities that extend beyond our Center's space and beyond the university campus. For us, engagement opportunities are symbiotic in that they allow us to engage with our local communities in unique ways while also providing opportunities for University students to learn and apply their skills in new contexts. It is our goal to be a contributing member of the village of our campus that helps students achieve their full academic potential.

REFERENCES

ACT, I. (2010). *What works in student retention? Fourth national survey. Public four-year colleges and universities report.* ACT, Inc.

Beal, P., & Noel, L. (1980). What works in student retention: The report of a joint project of the American College Testing Program and the National Center for Higher education Mangaement Systems. Boulder City.

Chickering, A. W., Gamson, Z. F., & American Association for Higher Education, Washington, DC. (1987). Seven principles for good practice in undergraduate education. *AAHE Bulletin*, 3.

Connors, R. J. (1997). *Composition-rhetoric: Backgrounds, theory, and pedagogy.* Pittsburgh, Pa: University of Pittsburgh Press.

Crowley, S., & Redman, G. (1975). Why teach writing? *College Composition and Communication, 26*(3), 279.

Eodice, Michele, et al. The Meaningful Writing Project: Learning, Teaching and Writing in Higher Education, Utah State University Press, 2017. ProQuest Ebook Central, http://ebookcentral.proquest.com/lib/knowledgecenter/detail.action?docID=4790023. Created from knowledge center on 2019-03-07 15:30:24.

Grimm, N. M. (1999). *Good intentions: Writing center work for postmodern times.* Portsmouth, NH: Boynton/Cook.

Griswold, G. (2003). Writing centers: The student retention connection. *Academic Exchange*, 277–281.

Habley, W. R., Bloom, J. L., & Robbins, S. B. (2012). *Increasing persistence: Research-based strategies for college student success* (First;1. Aufl.; ed.). San Francisco: Jossey-Bass.

Jackson, K. K. (2013). Don't knock the hustle: HBCU writing center life. *Academic Exchange Quarterly, 17(4)*, Retrieved from http://rapidintellect.com/AEQweb/t5406z3.pdf.

Kilgo, C. A., Sheets, J. K. E., & Pascarella, E. T. (2015). The link between high-impact practices and student learning: Some longitudinal evidence. *Higher Education,* 69(4), 525;509;-525. doi:10.1007/s10734-014-9788-z.

Lerner, N. (2003). Writing center assessment: Searching for "proof" of our effectiveness. Pemberton, M. A., & Kinkead, J. A. eds. (2003) in *The center will hold: Critical perspectives on writing center scholarship.* Logan: Utah State University Press.

Simpson, J. (1991). The role of writing centers in student retention. Wallace, R. and Simpson, J. (Eds.) The Writing Center: New Directions. New York: Garland. 102–109.

Tinto, V. (1993). Leaving college: Rethinking the Causes and Cures of Student Attrition (2nd ed.). Chicago: University of Chicago Press.

University of Nevada, Reno. (2014). University Mission, Vision and Values: Accreditation. Retrieved from https://www.unr.edu/accreditation/mission.

CHAPTER 19

The University Math Center

DANELLE CLARKE, M.S.

Danelle Clarke is the University Math Center Director at the University of Nevada, Reno. She earned her Bachelor's Degree in Mathematics and English (writing option) followed by her Master's in Mathematics at the University of Nevada, Reno. Previously, she was a lecturer in the Mathematics and Statistics Department.

Program History

The University Math Center (UMC) was established in 1994 with a grant for "math across the curriculum" initiative. At first, the UMC was mainly used as a resource for instructors wanting to teach in a computer lab and for student math placement testing. However, as grant money diminished, peer tutoring became a key service, and by 2000, drop-in tutoring was the UMC's main objective. Tutoring was seen as a complement to instructor resources so a formal tutor training program was never established. Students were hired based on grades and given a quick orientation about UMC operations. This method was functional when the UMC was smaller (8–10 tutors), as the program administrators could directly observe tutors and provide detailed feedback and mentorship. However, from 2010–2016 student usage of the UMC grew significantly as well as the number of student staff (45–50). This rapid growth required a more formal approach to tutor training, and in 2015 the UMC set out to develop a detailed, comprehensive training program. It took two years, but in August 2017 our training program was certified by the College Reading and Learning Association (CRLA).

Training Standards

After much discussion and research into other programs, the UMC decided to build a training program that would meet the guidelines and requirements of the CRLA. The CRLA's International Tutor Training Program is the standard for most tutoring centers in higher education. The curriculum focuses on: sound hiring practices, planned training experience, tutoring experience, and regular evaluation. The training experience has specific topic requirements each with its own set of standards, outcomes, and assessment plans. Learning centers have to choose a minimum of eight topics from fourteen different options.

Some topics include:

- Techniques for successfully beginning and ending a tutor session
- Adult learners, learning theory, and/or learning styles
- Assertiveness and/or handling difficult students
- Communication skills
- Active listening and paraphrasing
- Referral skills
- Study skills
- Critical thinking skills
- Modeling problem solving

Below is an example of a CRLA topic standard and outcome.

Study Skills

Standard: The tutor has developed a repertoire of effective study skills or strategies to utilize to enhance learning new information (e.g., effective time management, organization, note-taking, test taking, motivation, acquisition, retention, performance, anxiety reduction).

Outcome: The tutor articulates, models, and integrates a variety of appropriate study skills into the tutoring session and provides the tutee with content-specific tips and techniques to incorporate at key points, such as preparing for class; homework; preparing for exams; writing papers; etc.

Additionally, the CRLA also sets a minimum number of training hours and requires that training must be supervised, interactive, and in real-time. (A full description of their requirements can be found at www.crla.net.)

Training Content

When deciding on the content and delivery of our training program, we had to consider some of the UMC's unique challenges. First and foremost, the UMC is a drop-in tutoring facility, thus some of the CRLA's training topics were not applicable to our program (e.g. techniques for starting and ending a tutoring session). Also, being a math tutoring center, things such as plagiarism would not be an issue in our lab. In the end, we decided that the UMC would benefit the most from the following topics:

- Definition of tutoring and tutor responsibilities
- Basic tutoring guidelines/ tutoring do's & don'ts
- Assertiveness and/or handling difficult situations
- Communication skills
- Active listening and paraphrasing
- Referral skills
- Study skills
- Compliance with ethics and philosophy of the tutoring profession and/or compliance with sexual harassment concerns and/or compliance with plagiarism concerns.
- Leading review sessions
- Recognizing learning traits

The last two topics are ones we developed and are unique to the UMC. The UMC holds review sessions for every math course from beginning algebra (Math 095) to Linear Algebra (Math 330). In a single semester we will hold almost 300 review sessions. These review sessions are such a large part of the UMC services, so we decided that it was important to make it one of the main topics in our training curriculum.

Training Format

During training development, we mainly struggled with how to deliver the training material in a way that was valuable and effective. A credit bearing course was not possible for our program, and with over 60 undergraduate tutors, scheduling sessions during the regular semester is an impossible task. We tried a number of delivery methods: tutors working through material independently and then answering questions, and offering three different training times for the same sessions, videos, webchats, etc. None of these options produced the results we wanted. As mentioned previously, the UMC is a walk-in lab and there are typically 8–10 tutors on the floor throughout the day. Tutors work in tandem with one another and will often help groups of students together. With this dynamic, we determined that group work was essential to our training. We finally decided on two all-day training sessions (one in fall and one in spring) and two "focus sessions" (again, fall/spring). The material presented in the fall is different from the material presented in the spring, and in order for tutors to complete the training and earn a CRLA certificate, they have to attend all four sessions. However, even after earning a certificate, tutors are required to attend training sessions throughout their employment at the UMC. The response from the reviewers about our training program was positive.

> The emphasis on group work and collaborative learning throughout the training program is very impressive, especially considering the structure of the drop-in tutoring program... Very strong standards, outcomes, and assessment techniques to ensure high quality training sessions.
>
> —CRLA Program Reviewer

During the all-day sessions, tutors are divided into groups of five to six people and each group is led by a Shift Leader. A Shift Leader is a veteran tutor who helps the lab run smoothly. They direct tutors, handle small issues, provide weekly observations to the Director and Admin, assist with semester evaluations, and take part in the hiring process. Currently we have about 60 tutors and 10 Shift Leaders. In order to be considered for the position, student staff must complete all of their CRLA training.

Throughout the all-day sessions, the group of tutors work through the material presented in a packet. The packet consists of lesson plans with group exercises, occasional videos, discussion questions, and role play exercises. Shift Leaders' packets are annotated to ensure that specific topics are addressed in each group (the uploaded packets are the Shift Leader Versions). Additionally, different organizations from campus give presentations: Disability Resource Center, Counseling Center, Mathematics and Statistics Department, and University Campus Police.

The 3-hour focus sessions cover topics that are important to our program and require more in-depth training. Unlike the all-day sessions, during the focus session there is a short presentation of the material in a classroom like setting. After the presentation, tutors work in small groups to answer questions, participate in discussion, and take part in role play exercises.

Surprisingly, the in-depth training has been received very well by tutors. No one looks forward to all-day training, especially on a Saturday just before the semester starts. However, during each session the tutors were actively participating and engaging throughout the day and they, too, genuinely enjoy the training process.

At the end of each session, we ask the tutors for anonymous feedback. Here are some sample responses to the question: "In your own words, state the objective of tutor training at the UMC."

- To teach tutors some common methods and procedures used at the Math Center to promote student independence. It also provides a way to make tutors follow a uniform system so that they all may best be utilized towards that goal.
- The goal of tutor training at the Math Center is to standardize the type of help we offer to students. We want all tutors to be able to help students achieve in independent studies by training tutors to encourage certain habits.
- To both introduce crucial tutoring techniques and concepts to newer tutors as well as provide practice and refreshers to older tutors, as well as to ensure all tutors work together under the same principles.
- The objective of tutor training is to strengthen the skills of tutors and review/teach techniques of how tutors can do a better job at assisting students in becoming autonomous learners.

Impact

Experienced Tutors

Before the UMC began developing a training program in 2015, tutors were not very deliberate or conscious in their tutoring techniques. Students were getting help with their assignments, but they weren't learning *how* to solve problems on their own. Now, tutors learn how to be more intentional with their methods and techniques, thoughtfully modifying their approaches to different subjects as well as different types of students. Instead of applying methods repetitively, tutors are better suited to be dynamic in their tutoring, and able to consider potential nuances of students that may have seemed nonexistent before. Tutors are able to recognize when students need help beyond math concepts; they can identify when the student might need help with study skills, note-taking, organization, and test-taking strategies. They can also provide assistance in these areas or refer them to another resource on campus.

Our training program has changed not only how our tutors help students, but also how they perceive their role in students' education. Now, instead of helping students with a math problem, tutors recognize their objective is to assist students in becoming independent learners.

What is the role of a tutor at the UMC?

- The role of a tutor at the Math Center is to help students become more self-sufficient and independent when it comes to studies, as well as to help students in their pursuit of understanding course concepts.
- To teach students how to be independent in their studies, or to guide them through any difficulty they encounter in such a way that when they encounter the problem again they can overcome it independently.
- A tutor is meant to assist a student in developing their critical thinking skills and helping them with their process in order to promote independence.
- The tutor's main priority is to help the student achieve independence and self-sufficiency. To be more precise, the idea is we, as tutors, help foster an environment that would allow students to become independent learners.
- Tutors at the Math Center are meant to help facilitate a student's learning by teaching them to teach themselves—Math Center tutors don't teach or provide answers, but instead guide students along the process of solving problems. A tutor ensures that it is the student who gets the answer by his or her own work.

New Tutors

Another aspect of our training is New Hire training, which is separate from our fall and spring sessions. Because the UMC hires year-round, it is possible (and problematic) that a tutor will be hired after the semester training session. In order to ensure that new hires understand the role of a tutor, they are required to shadow senior tutors for a total 90 minutes. During this time, senior tutors will demonstrate and explain various tutoring techniques and the new hire is required to document the sessions and submit written notes to the director. After shadowing, the new hire is then observed by senior tutors for a total of 90 minutes. The senior tutors provide verbal feedback as well as written, formal feedback that is also submitted to the director.

Additionally, the group work in the all-day and focus sessions has proven very effective in bringing new tutors up to a comparable standard with older tutors. Even if we hire someone with previous tutoring experience, new tutors are often overwhelmed by the dynamic and hectic nature of the UMC. As they work together in groups with older tutors, they learn from their peers, and they can use strategies that others have successfully developed and refined. Our new employees are more prepared to handle common challenges and therefore feel more confident early on in their career (which directly translates to students' confidence in their ability to learn).

By exposing all the tutors (new and our most senior) to the same material, they learn a common set of terms and vocabulary. This gives tutors the tools to collaborate and address the types of problems that inhibit students' abilities to learn. Tutors use the activities, exercises, and role play scenarios from training to discuss and test out various strategies, and to develop a course of action to help students overcome these hurdles. As a result of our training process, the assistance that tutors provide is much more organized and the tutoring that students receive is more consistent.

Students

At the end of each semester the UMC sends out satisfaction surveys as a way to assess if we are meeting our objectives. While optional surveys are not definitive, they can be useful. Through consistent results each semester, we can make some conclusions about our program. Also, student surveys are widely used to assess tutoring programs as there is no other means of assessing certain aspects of student services (Norton 2012).

When reviewing specific questions of our student survey, we can see the tutor training has affected how students are getting help in the UMC.

Retention

There are many difficulties when assessing the impact that tutoring has on student performance and retention—this is especially true with walk-in labs.

- Students "self-select". They can be "A" students who just like the environment. They can be "D" students who would have failed without help. They could be students who only come in before exams.
- Students visit the UMC a varied number of times. (e.g. last Fall there were at least 10 students who visited the UMC more than 70 times.)
- Students can have a high number of visits but with irregular intervals

(e.g. every day for a month and then not again until the day before the final).

- Students visit the UMC for a variety of reasons. They come in for help with homework, to work on projects using the math/stats software we provide, to get help with an upcoming exam, and to study with friends.
- In a single visit, a student may be assisted by several tutors.
- Students stay in the lab for different lengths of time. They could stay for as little as 20 minutes or as long as 5 hours.

Furthermore, there are multiple factors that can impact student success. It would be inappropriate to insinuate that students' overall success (or failure) in math courses can solely be attributed to the UMC. That said, the following data is intended to illuminate how the UMC may contribute to students' success.

In the UMC's annual report, we compare student success of those students who visited the UMC and those who didn't. We focus on students enrolled in Math 126 and Math 181 (since these are the courses with the highest enrollment) and we report on one key aspects of students' performance: if students didn't take the final exam. This metric helps us assess course completion. In every course, and especially large lecture math courses, there is a certain drop-off rate: A number of students who have resigned themselves to the fact that they are going to fail the course and simply stop showing up. They don't withdraw, but they stop attending, turning in assignments, and taking exams. This affects FTE and formula-based state funds.

Figures 1 and 2 show the percentage of students who took the final exam in Math 126 and Math 181.

The results are consistent across years—students who visited the UMC in Fall 2012—Fall 2017 had a lower course failure rate and a higher course completion rate (i.e. taking the final exam) than those who didn't. Furthermore, the number of students who do well is not a small, select group—a significant proportion of students enrolled in these courses visit the UMC. Most recently, in fall 2017, 44 percent of Math 126 students, and 47 percent of students in Math 181 used the UMC.

TABLE 1. Student satisfaction survey results.

Question	UMC Objective	Spring 2016	Fall 2016	Spring 2017	Fall 2017	Spring 2018	Fall 2018
Tutors helped me identify ways to improve my note taking and/or study skills.	5a	3.08	3.49	3.21	3.55	3.21	3.57
Tutors refer to my in-class notes and/or text while helping me.	5b	3.57	3.9	3.65	4	4.14	3.98
Review Sessions help me identify new study techniques.	5c	3.69	3.74	3.49	3.95	3.58	4.11
After working with a tutor I feel that I am better equipped to work through other homework problems on my own.	5a	3.91	4.32	4.03	4.37	4.14	4.41

Conclusion

The UMC training program was submitted to the CRLA for review in August 2017, and in January 2018 our program was approved for Stage 1 certification. The feedback from the reviewers was very positive.

> This is by far the most thorough and comprehensive application I have had the pleasure to review.
>
> —CRLA Stage 1 Program Reviewer

There are three stages in the application/certification process. Our Stage 1 certification was good for one year, and in order to keep our certification we submitted a Stage 2 application in October 2018. The Stage 2 application process provides the opportunity to reflect and revise the training program and is good for three years. Since we spent two years

FIGURE 1. Percentage of Math 126 students who didn't take the final exam.

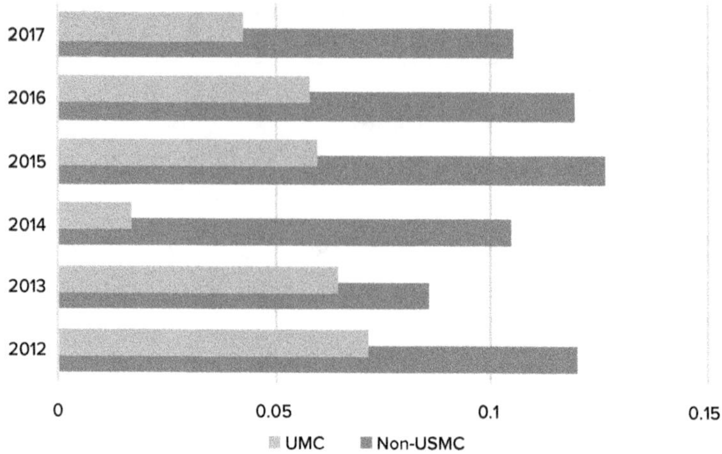

FIGURE 2. Percentage of Math 181 students who didn't take the final exam.

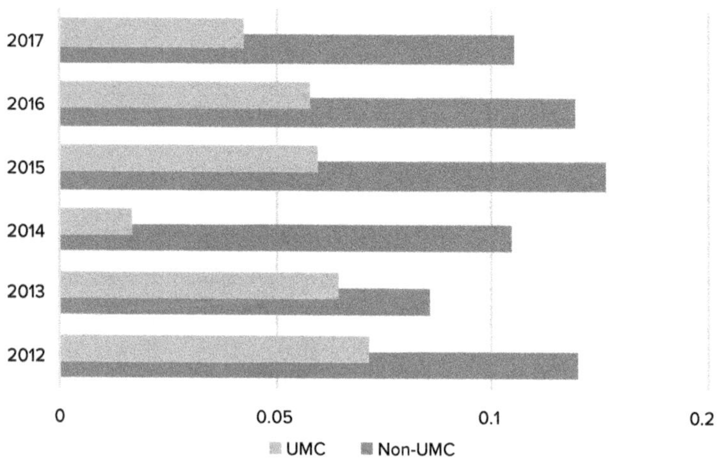

developing the training program before our first submission, very little changed when we submitted for Stage 2. In March 2019, the UMC's training program was were approved for Stage 2 certification, and again, the response we received was very positive.

> This program spent 2 years developing their program before seeking certification and has made some small changes (like swapping the order of sessions) to accommodate their needs. This program is so solid, clear, and well designed.
>
> —CRLA Stage 2 Program Reviewer

In 2021, we plan to submit for the last stage of the CRLA certification process. The Stage 3 application required further assessment and reflection of the training program and is valid for 5 years.

Beyond tutoring, the CRLA certification process has proven extremely valuable to the UMC. It provided us the opportunity to reevaluate and consider areas of our program that may have been previously overlooked. Through our attempts to develop a rigorous and relevant training program, we have achieved a greater degree of structure, organization, and guidance for the tutors, students, and the UMC as a whole.

Job expectations were heavily revised and clarified, we created a new employee manual, review session guidelines were developed, and tutors now complete a self-evaluation each semester.

Additionally, this process compelled us to develop UMC measureable objectives, and mission and vision statements.

Objectives

1. Hire qualified undergraduate tutors and staff.
2. Provide employment training and leadership opportunity for our student staff.
3. Coordinate with the Mathematics and Statistics Department faculty in order to provide students with relevant course information during tutoring and review sessions.
4. Maintain a friendly and respectful environment that encourages students to return.
5. Apply tutoring methods so that students feel that they are able to:
    a. Use a variety of strategies for learning, practicing, and reinforcing class material.
    b. Learn how to use academic resources for their classes.

c. Learn how to prepare for tests.

Mission

The University Math Center encourages undergraduate students to become independent learners by helping them to develop the skills, strategies, and behaviors necessary to succeed academically. We strive to provide a friendly and welcoming environment where students have access to highly qualified undergraduate tutors, frequent review sessions, and peer interaction. By promoting students' success in their math related courses, the University Math Center contributes to students' increased retention rates, their timely progress toward graduation, and the University's Core Theme of Learning.

Vision

The University Math Center will develop a rigorous and relevant training program for its tutors and staff that meets the requirements and standards set by the College Reading and Learning Association. We will continue to provide quality tutoring services to a growing student population. Additionally, the University Math Center endeavors to increase the visibility of its services through greater interaction with students and the campus community as a whole.

These goals and statements have helped propel our development over the past few years. The objectives give us very specific ways to assess our program, and the mission and vision statements provide us with overarching targets and goals. This vision statement was developed in early 2017 and we are happy to say that we have reached this goal. We look forward to developing a new Vision statement: one that will propel the UMC to the next level as we continue to support the success of our students.

REFERENCE

Norton, J. (2012). Evaluation of Tutoring and Tutor Training. In K. Agee, & R. Hodges, *Handbook for Training Peer Tutors and Mentors* (pp. 431–434). Mason, Ohio: Cengage Learning.

CHAPTER 20

Testing Out of Remedial Math

McKENNA CORTEZ and MARSHA URBAN, PH.D.

McKenna Cortez is an employee at the University Tutoring Center where she has worked as an Accuplacer Math Bridge Tutor, a Walk-in and Appointment tutor, a PASS Leader, and a Senior PASS Leader. She earned her bachelor's degree in Neuroscience at the University of Nevada, Reno with minors in Mathematics and Education. She will be attending Vanderbilt University in the fall of 2019 as a M.Ed. student studying Quantitative Methods.

Marsha Urban, Ph.D. is the director of the University Tutoring Center. She earned her bachelor's degree in English and Secondary Education from King's College (Wilkes-Barre, PA) followed by the master's degree in English Literature at the University of Nevada, Reno. She earned her Ph.D. in Seventeenth-Century British Literature at the University of Nevada, Reno, and in 2006 she published her dissertation: Seventeenth-Century Mother's Advice Books.

Introduction

Since I began running the University Tutoring Center (UTC) in 2003, remedial math has been a problem. Students have often referred to MATH 95 and 96 as "bone-head math" and vehemently declared they were bad at math. This belief impacted their performance in the classes because they believed no matter what they did, they would never succeed. The UTC has tried numerous ways to get students into tutoring. We have sent individual emails, conducted presentations, started a specific mentor program, and held special walk-in labs for classes. Each semester a few students would attend these programs, but we knew a much higher percentage needed help. Nothing seemed to work to get them involved. Students continued to fail remedial math and spend multiple semesters either retaking the classes or they would drop out. After talking to numerous students, I realized the psychological implications of taking a remedial math course impacted their chances far more than their ability.

Through conversations like this, the Las Vegas Office for Prospective Students (OPS) determined that the best thing for these students was to avoid remedial math all together. In the summer of 2017, (OPS) began a summer tutoring program in Las Vegas to address this same problem. They decided to run a free math tutoring program for incoming students slated to begin their University career in remedial math. OPS partnered with a third-party tutoring service to offer students in Southern Nevada summer tutoring for the Accuplacer exam. The Accuplacer exam is a standardized test offered by many universities to test math ability. When freshmen enter the University, they are placed into their fall math class using their SAT or ACT scores. The Accuplacer exam helps students test into higher math classes. If students can test out of remedial math it would enable them to avoid the psychological implications of being "remedial." Additionally, students starting university in a credit-bearing math class are more likely to graduate in four years.

At the end of the summer, 91 students attended OPS' tutoring program. Of those, fifty two (57 percent) were able to place into college-level math (including stretch classes) based on their Accuplacer score. Further analysis of their fall math class showed students participating in the program averaged 0.70 grade points higher in their math class than their peers. Participating in tutoring for the Accuplacer exam not only helped students pass the exam; it also helped them understand they could be successful in math with practice. Learning the importance of practice is a skill that is far more important to for success than innate math ability.

With such encouraging results, the University decided to expand the tutoring program the following summer to include Northern Nevada (Reno, Carson City and the surrounding area). The Math Tutoring for Accuplacer Success Series was jointly managed by 365 Learning and the University Tutoring Center. Student Services and the Provost's Office provided additional funding for the program. The main contacts in both departments were tasked with developing and managing the series.

The first step was to decide when to conduct the series. Since the students had just graduated high school, the series could not begin until mid-June. We decided to do a month-long series from mid-June to mid-July. As many students work in the summer, the scheduled had to give students a variety of times to attend. The final schedule included: two hours on Monday, Wednesday, and Friday mornings; two hours on Thursday and Friday afternoons; two hours on Sunday and two hours on Monday night. To help the last-minute students, we also included a week-long series two weeks before classes began. The student-friendly schedule was essential for success. 365 Learning created marketing material and sent out cards, emails, and letters to students inviting them to the series. Admissions and Records included information about the series in their letter to parents. The final step was forming the team and planning the tutoring.

The UTC included three handpicked tutors. Each tutor was selected not only for their ability in math, but also their non-judgmental approach to tutoring students who tested below college-level math. Their personal attributes included tutoring skills, approachability, math background, and focus. We met multiple times and devised a plan starting with a pre-test to capture information on baseline skills for each student. The test was composed of 42 Accuplacer preparation questions found online. Additionally, we organized the questions by topic to better understand what areas students understood and what areas needed improvement. Considering the students' fragile math egos, the tutors had the students use happy and sad faces as a representation of their confidence while taking the test. Students were encouraged not only to choose topics based on what they answered incorrectly, but also those concepts they felt unsure about. This enabled the students to see what they already knew and what they needed to learn within the broad topics: arithmetic, college-level math and elementary algebra. The test was administered on the first and last days of tutoring in order to help students gauge their improvement.

In addition to the practice test, we prepared several worksheets, each on one topic found on the Accuplacer exam. (Worksheets were primarily taken from https://www.kutasoftware.com/.) After students were given the practice test, they determined which topics they needed improvement and took the appropriate worksheet. Tutors tackled each topic by either "teaching" groups of students in a center style or by working with students individually (or in pairs) or circulating about the room. The method used was determined by how many students wanted to go over a specific topic at each time.

As the month long series progressed, we found we needed more tutors. Two additional tutors joined the group so they could break students into groups according to their needs. The UTC has individual rooms/areas enabling tutors to have new students take the pre-test away from the students working in groups and to break students into concept rooms. Some students took worksheets home to continue their work. When a student felt prepared to take the Accuplacer, they were given the pre-test to complete so they could see their own improvement and determine whether or not they felt confident enough to try to test into their goal class. As a thank you for attending the sessions, students were given passes to take the Accuplacer free.

Successful Elements to Continue in the Summer 2019

Building Confidence

The largest hurdle faced by students placed in remedial math is a lack of confidence. Typically, students have already decided that they are "not math people" and are therefore not able to learn math. With the accepting environment of the UTC, the non-judgmental nature of the tutors, and the knowledge that their peers were at a similar level gave students the confidence to speak up and feel proud of their accomplishments. Working with students who had the same difficulties with the material helped students understand they were not alone. Also, students saw how working on multiple problems and focusing on how math works benefited themselves and the others. Students began to help each other as their knowledge of math grew. As they began to understand the math concepts, their confidence grew—they could do math.

Trying Different Methods

Students who attended the Accuplacer series came from several different schools; they learned several math topics through utilizing different methods. One thing that was very successful during the Accuplacer tutoring sessions was the tutors approaching each topic with as many different methods as possible. This allowed students to either improve the method they were already comfortable with or try a new method they found easier to understand. Students entered the series believing there was one way to approach math. By showing students different methods, they began to understand there are multiple approaches to a problem; if they had difficulty with one method, they could try a different one.

Working Individually or with Friends

Some students chose to attend the series with their friends. Students who did this appeared to be more comfortable working together and asking questions. On the other hand, some students preferred to work alone. The UTC has separate areas so tutors we could work with students within their comfort zones. With the addition of two tutors we were able to work with students individually as well as in a group setting. The comfort zones enabled students to ask the questions that they may not have felt confident asking the group.

Things to Change

Creating Stricter Centers

For summer 2019 we will streamline our approach to each topic by organizing centers in one-hour topics areas. Students will choose what specific topic they want to work on for an hour and the tutor can concentrate on a particular topic. At the end of the hour, students can decide to remain in the area or go to another area. This will allow students more agency in their learning process and teach them to evaluate their knowledge. A schedule of centers will be made available to students so they can choose which two sessions they would like to attend per day.

More Materials

During the pilot, we were not sure what we needed so worksheets were quickly added at the last minute. Before the 2019 series begins, the tutors will meet to identify all the concepts needing be covered. Additionally, the program is being expanded to include math classes above remedial math. This inclusion will help students in STEM areas test out of pre-trigonometry and pre-calculus courses. Additionally, different pre-tests are necessary to ensure students are not memorizing one test, but understanding the concepts. Students will be working in topic rooms, and we will create small daily quizzes on each topic for students to assess their progress and decide if they should remain in the topic room or if they should move to another topic room. Ideally, a small quiz at the beginning of the hour can give them an idea of what they know before the session, and another small quiz at the end of the hour will help students to decide if they are ready to go on to another topic.

No Perks

During the series, 365 Learning provided food: fruit and cookies for each session and pizza on Sunday and Monday nights. They also provide different tchotchkes each week. The enticements were meant to make students feel more welcome and to enable working students to attend the series without worrying about food. Unfortunately, the enticements changed students' attitude. Rather than seeing the food as welcoming, student perceived it as an entitlement. Although we hoped to prepare them for college this had the exact opposite effect. In 2019 there will be no enticements. Students will come to the series to work and prepare for college.

College Prep

The most obvious concern in the pilot was with student professionalism and organization. We believed these skills are as essential in college as the math skills that they are learning. Before the beginning of the 2019 series, we will produce an "Introduction packet" to hand out on their first day. This packet will contain information on tutoring expectations including preparation for each day and studying outside of tutoring. The packet will include a daily reflection with these questions:

- "What did you learn today?"
- "What are you going to do between today and next time?"
- "What do you want to do next time?"

This will reinforce strong study habits students can use throughout their college career. The packet will also include tips and instructions on how to write a professional email, how to talk to professor, class expectations and time-management planning. These additional items will help in their professional growth.

Conclusion

Data Results from the 2018 Math Tutoring for Accuplacer Success Series

In summer 2018, 105 students attended the Math Tutoring for Accuplacer Success Series. The goal of the series was to help students enter college in a credit-bearing math class.

Some of the students who participated in the series chose not to take the Accuplacer exam before their fall math class. Additionally, fifteen of the students either did not attend the University or did not take a fall math class. The assessment below includes the results of the seventy five students who took the Accuplacer exam after or during the series and took a fall 2018 math class:

- Of the seventy five students who took the Accuplacer exam, 47 (62.7%) placed into college-level math (including stretch) and 28 (37.3%) placed into remedial math.
- The pass rate of the twenty eight students who took remedial math was 59 percent for MATH 95 and 71 percent for MATH 96.

- The students taking a fall, credit-bearing math class averaged .41 grade points higher (the difference between C- and C+) in their class than the general population.

For the last two weeks, we instituted a new (V2) version of Math Tutoring for Accuplacer Success Series for 2019. Setting college-level expectations from day one; creating a binder with pre-tests, homework and in-session worksheets; discontinuing perks; and reviewing at the end of the session has created a program focused on learning through practice. Students focus on their work and their success. Additionally, they are working together with the tutors and other students more than they did last summer. The structure and expectations are focused to allow students to learn math as a skill beginning the first minute they walk into the classroom.

Six students have taken the Accuplacer exam during the first 2.5 weeks of the program. Each one has placed into a credit-bearing class. One of the students have placed into calculus. Additionally, some parents in California have asked for a PDF of our Accuplacer binder so their student can either work on the binder themselves or see a tutor where they live.

The big problem we are experiencing is the changes in California concerning the Accuplacer exam. Only Los Angles and Sacramento are giving the Accuplacer. Some parents have brought their student here for one or two tutoring sessions and then taken the exam. We would prefer to see students working for weeks rather than days. That is why we are offering the binder to parents with the instructions to have the student work on the binder before they come in to take the exam.

The assessment of last year's program and the changes in the Math Tutoring for Accuplacer Success Series (V2) for 2019 is working beyond our expectations. The additional work of creating the binder is paying off exponentially. Creating a cohesive team of tutors with a student dedicated as the senior tutor has created a group focused on one goal: helping students avoid remedial math courses and beginning their college career in a credit-bearing math calls.

REFERENCE

Ferrell, B. B. (2015). *The Effects of Student Psychology on Remedial Math Success: A Case Study on Non-Academic Interventions* (Unpublished doctoral dissertation). University of Texas at Austin, Austin, Texas.

CHAPTER 21

Student Success at the DRC

Math 19—The Leap from Anxiety to Achievement

ANDREA JUILLERAT-OLVERA, M.F.A.

Andrea Juillerat-Olvera is the staff sign language interpreter and disability specialist at the Disability Resource Center at the University of Nevada, Reno. She holds a vocational degree in sign language from Seattle Central Community College, a bachelors degree in philosophy from the University of Washington, Seattle and a master of fine arts in Performance Art from the University of Nevada, Reno. Andrea's creative manifestations are informed by her daily exposure to a broad range of learning environments, time spent living abroad in Ljubljana, Slovenia and decades of political activism.

Anxiety about math is pervasive in higher education. The trepidation is so great that many students delay required math courses until the last possible moment of their academic journey. The incidence of math anxiety is even more concentrated for students receiving services at the Disability Resource Center. The problem was common enough that in 1996 the staff started considering different ways to assist students overcome their fears. Plenty of anecdotal evidence showed that many DRC clients found the barriers to passing Math 120 insurmountable. To prevent students from giving up and dropping out, a new format for learning math had to be invented.

Dyscalculia is math-related disability similar to dyslexia but instead of literacy, the problem regards numerical objects and functions (The Understood Team, n.d.). Dyscalculia can occur in a variety of contexts; sometimes it is an inability to process magnitude related to numbers themselves, other times it may be trouble with the mechanics of doing basic math. Dyscalculia frequently manifests as a co-occurring factor along with other disabilities. Students may have ADHD, a poor working memory, depression, anxiety, or mental health issues that compound their struggles and cause severe levels of anxiety related mathematics.

Some students may have anxiety surrounding expectations for math proficiency, others may have a formal diagnosis of dyscalculia, and some may have both. In 1996, students with learning disabilities made up the greatest percentage of the DRC's client population. With this in mind, the DRC approached the Math department and they agreed that an alternative route to success had to be developed. They took it upon themselves to garner approval from the curriculum committee and in 1996, the Math 19 equivalency course was added to the catalog.

The Math 19 course was designed to teach the same material as Math 120 and do it over the course of one full year instead of one semester. The choice to slow the pace and give students more time to absorb information was a positive one. The last century embraced a culture of math that valued rapid answers, drilling calculations over and over again, or competitive games that rewarded the fastest, loudest students. These strategies are ineffective and even damaging to non–traditional learners. Steve Chinn, who wrote *Maths Learning Difficulties, Dyslexia and Dyscalculia*, published his newest edition in 2019 and reinforces this concept with his "pragmatic mantra: take the intervention back to the beginning and then proceed at a pace and with a style to match the needs of the student." (Chinn, 2018, p. 10). In addition to the slower pace, the DRC offers a bridge course in the summer to prime students who will enter Math 19 in the fall.

For some DRC students, failure was the norm. Their inability to pass math classes was not due to a lack of trying; 58 percent of Math 19 students had at least one previous unsuccessful attempt. The DRC defines an "unsuccessful attempt" as a withdrawal or failure of Math 95, Math 96, Math 120, or any other Math course the student did not complete (see fig. 1). Of these students with previous attempts, many had tried and failed more than once. The sheer persistence and resolution displayed by these students is notable and speaks to the development of character that will serve them for the rest of their lives. While 43 percent had only one previous math course failure, 24 percent had three previous failures and 16 percent had four or more previous failures (see fig. 2). There were 3 percent of DRC students who had *six* previous failures and from that group, 100 percent graduated (see fig. 3). There is an old proverb that says, "success isn't measured by how far you got, but the distance you traveled to get there." These students took a journey longer than most, and while their success looks the same, what is not visible to the casual observer is the enormous strength and determination required to get there.

Math 120 represents a barrier that many of our students initially thought was insurmountable. Successful completion of Math 19 removed that barrier and enables the student to continue on toward their academic goal. From 2010 to 2017, 77 percent of students who took Math 19 were retained at least one-year post-completion (see fig. 4).

The DRC conducted interviews with a couple of the students who passed Math 19 and went on to achieve academic success. Their voices, both personal and passionate, speak to the value of this program. One such student was a non-traditional student by several metrics. As a single mom and dealing with multiple disabilities, the student has been pursuing her bachelor's degree for 20 years. The student spoke about her struggles and eventual success with great passion, "If it wasn't for this program, I would not have been able to graduate. But I am finally graduating in May of 2019. There's no way I could have done it without Math 19." The student explained that she has had math anxiety since she was a child:

> In the second and third grade I'd hide in the bathroom during long division practice. The teacher would have to find me. I did everything backwards in my mind. I couldn't do math the way everyone else did...and I don't know why.

Anxiety and fear are easily compounded by the perception of negative judgment. The student said she experienced isolation in other math courses. Instructors and students were too impatient to work with her. She explained how the summer bridge course enhanced her chances for success:

> The bridge course gave me some preparation, similar to the college prep courses in high school. Having the bridge program meant that I could 'ACE' Math 19 later on. Because of the bridge course, I knew what to anticipate. I already know the areas that were going to be difficult for me. When those topics came up, I was ready.

But, the students highest praise was reserved for her instructor:

> The instructor was great! He had this enormous task to keep everyone's attention on math. We had autistic kids and others with different disabilities. Each student was unique, and we were all part of the same ilk. Some were brilliant, but had other issues, some

FIGURE 1. Previous math course failures before taking Math 19.

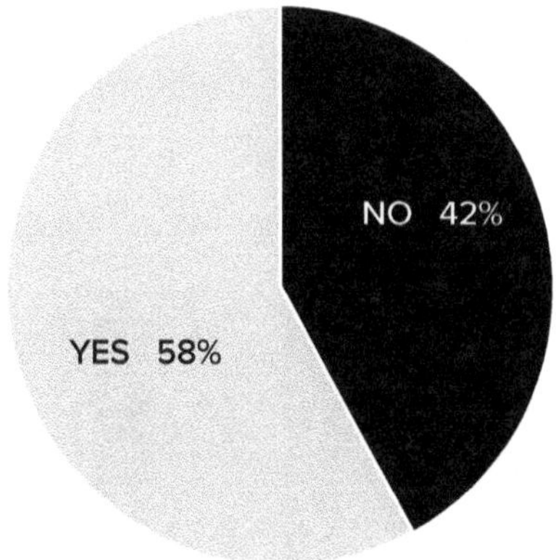

FIGURE 2. Number of previous math course attempts prior to taking Math 19.

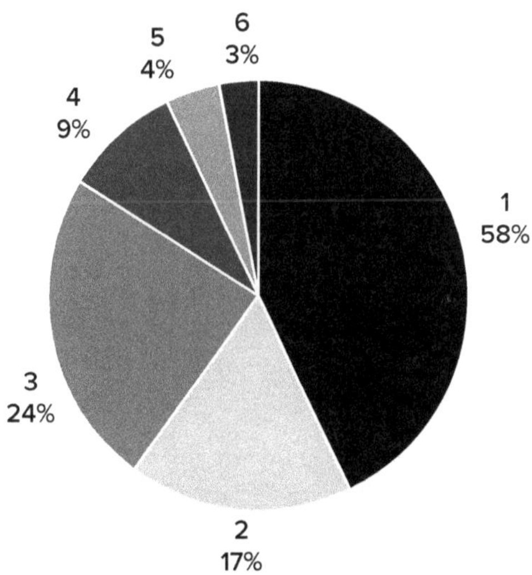

were partially deaf, someone was missing an eye, everyone had some kind of disability, whether it showed or not. If you came in 15 minutes early, you could chat with the instructor and the others; it was safe. Everyday we'd start by going over homework. We'd swap papers, grade and review them. Nobody judged, we were all in the

FIGURE 3. Graduation rates for students with previous math course failures.

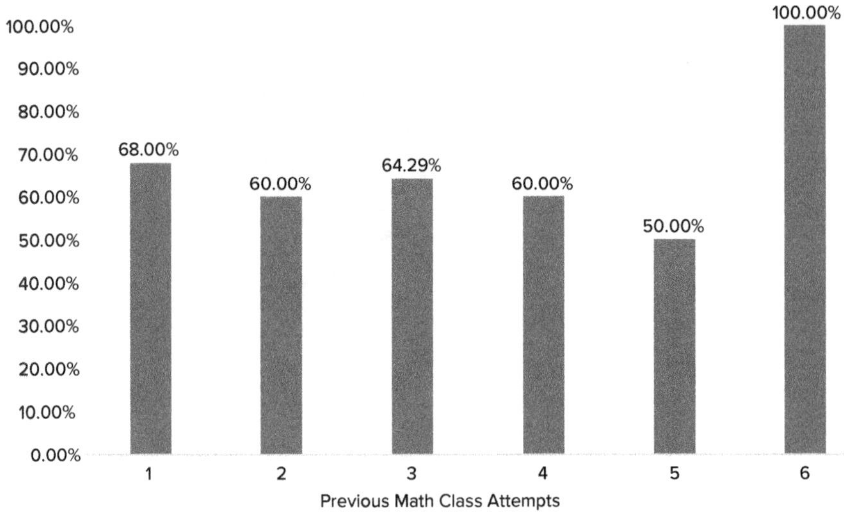

FIGURE 4. Percentage of Math 19 students retained (at least one year post-completion of math 19).

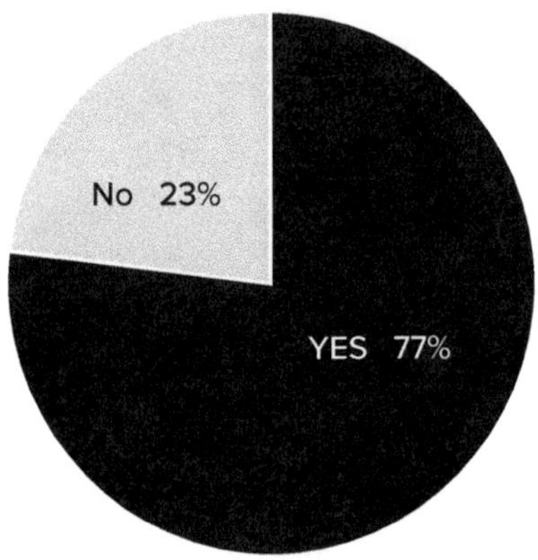

same boat. The instructor didn't criticize; he didn't shame you for getting it wrong. 'You learn from your mistakes' and you move on. That's how he taught and if you didn't get it, they had tutors. I felt like I belonged there, no stigma, no judgement . . . and that's really my biggest fear walking into a math class: judgement.

When asked about how her math skills, after taking Math 19, The student said, "I can use formulas in my job; I can look at math now and figure it out."

Another non-traditional student returned to school in her thirties as a mother of four children. Like the aforementioned student, she struggled with math anxiety since grade school. At UNR she took Math 95 and failed it on the first try. She succeeded the second time, but then had to withdraw from Math 96. The goal of passing Math 120 was daunting, so she was referred to the Math 19 program. The student stated:

> The professor was great! His explanations were easy to understand, the slower pace was helpful. He didn't use MyMathLab and we had a different math book. I liked that the quantity of homework was a bit less than other courses; we had time. The instructor was an ally, he told us 'we will do whatever it takes for you the pass this class, so you can graduate.' In all ways, he was very accommodating.

Regarding the other students and classroom atmosphere, The student stated, "Other people I met in the class made me realize I wasn't at the bottom, in fact, others were worse off than me." Regarding her anxiety levels, she explained, "The professor was a calming presence with a good demeanor. He knew how to work with people like me. He wasn't intimidating at all." When asked about how her math skills are now, she said, "Now I'm taking statistics and I'm not having any difficulties. The skills from class definitely help. Who knows how many times I would have tried and failed, in a standard classroom." The Math 19 program supports student success by enabling those for whom math felt insurmountable to find their way to the summit.

REFERENCES

The Understood Team. (n.d.). "Understanding Dyscalculia". Retrieved from https://www.understood.org/en/learning-attention-issues/child-learning-disabilities/dyscalculia/understanding-dyscalculia.

Chinn, S. (2018). Maths learning difficulties, dyslexia and dyscalculia: Second edition. Retrieved from https://ebookcentral.proquest.com.

PART V

Success Through Undergraduate Research

Undergraduate research is a critical component for any university seeking a research Carnegie classification. Undergraduate research helps students go beyond the expectations of receiving the college degree by providing publishing opportunities; a unique component that enhances the likelihood of a student pursuing research intensive graduate education. University curriculum also promotes students abilities to take part in co-curricular activities that bridge what students learn from the classroom setting to the real world. Through building curriculum that bridges academics with co-curricular experiences, the Office of Undergraduate Research, the Honors program, and schools like the School of Journalism, the University encourages students to partake in co-curricular activities, undergraduate research, and promote undergraduate publishing to enhance their ability to reach their graduate school and career goals.

CHAPTER 22

The College Completion Gap

A Nationwide Snapshot

JENNIFER LOWMAN, PH.D.

JENNIFER LOWMAN, PH.D., is the Director of Student Persistence Research at the University of Nevada, Reno. Her research focus is on educational and occupational pathways from a perspective of structural social psychology. She supports campus climate and co-curricular assessment; consults on assessment design and analysis; conducts longitudinal persistence research; and encourages the development of a data savvy faculty and staff. She is a former first-generation and community college transfer student. She credits her mother's nagging with her educational persistence.

Rates of retention and graduation are the top two *institutional indicators* of student success in higher education. At four-year institutions specifically, the key performance indicators are freshmen to sophomore retention and the four-year cohort graduation rate (i.e. the proportion of first-time degree-seeking students who enter the institution at the same time and who graduate within four-years). From an institutional perspective, it is more cost-effective to retain students than continually replace them with new students (Herzog & Stanley, 2013). That said, it was not until the early 21st century that increased scrutiny and legislative changes to state funding formulas drove institutions of higher education to be accountable for graduating the students they enrolled (Baum, Kurose, & McPherson, 2013; Kirwan, 2007).

As accountability has increased nation-wide, an important qualification against which to interpret retention and graduation rates is whether such rates reveal equitable outcomes for students from different backgrounds. Those groups considered historically underrepresented, Hispanic or Latino, Black or African American, and American Indian or Alaskan Native, have proportionately lower educational attainment

TABLE 1: Bachelor's Degree graduation rates nation-wide by sex, race or ethnicity, and time to completion.

	4-years	5-years	6-years
Asian, men	39%	61%	68%
Asian, women	49%	69%	75%
White, men	33%	54%	59%
White, women	45%	61%	65%
Hispanic, men	21%	41%	49%
Hispanic, women	30%	51%	57%
Pacific Islander, men	23%	44%	50%
Pacific Islander, women	33%	50%	55%
Black, men	13%	29%	35%
Black, women	22%	38%	44%
American Indian/ Alaska Native, men	14%	27%	33%
American Indian/ Alaska Native, women	21%	35%	39%

as a group (U.S. Census Bureau, 2015) and complete fewer degrees after enrollment in college by cohort (NCES, 2017, Table 326.10). The difference in graduation rates between historically underrepresented minority groups and their white peers is referred to as the *college completion gap.*

Table 1 depicts graduation rates from first institution attended for first-time, full-time bachelor's degree-seeking students at four-year *public* institutions of higher education, by sex, race or ethnicity, and time to completion for the 2010 entry cohort (NCES, 2017, Table, 326.10). Across all race and ethnic groups, more women than men complete bachelor degrees after four, five, and six-years of enrollment. Asian men or women and white women are most likely to complete degrees, while Black men and Native American or Alaskan Native men or women are least likely to complete degrees.

Evaluation of the college completion gap over time shows that it is narrowing, though much more quickly for some groups than others. According to the most recent *Digest of Education Statistics* (NCES, 2017: Table 322.20), the percent change in bachelor's degrees awarded between 2006 and 2016 was positive for Hispanic or Latino students (+118 percent) and Black students (+35 percent), but negative for American Indian or Alaskan Native students (−11 percent). Most notable were the gains made by Hispanic or Latino students, though educational attainment remains very low at 28 percent for this group overall (U.S. Census Bureau, 2015).

Even with added accountability and scrutiny of graduation rates, identifying the structural and systemic inequities that push historically underrepresented students out before graduation has proven difficult for institutions. A limiting factor may be that research on college success and completion has continued to focus on the *college readiness* of underrepresented students and paid far less attention and research on the effects or impacts of programs and systems of support for students already enrolled in college. Essentially, the focus of research on college readiness has failed to help administrators and faculty identify how to help students succeed once enrolled. For instance, high school GPA is well-documented as the best indicator of degree completion (Jackson & Kurlaender, 2013), but college programs that support student success have not been able to translate such information into successful programmatic interventions that increase retention.

One reason for this failure may be that college retention programs focus too much on trying to turn less "ready" students into their ideal students. In "Becoming a Student-Ready College," Tia Brown-McNair and her colleagues (2016) ask a more actionable question, *how are colleges supporting the students they have, instead of the students they wished they had?* A student-ready college consists of a healthy ecosystem of programs and services from admissions to the classroom that are committed to holistic student development. Beyond academic achievement, a student-ready college is intentionally designed to empower students and foster students' agency.

The programs and services described in this book are the result of a campus community working in collaboration to become student-centered and student-graduation ready. In the 21st century, we aspire to go beyond aspirational statements of inclusion and diversity and focus on closing the college completion gap through practical solutions and attention to the needs of historically underrepresented students at the University of Nevada, Reno.

REFERENCES

Baum, S., Kurose, C., and McPherson, M. (2013). An overview of American Higher Education. *Future of Children*, 23, 1, www.futureofchildren.org.

Brown-McNair, T., Albertine, S., Cooper, M. A., McDonald, N., Major, Jr., T. (2016). *Becoming a Student-Ready College: A New Culture of Leadership for Student Success.* San Francisco, CA: Wiley & Sons, Inc.

Kirwan, W. E. (2007). Higher education's "accountability" imperative: How the university system of Maryland responded. *Change*, 39, 2, 21–25.

Herzog, S., & Stanley, J. (2013). *Identifying at-risk students to raise retention and revenues.* Presentation to the annual American Institutional Research association meeting in Long Beach, CA. Retrieved from http://www.unr.edu/ia/research.

Jackson, J., & Kurlaender, M. (2014). College Readiness and College Completion at Broad Access Four-Year Institutions. *American Behavioral Scientist*, 58(8), 947–971.

U.S. Census Bureau (2016). Educational Attainment in the United States: 2015. Retrieved from https://www.census.gov/library/publications/2016/demo/p20-578.html.

National Center for Education Statistics (2018). Digest of Education Statistics: 2017. Retrieved from https://nces.ed.gov/pubsearch/pubsinfo.asp?pubid=2018070.

CHAPTER 23

Assessment and Success

The Role of Foundational Competencies

RUSSEL STONE, PH.D.

Russel Stone oversees the assessment of the University of Nevada, Reno's, competency-based general education curriculum and is responsible for institutional assessment of UNR's strategic plan. He also serves as the University's accreditation liaison officer. Trained as a medievalist at the University of Toronto, where he received his master's, and UCLA, where he received his Ph.D., he taught general education humanities courses for nearly a decade before joining the Office of the Provost. As an administrator, he relies on his experience in the classroom to inform his work in the assessment of student learning. He is a Mission Fulfillment Fellow with the Northwest Commission on Colleges and Universities, and his current research interest is the impact of civic and campus engagement on student learning and success, particularly among transfer-ins and first-generation students.

Introduction

Any educator who has been involved in designing and teaching a general education curriculum can appreciate that it is a democratic learning experience for students. Regardless of their academic and personal backgrounds or their majors and career goals, all students travel together through a series of competencies-based, often topical classes in which they encounter the literary canon, fine arts, social sciences, and natural sciences; in the process, they learn how to write and speak effectively, how to collaborate with their peers, and how to think creatively and analytically. These all comprise "crosscutting skills" that some argue are more valuable to one's chosen career than disciplinary knowledge (Pasquerella). In teaching writing- and literature-centric general education classes for many years at two public universities, I encountered all manner of individuals, including first-generation students, athletes, single parents, and veterans. Some individuals were non-traditional students seeking a college education later in life, while the background of other students ranged from underfunded rural high schools to well-heeled preparatory schools. While some students were from underrepresented groups, still other students had parents who were physicians, engineers, and even college faculty members. In order to effectively teach such a varied group of students, I had to learn to become pedagogically adaptable and to tailor my office hours towards mentoring those who needed assistance in structuring theses or relying on textual evidence to support arguments or comparing and responding to cross-cultural ideas. It was a transformational learning experience, perhaps more for myself than for the students, and I often found myself wondering about the very questions that occupy administrators and those of us who report on student learning and student success to accreditors and external agencies. What does success mean to these individual groups of students? How do they learn, and how do we know whether they have or to what extent they have learned? Have we done all that we can to prepare them for future classes and semesters or even further education and careers?

Tracking Student Success

Tracking student success metrics and assessing students' demonstration of learning outcomes have long preoccupied siloed, but parallel agendas within institutions of higher learning, and both have elicited critical discussions in recent years. While colleges and universities report success data to national repositories (e.g., first-to-second year retention and four- and six-year graduation rate to IPEDS), these metrics suggest goals for an anonymous, aggregate cohort of students successfully navigating and finishing the required number of credits semester to semester, year to year. What this tracking does not account for is the quality of the education that these students received, or what they learned—both in terms of a specific body of disciplinary knowledge and a universal set of such skills as communication and critical thinking—as they completed their courses and accumulated the requisite number of credits. At the beginning of the decade, when the Lumina Foundation, a private foundation dedicated to fostering higher educational opportunities among the American public, established the goal of helping 60 percent of adults in the United States earn a postsecondary degree or credential by 2025, it was not long before representatives of higher education raised the question of quality of learning. The National

Institute for Learning Outcomes Assessment (NILOA) at the University of Illinois at Urbana-Champaign suggested, for example, a secondary complementary goal:

> it was soon clear that achieving this landmark would be a hollow attainment if the quality of the learning was substandard, the non-negotiable target became high-quality credentials in the form of degrees and certificates with well-defined and transparent learning outcomes that provide clear path—ways to employment and further education (Ewell 4).

Now, at the end of the decade, the anxiety over discerning educational quality and showing evidence of learning alongside the standard metrics of student success has led to a more nuanced concern about how universities foster and report on student achievement. Beyond compliance (reporting quantitative data), accountability requires that an institution consider who its students are, what they need to be successful, and what it offers all students equitably to ensure their education (Ikenberry and Kuh 49). As the contributions to the present volume attest, there are many types of students and many impacts upon their success. In this chapter, I will discuss the third of these three considerations through the lens of both expectations for higher education accreditation and through emerging trends in assessing student learning. I will also ask how in light of these trends we might design assessment of student learning activities so that they supplement student success metrics, and, more importantly, support student success itself.

Assessment and Accreditation, Then and Now

Assessment of student learning involves a seemingly straightforward research agenda that asks innocuous and much needed questions. As Barbara E. Walvoord posited in her seminal guide to assessment design, institutional administrators and faculty should ask themselves what information about student learning is necessary to inform action and how they will go about collecting and interpreting that information (Walvoord 11). Challenges arise not in articulating such questions, or even in the collection and interpretation phase, but in the crucial next step: making use of one's findings to inform curricular reform, for example, or employ new teaching strategies. Use of evidence, specifically use of evidence toward improvement in a program or even the University itself, is the gold standard not easily attained. As Stanley O. Ikenberry and George D. Kuh have argued, "harnessing evidence of student learning, making it consequential in the improvement of student success and strengthened institutional performance" is necessary for "the long-term health and vitality of American higher education and the students and society we serve" (Ikenberry and Kuh 4). An idealistic goal, to be sure, but an imperative for all of us responsible for student learning and success.

The primary motivation for assessment of student learning comes directly from the country's seven regional accrediting bodies and indirectly from the U.S. Department of Education, which effectively deputizes these bodies by requiring that an institution of higher learning must be accredited if its students are to be eligible for federal financial aid. Although the federal government has revised the roles of these regional accrediting bodies since the passage of the Higher Education Act in 1965, assessment became a far-reaching concern for institutions of all types and missions only in the late 1980s, when the Department of Education first mandated that, along with retention and time-to-degree metrics, accreditors procure from their member institutions educational quality and a demonstration of their "effectiveness through evidence of learning" (Ewell and Jankowski 149). A generation later, "A Test of Leadership: Charting the Future of US Higher Education" (colloquially known as the "Spellings Report," after then Secretary of Education, Margaret Spellings) lamented that graduates of American colleges and universities were underprepared for the modern workforce and lacked sufficient knowledge and skills necessary for successful employment in the new century. The deliberation that led to the report also revealed a widening chasm between educators and the private sector and their views on the higher education enterprise, as it became apparent that the latter was as concerned as ever that universities were not held accountable for demonstrating the learning and success of their students and that educators were out of touch with the demands of the job market (Nunley 6). Although the federal commission behind the report did not call for institutions to employ standardized testing, a proliferation of out-of-the-box testing products soon followed in response to the report but did not generally provide universities with useful information about their unique students, curricula, and missions (Kinzie et al. 168). The next federal attempt to shed light on accountability for colleges and universities through a national database was the so-called "College Scorecard," implemented in President Obama's second term and intended to make readily available to potential students a myriad of data, ranging from location, size of student body, and majors offered to costs, graduation rate, loan default rate, average amount borrowed, and employment rates. The goal of the online tool was to "highlight . . . key indicators about the cost and value of institutions across the country to help students choose a school that is well-suited to meet their needs, priced affordably, and is consistent with their educational and career goals" ("Education Department").

Finally, in the last few years, even as the Department of Education seeks to become less prescriptive in its oversight of the regional accrediting bodies, and as six years have passed since the Higher Education Act was due for reauthorization (Kelderman), accreditors have become holistic in their scope and mission and have granted more autonomy, or, we might say, creative control, to their member institutions in reporting on student learning and student success. In 2016, the Council for Higher Education Accreditation (CHEA), an advocacy group for accrediting bodies and institutions of higher learning, announced its intent to reconfigure the accreditation process as one that would benefit students, society at large, and the American public interest by ensuring the legitimacy of the education offered by the country's colleges and universities (Gaston 7–8). In the same year, the Council of Regional Accrediting Commissions (C-RAC) published a caveat that graduation, employment, and loan repayment rates were reported "due to a national completion agenda driven by real concerns about whether students are being educated to support a thriving and sustainable economy" but were insufficient metrics of institutional effectiveness without evidence that students had mastered both disciplinary knowledge and "the broader knowledge, skills, and attitudes that are associated with being 'an educated person'" ("A Statement from the Council"). Defining the intellectual scope of such a person, C-RAC called for a renewed emphasis on the skills taught universally across all institutions of higher learning, including communication and critical thinking, as well as the ability to integrate and apply learning across the disciplines and within one's chosen field of employment and indeed life as an informed citizen (the last is reflective of what is often termed "lifelong learning") (Gaston 8–9).

These national responses have helped inform three current trends in accreditation and its expectations for evaluating and reporting on student learning and success: (1) an emphasis on soft skills, or what University of

Nevada, Reno, and many other institutions designate as 'fundamental competencies' (communication, quantitative reasoning, critical thinking, and information literacy); (2) the recognition of and appreciation for the multiple places in which learning occurs during a student's time at the University; (3) a move away from reporting on retention rates, for example, or performance on a Capstone assignment for the anonymized, average student at the University (the proverbial 'everyman' of the student body) towards an analysis of success metrics and demonstrations of learning among specific student groups. The three are inherently related. For example, a consideration of the multiple places in which students learn is relevant to general education and the aforementioned fundamental competencies and the lure of an integrative learning experience, in which students apply and hone the communication, quantitative, and analytical skills to their major, but acknowledges learning beyond courses and curricula as well. Careful consideration must also be given to the "rich array of learning experiences [needed] to complete a degree" and the "type of learning [that] cannot be achieved without collaboration among campus units" (Malenfant and Brown 20–21). The possibility that students may hone these foundational skills through a host of co-curricular experiences, including, for example, civic engagement, internships, student leadership, employment, or clubs and organizations is vital to understanding where, how, and why they become more effective thinkers and communicators, but assessing these factors, rather than adhering to assignment-based evaluations of student performance, poses a considerable challenge. The proliferation of students involved in these activities has cast considerable doubt on an assessment concept that became fashionable in reaction to the Spellings Report: the notion of value-added, or measuring a student's improvement in fundamental skills from first-year general education classes to the senior year in the major. As more students become involved in more co-curricular activities, too many external factors may impact their intellectual maturation and render a traditional, class-based, value-added assessment impractical (Suskie 110). The access to various avenues of learning that students have within and beyond general education and major curricula is also indicative of the different types of learning that they encounter—and likely desire—during their college career. Passive learning, the traditional setting of students sitting through lecture-based instruction, is increasingly supplemented, if not supplanted, by online and hybrid instruction, flipped classrooms, integrative learning as described above, and active, applied, and experiential learning in which students employ their skills through research, internships, and service learning, as well as the other, aforementioned co-curricular experiences (Dugan and Hernon 8).

Students seeking out unique co-curricular experiences and learning in various ways during their college career has led, in part, to the third trend in accreditation and the expectations for assessing student learning and success, the need to consider specific groups of students. In recent years, a consensus on what constitutes the twenty-first century student has arisen between accreditors and educators:

- A student increasingly mobile who may complete courses and credits at more than one institution; and who can increasingly learn beyond the traditional lecture setting
- A student who faces a shortened shelf-life of the educational experience and the degree in which it culminates, as technology drives knowledge and the needs of the workforce
- A student who seeks out experiential and applied learning experiences reflective of a real-world environment (Ramaswamy);
- A student who undergoes the higher education experience during a time of skepticism of the value of that experience among the public at large (Kuh et al. 9);
- A student who will complete a degree and enter a "harsher, less forgiving economic environment that will place a greater premium on evidence of what students know and are able to do" (Kuh et al. 225).

At the same time, the demography of the American student body continues to change, and evidence of student learning and success must account for students of color, first-generation students, first-generation Americans, transfer students, and a number of other groups who will not only find multiple avenues of learning once they matriculate but will also be informed by disparate levels of prior knowledge, cultural experiences, and attitudes towards and familiarity with types of learning (Suskie 22–23). This has led to a recent emphasis on individual student-based assessments and accountability not simply for a given year's cohort of students or for the undergraduate or graduate body at large, but for the diverse types of students who populate a university campus. For the last decade or so, this attention to student groups, especially those of underrepresented students, has driven the concept of equity in assessment and what is known as "culturally responsive" assessment, strategies that I will propose below as models for evaluating student learning at UNR.

Both are rooted in classroom assessments. Equity in measuring student learning asks educators to consider whether one type of assessment for a given competency is sufficient for all students or whether multiple options of assessments for various types of assignments would better allow students to demonstrate their learning. In similar fashion, "culturally responsive assessment," originating in culturally responsive teaching (a type of pedagogy that acknowledges and is inclusive of the cultural backgrounds of students), proposes that educators should select "appropriate assessment tools or approaches that offer the greatest chance for various types of students to demonstrate their learning so that assessment results may benefit students from all backgrounds" and seeks to counter "an assumption that hinders consideration of diverse learner needs within assessment—that while learners may take multiple paths to and through learning, they must demonstrate their knowledge and skills in the same way" (Montenegro and Jankowski 5). The first step in this approach to assessment is thus to identify the students whose work is being evaluated and consider their performance across various academic and demographic populations—to expand on an institutional scale an attention to students' prior knowledge and needs that many instructors exhibit in the classroom. Moving beyond assessment techniques for classes and programs, an institutional model for utilizing a culturally responsive assessment strategy on this larger scale lay in the disaggregation of student success metrics, particularly at Minority-Serving Institutions. Vuong and Hairston recently argued, "Traditional data points such as graduation rates . . . do not always show the complete picture of [these schools'] successes, as they do not always adequately measure [their] unique educational experiences and targeted missions" (2). In response, some such institutions have begun to collect impactful data throughout students' college careers from matriculation to graduation, including prior educational experience, students' stated goals for a college degree, points in the institution's curricula that hinder persistence and completion, contact with faculty, learning (especially in fundamental competencies), and involvement in student leadership, activism, and engagement (Conrad et al. 4–5).

A New Model of Student Learning Assessment at UNR

In fall 2016 the University implemented a new competencies-based general education curriculum, in which undergraduates complete fourteen learning objectives offered across classes both within traditional, lower-division, general education groupings (e.g., natural sciences and fine arts) and their respective majors, in which students encounter more focused competencies (e.g., diversity and equity, global contexts, ethics) taught from a disciplinary perspective. This new Core Curriculum thus introduces three innovative features to the general education program at the University. First, as co-owners of the curriculum, faculty in academic departments teach general education competencies on their own disciplinary terms and often at multiple levels, as departments are encouraged to offer classes that simultaneously fulfill general education and major requirements. All classes proposing to satisfy a given objective are also vetted by faculty committees at various levels, and all such classes must be assessed by faculty in the department offering them. Finally, both the general education curriculum and the assessment of student learning within it are designed to foster the development of three fundamental competencies—communication, quantitative reasoning, and critical thinking/use of information—from first-year Core Writing and Core Math classes, through the remainder of the Core Objectives, to a senior Capstone (rebranded as "Integration and Synthesis" in the new Core), as well as any other moments of experiential or applied learning. The integration of Core Objectives within the major ensures that students have multiple opportunities to hone their soft skills within both the general education and major curricula. As at many institutions, UNR's goals for this revised general education are to provide students with a breadth and depth of knowledge, skills, and values, to prepare them for careers or further education, and to train them for global citizenship, as the University's mission statement articulates.

The University implemented this new general education curriculum following a period of unprecedented growth among the undergraduate student population. This population had been changing, too, in ways reflective of the aforementioned 'twenty-first century student.' Just over one-third of the graduating class in that 2016–17 academic year began their UNR career as transfer-ins, evidence of the mobility of students in the region and state. Diversity among the student body was also increasing, as the number of Hispanic students had grown by nearly 50 percent since fall 2013, when the surge in enrollment began in the wake of the Great Recession, and students of color and multi-ethnic students accounted for over 40 percent of the total undergraduate population in fall 2017. At the same time, UNR matriculants were gravitating towards the professional disciplines (namely health sciences, engineering, and business), and graduates were encountering a rapidly changing city beyond the confines of campus, with Reno benefiting from sustained economic development, particularly in the tech industry. General education reform was thus implemented at a critical transitional phase in the demography of the University's students and the career prospects that they would face upon graduation. As the student body evolves, teaching, learning, and assessment will have to evolve in turn, and as UNR welcomes, in particular, large cohorts of transfer-ins and underrepresented students, faculty and administrators alike will benefit from a more nuanced understanding of where and how students develop skills across their college careers. Universities that have implemented culturally responsive assessment strategies offer a viable model for the future of both general education and the assessment of student learning therein.

Completion of general education classes and development of the fundamental competencies are crucial to retention and learning, respectively, but the ramifications for student success are often more glaring. For example, if students struggle in an introductory mathematics course required for STEM majors, they may have to declare an alternative major or, in a worst-case scenario, leave the University. Still another outcome for students who struggle in the prerequisite mathematics course is an ongoing struggle throughout the STEM major with the concepts taught in Core Math, to the point that students run the intellectual risk of failing to master the necessary competencies in the discipline and the psychological and financial risks of expending time and money on a desired degree that they may not attain at all. A parallel, albeit more sublte scenario is conceivable in the other fundamental competencies of communication, critical thinking, and information literacy. If students struggle to construct a thesis, support an argument with appropriate sources, respond to the opinions and arguments of others, analyze problems, or demonstrate any of the many other soft skills encompassed by these broad competencies in introductory, general education courses, how might we expect them to apply these skills in their majors, much less their careers? How might we know their strengths and weaknesses in demonstrating these skills at various points in the curricula? And are we not doing our students a disservice if we do not consider where in the general education and major curricula they need help in honing these skills? Moreover, to what extent do students learn and demonstrate their learning in different manners?

In spring 2019, the Office of the Provost and representatives from the UNR's Writing and Speaking Initiative will undertake with these questions in mind the first of three institutional-wide assessments of UNR's fundamental competencies for general education. Drawing student writing samples from across various disciplines and evaluating them on a standardized rubric, the assessment designers will forego a traditional assessment of randomly selected student work intended to represent the performance of the "typical" UNR undergraduate and take into consideration the academic and personal backgrounds of the students. This project will consider whether a host of factors (e.g., major, ratio of completion of online compared to face-to-face classes, first-generation status, involvement in engaged learning activities) can and do impact students' proficiency at written communication. At the same time, student writing artifacts will be evaluated based on types of and expectations for writing, determined by the class level and the criteria for the assignment defined by the instructor, whether it be for a critical analysis of a text in a lower-division general education class or constructing a research proposal for a senior-level, applied learning class or thesis. This will allow the evaluators to construct an alternative to traditional models of value-added assessment that attempt to measure progress or regression from a student's first to final year in a program or at the University. Instead of tracking a single student over successive years (a methodology that often neglects non-curricular impacts on student learning), the assessment designers will (1) assemble a cohort of student writing samples that offers a statistical representation of the UNR undergraduate student body in terms of academic level, demographic background, and co-curricular activity; (2) score these anonymized samples by a series of standardized rubrics; (3) analyze the results to determine if, in fact, these various factors impact students' performance on lower-, intermediate-, and higher-level writing assignments. If successful, the design of this project can adhere to another foundational principle of equity in assessment—that all students be given multiple and varied opportunities to demonstrate their mastery of competencies—and thus be applied to oral communication, quantitative reasoning (the second fundamental competency), and the many manifestations of critical thinking (the third such competency), including analysis, synthesis, problem solving, and the ability to distinguish facts from opinions (Suskie 85).

In implementing this assessment, I advocate for adopting and adapting the initiatives of Minority Serving Institutions that examine the several curricular, co-curricular, and life experiences that determine retention and graduation or employ classroom techniques to understand how to make courses and curricula more responsive to all groups of students. In either case, the objective is "to empower students, create clear transparent pathways, and ensure that credits and credentials are awarded by demonstration of learning, in whatever form that may take" (Montenegro and Jankowski 16). Translated into local terms, a university must ensure that transfer-ins fully develop fundamental competencies and effectively integrate them within their major, and that first-generation, underrepresented, and English as a second language students receive an equitable, competencies-based education. Thus, an ideal opportunity for a similarly equitable assessment of student learning is upon us.

REFERENCES

Conrad, C., Gasman, M., Lundberg, T., Nguyen, T-H., Commodore, F., and Samayoa, A. C.

"Using educational data to increase learning, retention, and degree attainment at Minority Serving Institutions (MSI)." Philadelphia: Penn Center for Minority Serving Institutions, 2013. https://www.gse.upenn.edu/pdf/cmsi/using_educational_data.pdf.

Dugan, R. E., and Hernon, P. "Institutional mission-centered student learning."

Revisiting Outcomes Assessment in Higher Education. Edited by Hernon, P., Dugan, R. E., and Schwartz, C., Westport, CT: Libraries Unlimited, 2006.

Ewell, P. T. "The Lumina Degree Qualifications Profile (DQP): implications for Assessment" *National Institute for Learning Outcomes Assessment, Occasional Paper 16*. Champaign, IL: NILOA, 2013.

Ewell, P. T. and Jankowski, N. A. "Accreditation as opportunity: serving two purposes with assessment." *Using evidence of student learning to improve higher education*, edited by Kuh, G. O., et al. San Francisco: Jossey-Bass., 2015.

Gaston, P. L. "Assessment and accreditation: an imperiled symbiosis." *National Institute for Learning Outcomes Assessment, Occasional Paper 33*. Champaign, IL: NILOA, 2018.

Ikenberry, S. O., and Kuh, G. O. "From compliance to ownership: why and how colleges and universities assess student learning." *Using evidence of student learning to improve higher education*, edited by Kuh, G. O., et al. San Francisco: Jossey-Bass, 2015.

Kelderman, E. "Cutting oversight of accreditation will spur innovation, says education dept. Critics say not so fast." *The Chronicle of Higher Education*, vol. 65, no. 18, 2019. https://www.chronicle.com/article/Cutting-Oversight-of/245429.

Kinzie, J., Ikenberry, S. O., and Ewell, P. T. "The bigger picture: student learning outcomes assessment and external entities." *Using evidence of student learning to improve higher education*, edited by Kuh, G. O., et al. San Francisco: Jossey-Bass, 2015.

Kuh, G. D., Ikenberry, S. O., Jankowski, N. A., Cain, T. R., Ewell, P. T., Hutchings, P., and Kinzie, J. "Making assessment matter." *Using evidence of student learning to improve higher education*, edited by Kuh, G. O., et al. San Francisco: Jossey-Bass, 2015.

Kuh, G. O., Ikenberry, S. O., Jankowski, N. A., Cain, T. R., Ewell, P. T., Hutchings, P., and Kinzie, J. *Using evidence of student learning to improve higher education*, edited by Kuh, G. O., et al. San Francisco: Jossey-Bass, 2015.

Malenfant, K. J., and Brown, K. "Creating sustainable assessment through collaboration: a national program reveals effective practices" *National Institute for Learning Outcomes Assessment, Occasional Paper 31*. Champaign, IL: NILOA, 2017.

Miller, M. A. "From denial to acceptance: the stages of assessment." *National Institute for Learning Outcomes Assessment, Occasional Paper 13*. Champaign, IL: NILOA, 2012.

Montenegro, E. and Jankowski, N. A. "Equity and assessment: moving towards culturally responsive assessment." *National Institute for Learning Outcomes Assessment, Occasional Paper 29*. Champaign, IL: NILOA, 2017.

Nunley, C., Bers, T., and Manning, T. "Learning outcomes assessment in community colleges." *National Institute for Learning Outcomes Assessment, Occasional Paper 10*. Champaign, IL: NILOA, July 2011.

Pasquerella, L. "In pursuit of quality and deliberative democracy." *Liberal Education*, vol. 104, no. 2, 2018. https://www.aacu.org/liberaleducation/2018/spring/president.

Ramaswamy, A. "Are you ready?" *The Beacon*, vol. 1, no. 2, 2018. http://www.nwccu.org/the-beacon/.

Suskie, L. "Assessing student learning: a common sense guide." San Francisco: Jossey-Bass, 2004.

U.S. Department of Education Press Office. "Education department releases college scorecard to help students choose best colleges for them." U.S. Department of Education. February 13, 2013. https://www.ed.gov/news/press-releases/education-department-releases-college-scorecard-help-students-choose-best-college-them.

Vuong, B. and Hairston, C. C. (2012). "Using data to improve minority-serving institution success." Institute for Higher Education Policy: Washington, D.C., 2012. https://eric.ed.gov/?id=ED537368.

Walvoord, B. E. "Assessment clear and simple," San Francisco, Jossey-Bass, 2010.

WASC Senior College and University Commission. "A statement from the Council of Regional Accrediting Commissions on student outcomes." *WASC Senior College and University Commission*, 2016. https://www.wscuc.org/annoucements/statement-council-regional-accrediting-commissions-student-outcomes.

CHAPTER 24

The Undergraduate Research Program at the University of Nevada

JAMES BEATTIE, PH.D., TANNER LYON, KAPREACE YOUNG, TYLER EWING, and SCOTT MENSING, PH.D.

James Beattie is the coordinator for First in the Pack, an academic outreach program for first-generation students. The program utilizes a proactive advising approach to work with students to reach their academic, personal, and career goals. He returned to school to pursue a masters in Sociology and a Ph.D. in Educational Leadership after a successful, yet unfulfilling career in the private sector. He found his passion in higher education while developing and implementing a mentoring program for first-generation and low-income college students for the Dean's Future Scholars Program. His research interests include successful characteristics of academic outreach programs, college access, retention, and graduation for underrepresented students, as well as organizational theory.

Tanner Lyon is a graduate student in Philosophy with a specialization in Psychoanalysis at The New School for Social Research in New York City. Before graduating from the University of Nevada, Reno in the spring of 2019, he served as a senior co-editor for the *Nevada State Undergraduate Research Journal*, as well as a writing consultant for the Nevada GEAR UP program. He plans to attain a Ph.D. in philosophy and hopes that he can apply his studies to a professorship position at a research institution. His research interests include nineteenth and twentieth century continental philosophy, political economy and psychoanalysis; his projects focus on the effects of global social institutions on individual psychology.

KaPreace Young is the graduate assistant for the Undergraduate Research Department. She is a master's student in the Educational Leadership program and is focused on the retention and success rates of Black students at Predominately White Institutions. She is passionate about bridging a gap between the University of Nevada, Reno and the Reno community. She is the co-founder of a women's empowerment group and plans to use her knowledge and experience to feed back into her community and University.

Scott Mensing has served as director of Undergraduate Research for the University of Nevada since 2015 and is Gibson professor of Geography and a Foundation professor. He is interested in supporting all avenues of undergraduate education and has been awarded the F. Donald Tibbitts Memorial Distinguished Teaching Award, the Nevada System of Higher Education Regents Teaching Award, and the CASE Nevada Professor of the Year from the Carnegie Foundation of Advancement of Teaching. His research focuses on reconstructing past environments and the impact of both climate and human activity on landscape change during the last few thousand years. He has worked on sites across western North America as well as in Italy. His projects are collaborations with researchers in History and Archaeology in an effort to better integrate an understanding of the role of humans in ecological processes through time.

Introduction: History and Development

The Vice President for Research (VPR) at the University of Nevada, Reno established the Undergraduate Research office in the early 2000's. The office was established to award and distribute funding to undergraduate students who had submitted independent research proposals under the guidance of a faculty mentor. Two funded programs were initially developed, the Honors Program (discussed in Part 5, Chapter 25 of this book), and the General Undergraduate Research Award (GURA) which eventually became the Nevada Undergraduate Research Award (NURA). Funding for these two awards was initially provided by the VPR from indirect cost recovery monies accrued from externally funded grants. These monies were distributed annually to undergraduate students through a competitive review process and an annual research symposium was established to allow all undergraduate researchers to present their work in a public forum. Initially, between fifteen and twenty-five students per year were supported through this funding.

In 2012, the Associated Students of the University of Nevada (ASUN) passed legislation to financially support the National Undergraduate Research Award and in 2015 they subsequently passed legislation to support international research in partnership with the Undergraduate Research, which became known as the International Research Experience (IRE). In 2016, the Undergraduate Research office sequentially created two additional undergraduate research opportunities: the Community-based Award and the Pack Research Experience Program.

In 2018, an agreement between the President of the Associated Students and the President of the University of Nevada, Reno established a new funding structure that substantially increased the money available for undergraduate research. Additionally, this new structure provided a sustainable funding formula that also allowed for the expansion of each of these new programs. Today, more than 150 students are funded annually through a partnership between Undergraduate Research and ASUN. Three research symposia are held throughout the year to showcase student work and all students who receive funding are required to present in at least one of the symposia held throughout the year. Undergraduate Research is currently directed through a part-time administrative appointment to an academic faculty member on campus who is supported by a full-time administrative assistant and a part time graduate student assistant.

Research Program Components

Undergraduate research is an invaluable experience that provides students with opportunities to examine critical questions, engage in the research process, showcase their findings in meaningful ways, and build strong relationships with faculty members. Students interested in answering critical research questions may lack the experience and resources to pursue an answer to these questions in a well-defined and structured manner. Faculty mentors can provide the expertise to help guide students. Additionally, building a relationship with a mentor or an expert in the student's field of interest is reportedly the most important part of participating in undergraduate research (Mabrouk and Peters). Not only does the mentor serve as a guide for the research, they often provide the level of support necessary for future success. Faculty mentors are an important source of information in regard to their field of study and can facilitate a student's transition into the workforce or in the pursuit of post-baccalaureate education.

Mentorship Programs

Mentorship programs allow undergraduate students to conduct research under the supervision of academic faculty. Undergraduates may assist faculty with their current research or create a proposal that incorporates their individual ideas. These projects can be incentivized with a research award or with course credit. Mentorship programs give undergraduates an introduction to conducting research within their field, as well as providing an experience working alongside a professional researcher.

Summer Research Programs

Summer research programs have a similar structure to mentorship programs. They typically take place over a ten-week period during the summer and may include a larger stipend as students are expected to dedicate a majority of their time to the program during the award period. Many summer programs also offer graduate school preparation resources during the award period that can include GRE preparation courses or various workshops addressing application materials. One example is the Ronald E. McNair Baccalaureate Achievement Program explored in (Part 3, Chapter 16). In some variations, such as the International Research Experience at the University of Nevada, Reno, the research program is hosted by partnering institutions abroad. By hosting programs such as these, students can develop knowledge and relationships that may assist them in future graduate studies. Many of these programs are specifically aimed at student populations that are underrepresented in graduate school demographics.

Funding

Research funding can be accessed in multiple ways such as general research awards, community-based awards, travel awards, and video awards. General research awards provide students, and potentially their faculty mentor, with funding for materials, travel or stipends. General awards can be state or institution-wide and might have different tiers for upper and lower classmen. Community awards offer funding for research projects of public interest, rather than the student or faculty's individual research interests. In addition to a faculty mentor, students may be matched with a local organization to facilitate the research project. Travel awards are offered to undergraduates that have already been accepted to present at external conferences. Travel awards often act as an incentive to undergraduate students to seek out external presentation opportunities that they may have otherwise overlooked. In addition, video competitions often provide monetary awards to undergraduate students that compose a short, accessible video explaining their research. These programs allow students to showcase their research to a wider audience in multiple platforms. Amounts for any given award can span from hundreds to thousands of dollars, depending on institutional funding and span of the research project.

Symposia

Symposia and conferences give undergraduates the opportunity to present their research or creative activity in a formal, academic setting through multiple methods; oral presentation, poster, exhibit, or performance. Institutions with high research activity, such as the University of Texas at Austin, may offer a "research week" in which student presentations are scheduled throughout five days (University of Texas at Austin School of Undergraduate Studies). Public research presentations give undergraduates an exercise in presenting their work in a concise manner accessible to a public audience.

Undergraduate Research Journals

Undergraduate research journals provide students with peer-reviewed publication opportunities within their home institution or state. Typically, these journals are student-led, with oversight from faculty or staff and reviews provided by fellow undergraduate students, graduate students, and faculty. Journals may or may not have an International Standard Serial Number (ISSN), a unique label for object identification, or assign Digital Object Identifiers (DOI) to the published research, which provides stable metadata for future use of the research article. As these journals are less competitive than national or discipline-specific journals, they are an ideal resource for familiarizing undergraduates with the peer-review process and the significance of publication in the research community.

Research Workshops

Workshops can be directed at undergraduates or faculty. Student workshops can focus on any aspect of the research process: starting a project, conducting research, the writing process, presentation via symposium/conference, or publication, etc. General guides to the research process can be very helpful for beginners that may be hesitant in regards to approaching research, as well as provide additional clarity for those that are already involved in research. Faculty workshops are typically centered on how to facilitate the research process for beginning researchers or recruiting undergraduates for various research-related positions. Faculty may have extensive experience working with graduate students, postdocs, and colleagues; however, facilitating undergraduates can pose unique challenges. Due to these differences, faculty-oriented workshops can help hesitant faculty members become confident undergraduate student mentors.

Skeletal, Limited, and Strong Undergraduate Research Programs

After examining Undergraduate Research programs at selected land-grant, Ivy League, and state institutions across the nation we developed a working model to categorize programs. Our model suggests three program levels; skeletal, limited, and strong. Each level has varying degrees of support from the institution including, but not limited to grants, staff, symposia, and workshops. In addition to listing the resources typically offered, we will provide an example of an institution that exemplifies each model level.

Skeletal Programs

Skeletal programs typically have limited in-house resources with little to no funding but are able to maintain a universally accessible list of resources online, generally external to the institution. The list may include opportunities such as scholarships, conferences, research awards, and summer research programs; unfortunately, external opportunities are often more difficult for students to secure than internal equivalents.

The University of Wyoming is an example of a skeletal program. Although the institution has an active IDeA Networks of Biomedical Research Excellence (INBRE) presence, the university lacks internal funding for undergraduate research (University of Wyoming, 2019). The online list of resources features links to McNair, INBRE, EPSCoR, and Wyoming NASA Space Grant opportunities. There is also no indication of professional staff dedicated to undergraduate research.

Limited Programs

Limited programs have multiple resources but may not include all of the opportunities housed within strong programs. An average limited program offers an online list of resources, a research award, a symposium, and various workshops. The research award may also take the form of a mentorship program. Funding for these resources is often managed by the office of the provost or vice-provost. Limited programs are generally managed by a small staff dedicated to undergraduate research or might be located within another department, such as student affairs or an office of undergraduate studies.

The University of Southern California has a structure in-line with the definition of limited programs. The Provost funds multiple fellowships, which includes general and travel awards, as well as the undergraduate research symposium (USC Undergraduate Programs). Additionally, students can receive a research distinction for graduation. These resources can be found on their online list of undergraduate research opportunities. USC does not have a staff that is dedicated to undergraduate research.

Strong Programs

Institutions with strong undergraduate research programs offer at least one form of mentorship/summer program, undergraduate and graduate workshops, research award, conference/symposium, undergraduate research journal, and have staff dedicated to undergraduate research. These programs necessarily have a dedicated budget within the upper administrative offices (such as the office of the provost) due to the presence of multiple internal research awards and an employed staff dedicated to undergraduate research.

The University of Minnesota, Twin Cities has one of the most impressive undergraduate research programs in the country. The Office of the Provost funds the Undergraduate Research office, which manages the Undergraduate Research Opportunity Program ($1,500 mentorship program), the International UROP (up to $2,000 international mentorship program), the Grand Challenges Undergraduate Research Opportunities Program (Community award), the Undergraduate Research Scholarship ($1,400 award for lower classmen), and the Multicultural Summer Research Opportunities Program ($4,000 summer research program for underrepresented students) (University of Minnesota Office of Undergraduate Research). The staff organizes the undergraduate research symposium, advises students in finding faculty mentors, holds three workshops per year, and maintains a comprehensive list of past and ongoing undergraduate research projects, as well as a list of paid research positions. The undergraduate research website provides abstract examples, poster templates, and discipline-specific proposal examples. The Minnesota Undergraduate Research Academic Journal has a staff of four undergraduates, with supervision by the coordinator for Undergraduate Research; the journal itself has a dedicated International Standard Serial Number (ISSN), but does not distribute Digital Object Identifiers (DOIs). Additionally, the Twin Cities staff also assist the Duluth campus. In the future, the office plans to provide a list of faculty members that can mentor undergraduates.

Components of Undergraduate Research at the University of Nevada, Reno

Nevada Undergraduate Research Award (NURA)

The Nevada Undergraduate Research Award (formerly General Undergraduate Research Award—GURA) is the oldest such program at UNR and is designed to provide financial support to undergraduate students who conduct independent research under the mentorship of a faculty member. The award requires students to submit a two-page research proposal, academic transcript, and mentor support letter in one of four subdisciplinary areas, STEM, Social Sciences, Arts or Humanities. Review panels of faculty from these respective sub-disciplines and undergraduate students (ASUN senators, previous award recipients, and students on the dean's list) rank proposals, considering the intellectual merit, project feasibility, student preparedness and mentor support, and funding decisions are made based upon the panel recommendations. The student award may be used for materials and supplies, travel to conduct research, or salary at a fixed rate. Between sixty and seventy awards are made annually through two solicitations, in fall and spring semesters.

International Research Experience (IRE)

The International Research Experience was designed to provide STEM students greater opportunities for an international experience. All academic indicators suggest that an international experience adds value to an undergraduate degree, however, research abroad programs traditionally provide limited offerings for those in the STEM disciplines. This program is a collaboration facilitated between the Undergraduate Research office and the University Study Abroad Consortium to help fill this gap. Faculty mentors at participating programs propose research projects suitable for undergraduate students. Students apply to work with specific faculty mentors and those faculty mentors select the students. Students spend ten weeks during the summer taking language classes and conducting research in the mentor's laboratory. Students must pay for their program; however, they receive a discounted program rate and Undergraduate Research and ASUN provide generous scholarship support to help subsidize costs. Between ten and twelve students receive this award annually. The program also works as an exchange program, with students from international partner institutions traveling to UNR during the summer to conduct research with our faculty.

Community-Based Research Award (CBR)

The Community-based Research Award program supports the universities goal to be a community engaged institution. Undergraduate Research solicits research problems from organizations within the Reno/Sparks/Carson City community that can be addressed during an academic semester by an undergraduate student working with a faculty mentor. Community representatives select the most appropriate applicant, and in an initial meeting with the Director of Undergraduate Research, organizational representative, undergraduate student, and faculty mentor, the research plan is refined, and a deliverable is agreed upon. The student under the guidance of their mentor, and in collaboration with the representative spend one semester conducting research to help solve the problem. Large and complex problems are phased over multiple semesters and students. Students are paid as student workers by Undergraduate Research, providing them with an on-campus research job. Solicitations are held each fall and spring semester, supporting about twelve students each semester and twenty-four projects per year.

Pack Research Experience Program (PREP)

The PREP program was implemented in response to our University's initiative to further diversify the campus and increase the participation of students from underrepresented groups and first-generation families in undergraduate research. The program is open to freshmen and sophomores. We work in collaboration with the McNair Scholars program, including requiring participation in select McNair outreach workshops to enhance potential recruitment into that program. Select faculty mentors across a broad range of disciplines are invited to submit research projects they feel suitable for lower division students. Mentors select from among applicants, and those students that best fit the criteria are then hired by Undergraduate Research to work one semester as a student researcher, under the mentorship of the faculty member on the designated research project. This solicitation is held once per year and funds up to twelve students per year.

Travel Awards

In an effort to provide undergraduate researchers an opportunity to present their work off campus, Undergraduate Research provides a set amount of travel funds to any student who has had an abstract accepted at a professional conference. This opportunity is open to any student on campus, regardless of whether their research was sponsored by Undergraduate Research. We support up to twenty students per year through this opportunity.

Nevada State Undergraduate Research Journal (NSURJ)

The Nevada State Undergraduate Research Journal was established in 2012 to provide a unified, peer-reviewed publication resource for undergraduates at all NSHE institutions and Sierra Nevada College, as well as international students conducting research at any of these institutions. By introducing undergraduates to publishing, they can become familiarized with the peer-review publication process that will become central in graduate school and research-related employment. NSURJ requires all submissions to be original and thesis or hypothesis driven. Upon initial review and acceptance by the Senior Editors, submissions are assigned to an Associate Editor, an undergraduate that reviews submissions for grammatical and structural errors. Upon application of these edits, the submission is subsequently reviewed by a professional researcher in the submission's respective field; professional referees are typically faculty members with the terminal degree in their field of research. Following application of the referee's suggestions, the submission goes through a final acceptance and is edited once more by the Associate and Senior Editors. Published articles are assigned a Digital Object Identifier and are physically and digitally printed in the annual journal.

Student Government Engagement

A unique aspect of Undergraduate Research at the University of Nevada, Reno is the level of engagement and dedication of the Associated Students of the University of Nevada (ASUN) student government. ASUN not only initiated and continues to fund the Nevada State Undergraduate Research

Journal, they also invest tens of thousands of dollars annually for the Nevada Undergraduate Research Award and the International Research Experience (IRE).

In 2012 the Senate of the Associated Students passed legislation to allocate no less than $25,000.00 and up to $50,000.00 a year to Undergraduate Research beginning in fiscal year 2014 to assist in funding the NURA awards. Subsequently, the President of the Association entered into an ongoing agreement with the Assistant Vice President for Research (VPR) to provide annual funds for these awards to Undergraduate Research. The NURA funding is transferred to Undergraduate Research and when applications for those funds are closed, ASUN senators from varying disciplines collaborate with Undergraduate Research in reviewing applications and allocating funds.

In 2015, the Senate of the associated students passed additional legislation to allocate $10,000.00 for the intended purpose of the aforementioned International Research Experience. Each year, Undergraduate Research provides completed applications to the student senate Chair for the Subcommittee on Academics. The Chair then selects a group of senators and creates a rubric to determine the priorities of funding that guides the allocation amounts. Once allocations have been decided, the money is transferred to the University Studies Abroad Consortium who then works directly with the awardees to facilitate payment.

Nevada State Undergraduate Research Journal

In 2012, the Senate of the Associated Students passed legislation to create and fund The Nevada State Undergraduate Research Journal. Each year, the ASUN president submits a budget to the student senate body for confirmation to fund the journal. In 2019, allocations for the journal were $21,789.00. Allocated funds provide the wages ($12.600.00) of two student senior co-editors that facilitate the publication process and creation of the journal. In addition, travel funds in the amount of $2000.00 dollars provide the senior co-editors with the opportunity to travel to various institutions of higher education across the state to market the journal and solicit submissions. Senior co-editors are provided with a $6000.00 dollar operating budget that funds NSURJ promotional items, physical copies of the journal, and software subscriptions to create and maintain an online presence. Finally, $2000.00 is allocated for hosting to provide food for workshops, host student government officers from other institutions, and organize a launch party to celebrate the release of the journal at the senior co-editor's discretion. Other support systems provided include Center for Student Engagement staff advising, inkblot marketing services, working space and infrastructure, as well as, a robust network of student government officers and their respective social and cultural capital within the system. In return for this support, the senior co-editors provide regular updates on expenditures and information regarding the journal to the senate body.

Data

Undergraduate research data for all awards (Community Based, Honors, International, and Nevada Undergraduate) are summarized from records collected since 2005. Demographic data from 2005 to 2019 are self-reported from student applications. Although the demographic composition of the University has changed over this time period, we compare our total awardee statistics to the current academic year, 2018–2019. Due to staff changes and changes in the application process over time, loss of identifier information (email, NSHE ID, middle initial) has resulted in some demographic data loss.

Overall, the percentage of applicants and awardees identifying as Asian American or Multi-ethnic is higher than the University population, whereas those identifying as White non-Hispanic, and Black non-Hispanic are somewhat underrepresented (fig. 1). Those identifying as Hispanic are

FIGURE 1. Demographic data for undergraduate research applicants and awardees for the period 2005 to 2018, compared to unr 2018–19 demographic data.

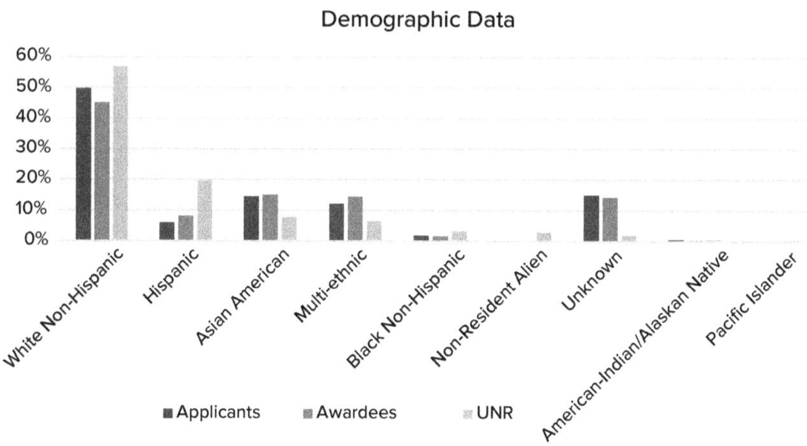

FIGURE 2. Applicant and Awardee data for the General Undergraduate Research Award (GURA, 2005–2015) and Nevada Undergraduate Research Award (NURA, 2016 to present).

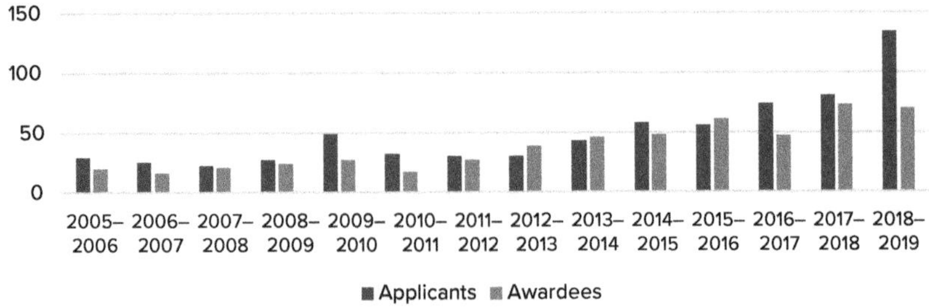

clearly underrepresented. While nearly 20 percent of UNR students identify as Hispanic, only 5 percent of applicants and 8 percent of awardees are Hispanic. Unknown represents students for which no data were collected by Undergraduate Research.

Among those identifying as White Non-Hispanic, the UNR population is 57 percent, while 50 percent of our applicants and 45 percent of award recipients were in this category. The Black non-Hispanic population at UNR is low, about 3 percent, and about 1 percent of applicants and award recipients are in this category. The Native American population is also very low, but our percentages of applications and awards are equivalent to the University percentage. Asian Americans are overrepresented, with 15 percent of applicants and award recipients in this category, compared with only 8 percent of the University population. Similarly, multi-ethnic students are funded at a higher rate than the total population, with 11 percent of our applications and 13 percent of our awards given to these students, while the University population is about 6 percent. The multi-ethnic population is a combination of the following self-identified groups; American Indian, Alaskan Native, and White; Asian and Black; Asian and Hispanic; Asian, Native Hawaiian and other Pacific Islander; Asian, Native Hawaiian, other Pacific Islander and White; Asian and White; Hispanic, Latino and White; White and Black; White, Hispanic, Latino, American Indian and Alaskan Native; White, Native Hawaiian, Other Pacific Islander, Not Hispanic and Latino; White, Asian, Hispanic and Latino. The two demographic categories (both with small populations) that the Undergraduate Research department has not had applicants and/or awardees are Non-resident Alien and Pacific Islander (as a single demographic, not multi-ethnic).

The number of awards given has increased since 2005 (fig. 2). When awards were first created in 2005, the General Undergraduate Research Award (GURA) was the only funded solicitation. Through 2012, on average twenty to twenty-five awards were given, supported by funds from the Vice President for Research and Innovation (VPRI) office. Beginning in 2013, additional funds were contributed by the ASUN, raising the total number of awards possible. In 2016 the award name was changed to the Nevada Undergraduate Research Award (NURA). Beginning in 2017, the source of funding changed from the VPRI office to the University, through an agreement related to tuition increases and the ability of the University to retain some tuition monies. Once again, this allowed the number of awards to increase, as well as provided the opportunity to move from one solicitation per year in spring, to two per year, in both fall and spring semesters. In 2018, the amount of the award increased and a stipend was provided for mentors. The increase in award size plus addition of faculty stipend led to a slight reduction in total number of awards provided. As of 2019, between seventy and seventy five awards are funded per year.

With the increase in funding, several other new awards were also created, including the International Research Award (fig. 3) initiated in summer 2016 and supporting on average eight students per year, and the Community Based award (fig. 4), initiated in fall of 2016 and now supporting between twenty and twenty four students per year. Not graphed is the Pack Research Experience Program (PREP), which began in spring 2019, with 11 students in the inaugural group.

The distribution of awards by student major sub-discipline and department (fig. 5) shows that by far, the largest number of awardees come from

FIGURE 3. Data for the International Research Experience award, first funded in 2016. Total number of applicants and awardees for the International Research Experience Award.

FIGURE 4. Data for the Community Based research award, first funded in 2016. Total number of applicants and awardees for the Community Based Research Award.

the STEM disciplines. Following STEM, in order of number of awardees is the Social Sciences, then Arts and Humanities.

A total of twenty one awards have been received within the Arts subdiscipline (fig. 6). Of those, students in the Art Department have received the highest number of awards (9) followed by Fine Arts (4), Music (3), Photography/Videography (2), Theater and Dance, (2) and then Art History (1).

A total of sixteen awards have been received by students in the Humanities (fig. 7). Of those, students in English Literature and History have each received five awards, World Languages and Literature have received four, and Philosophy and Linguistics each one.

A total of eighty awards have been received within the Social Sciences sub-discipline (fig. 8). Of those, students in the Psychology Department have received the highest number of awards (40) followed by Political Science (10), Anthropology, Sociology and Speech Pathology (6 each), Criminal Justice (5), Community Health Sciences (4), Economics, Human Development and Family Studies, Journalism (2 each), and Basque Studies, Behavior Analysis, Marketing and Communications, Public Health, and Social Work (1 each).

The STEM departments are historically the most active in both submissions and awards for undergraduate research. Within STEM, the biological sciences and engineering receive the most awards, followed by Medicine and Health Sciences, Chemistry, Biochemistry, Earth Sciences, Natural Resources and Environmental Sciences, Physics, Agricultural Sciences and Mathematics and Statistics. Total numbers of awards by department are given in Table 1.

FIGURE 5. Total awards given by subdiscipline from 2005 to 2019.

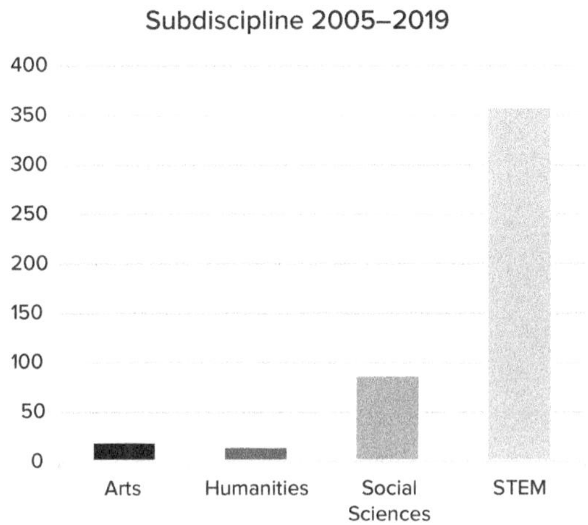

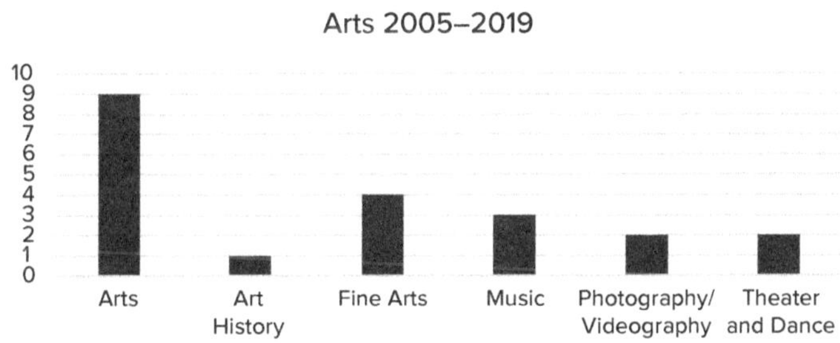

FIGURE 6. Distribution of awards between departments within the Art subdiscipline from 2005 to 2019.

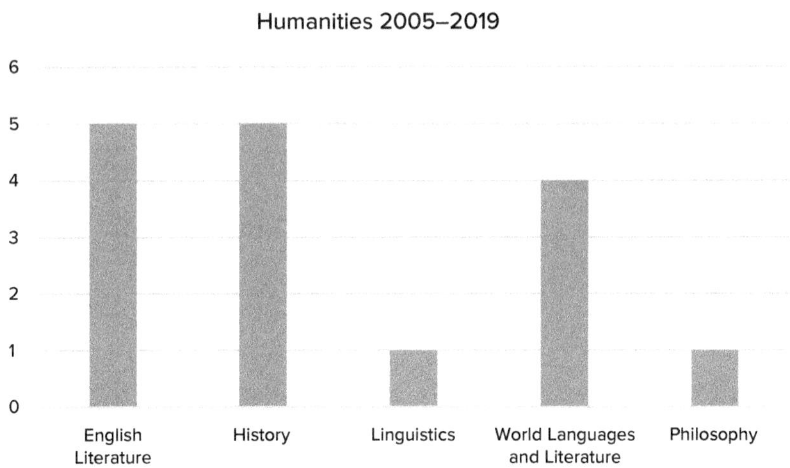

FIGURE 7. Distribution of awards between departments within the Humanities subdiscipline from 2005 to 2019.

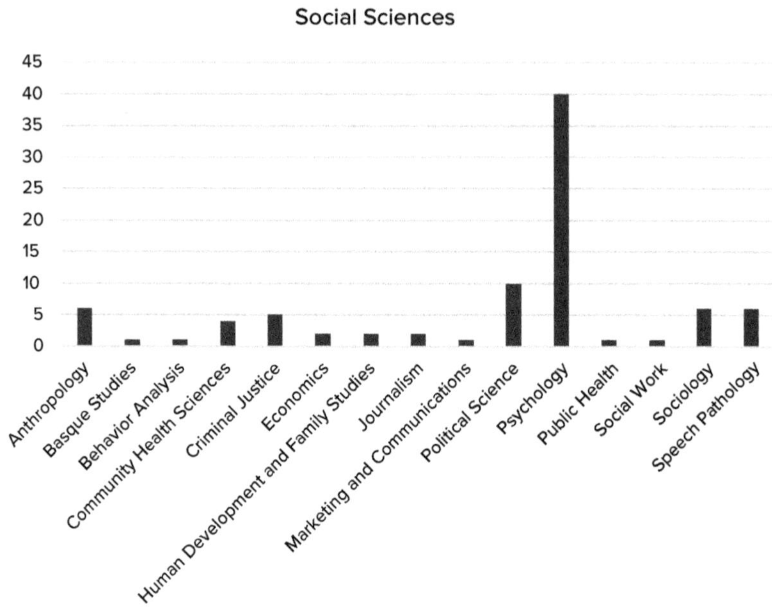

FIGURE 8. Distribution of awards between departments within the Social Sciences subdiscipline from 2005 to 2019.

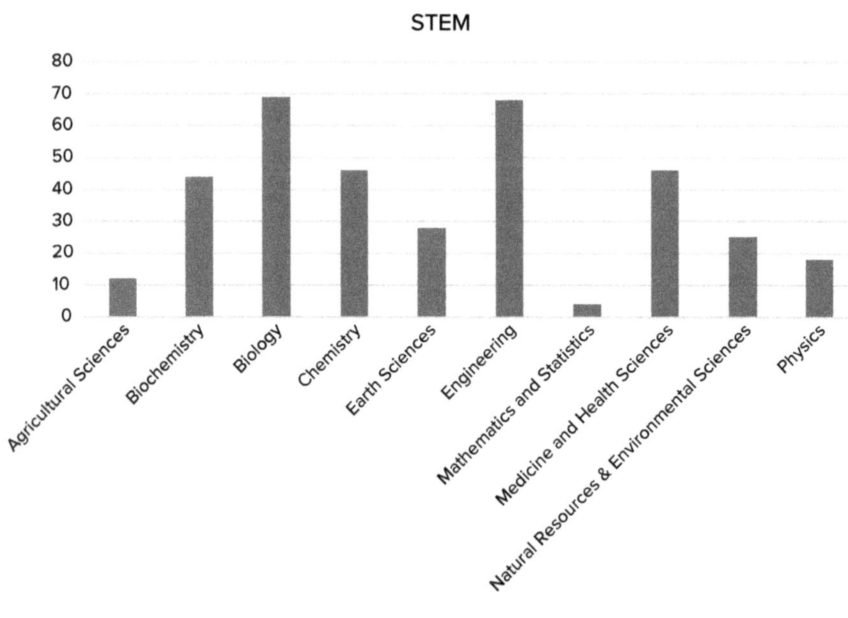

TABLE 1. Distribution of awards between departments within the STEM subdiscipline from 2005 to 2019.

Disciplinary Category and majors	Awardees	Disciplinary Category and majors	Awardees
Agricultural Sciences	**12**	**Mathematics and Statistics**	**4**
Agriculture, Nutrition and Veterinary Science	9	Mathematics	1
Animal Biology	3	Mathematics and Statistics	3
Biochemistry	**44**	**Medicine and Health Sciences**	**46**
Biochemistry	24	Gerontology	1
Biochemistry and Molecular Biology	20	Medicine	10
Biology	**69**	Microbiology and Immunology	3
Biology	64	Neuroscience	1
Biotechnology	5	Nursing	1
		Nutrition	4
Chemistry	**46**	Pharmacology	22
ACS Chemistry	1	Physiology and Cell Biology	4
Chemistry	44		
Professional Chemistry	1	**Natural Resources & Environmental Sciences**	**25**
		Echohydrology	2
Earth Sciences	28	Natural Resources & Environmental Science	22
Geography	21	Wildlife Ecology and Conservation	1
Geological Engineering	2		
Geological Science	4	**Physics**	**18**
Geophysics	1	Atmospheric Science	1
		Physics	17
Engineering	**68**		
Chemical and Materials Engineering	11		
Chemical Engineering	9		
Civil and Environmental Engineering	5		
Computer Science and Engineering	14		
Electrical and Biomedical Engineering	5		
Electrical Engineering	4		
Materials Science and Engineering	5		
Mechanical Engineering	15		

Reinforcing and Extending the Program: Future Practices for Undergraduate Research

While the opportunities provided for undergraduate research at the University of Nevada, Reno exceed the necessary criteria in order to meet the conditions of a "limited program," undergraduate research practices still fall short of the conditions recommended by our analysis to meet the criteria of a "strong" program. There are a number of potential avenues the Undergraduate Research office at the University of Nevada could pursue to enhance the culture and opportunities for undergraduate research, maximize engagement in research, and serve as many student populations as possible. The recent budget increase suggests that the budget will likely not increase in the foreseeable future, thus any new programs need to carefully consider the potential cost. No-cost programs that will enhance the scope of undergraduate research across campus will have the greatest chance of success.

Potential enhancements

Programs that can be done with little or no funding:

1. Workshops instructing faculty on facilitating undergraduate researchers in order to involve more members of the faculty in undergraduate mentorship programs.
2. To capture undergraduate research happening within classes, but currently not documented at the university level, develop a 'Research' designation that can be assigned to a class, vetted through the current university course development structure, and appear on a student's transcript. Such a process would create a structure to ensure that undergraduate research within the classroom setting meets an agreed upon standard and can be easily tracked through existing university data gathering mechanisms.
3. To capture funded research across campus that does not originate from the Undergraduate Research Office two things are recommended. First, canvas programs across campus and better integrate such programs (e.g. INBRE, NSF REU etc.) with Undergraduate research. Second, work with Human Resources to obtain names of those students being paid from grant accounts to then determine how many of these are doing research with faculty under individual grants.

4. As the Honors program transitions under a new director, work closely to identify potential synergistic opportunities to enhance undergraduate research across campus.
5. Strengthen outreach to the Arts, Humanities, and Social Sciences sub-disciplines with a purposeful and deliberative marketing campaign, in order to expand the number of applications submitted by students in these disciplines.
6. Strengthening relationships with other offices on campus involved in learning beyond the classroom (e.g. internship programs and service learning).
7. Creating a more visible space on campus for Undergraduate Research, such as a table in the Pennington building several days a week.
8. Expanding our assessment program to include exit surveys and follow-up with students after graduation.

Proposals that may require new funding:

1. A video competition to encourage concise, accessible research presentations and to introduce undergraduate's research to a diverse population.
2. Development of a team-based undergraduate research competition.
3. Expanded international research opportunities that take advantage of existing departmental and faculty relationships with other institutions.

Conclusion

Undergraduate Research at the University of Nevada, Reno has grown significantly over the past decade and now serves a diverse community with a number of different undergraduate research opportunities. There is still room for growth to become a 'strong' program as defined through our analysis of selected programs across the country. There are multiple avenues by which to grow even without an increase in funding, as outlined in this chapter. The history of the program has resulted in focusing on providing funded research opportunities to students conducting research on campus, within the community, or internationally. Future efforts that can expand opportunities within the existing budget could focus on doing a better job of identifying all other types of research already being conducted on campus and developing the mechanisms for better tracking these activities. This will require better coordination with Admissions and Records, the Provost's office, and the department of Human Resources. Undergraduate Research has a strong working relationship with ASUN and this needs to be maintained. A stronger working relationship can be built with Student Services as well as the Honors program. Currently, there is no coherent structure for the various opportunities across campus for learning experiences beyond the classroom, however, helping create such a platform would be another way to strengthen the culture of undergraduate research at UNR.

The multiple avenues for engaging in Undergraduate Research at the University of Nevada Reno provides hundreds of students with research opportunities each year. Our goal is to enable every student interested in research to have a directed research experience as part of their academic experience. We are confident that such an experience is an important element of student success.

REFERENCES

Mabrouk, P.A., Peters, K, "Student perspectives on undergraduate research (UR) experiences in chemistry and biology." 2000. https://confchem.ccce.divched.org/sites/confchem.ccce.divched.org/files/2000SpringConfChemP2.pdf.

University of Minnesota Office of Undergraduate Research. "Conducting Your Research." n.d. https://ugresearch.umn.edu/node/5366.

University of Minnesota Office of Undergraduate Research. "Find a Mentor." n.d. https://ugresearch.umn.edu/home-1.

University of Minnesota Office of Undergraduate Research. "Find an Opportunity." n.d. https://ugresearch.umn.edu/find-anopportunity.

University of Texas at Austin School of Undergraduate Studies. "Research Week." n.d. https://ugs.utexas.edu/researchweek.

University of Wyoming. "Research Opportunities and Projects." n.d. http://www.uwyo.edu/wyominginbre/research/uw-undergraduate-research.html.

USC Undergraduate Programs. "Research & Discovery." n.d. https://undergrad.usc.edu/experience/research/.

USC Undergraduate Programs. "Undergraduate Symposium." n.d. https://undergrad.usc.edu/experience/research/symposium/.

CHAPTER 25

On the Road to Success

Achieving an Honors Education at the University of Nevada, Reno

TAMARA VALENTINE, PH.D.

Tamara M. Valentine is currently professor of Linguistics in the English Department at the University of Nevada, Reno. She held the position of director of the Honors Program at the University of Nevada for over fourteen years. She has published and presented numerous research papers on topics related to world Englishes, South Asian languages and linguistics, discourse analysis, language and gender, and cross-cultural communication. Her book *Language and Prejudice* is a collection of readings addressing issues related to the power of language in shaping a speaker's worldview. A Fulbright Scholar, Valentine has been awarded grants to conduct fieldwork in India, has held a series of lectureships in Lithuania, and has traveled extensively throughout South Asia, Southeast Asia, and Eastern Europe. She earned her Ph.D. in linguistics from the University of Illinois, Urbana-Champaign focusing on the relationship between language and gender in South Asia.

Introduction

It is unsurprising that academically outstanding undergraduates who elect to participate in an honors program at the college level display distinct academic, behavioral, and social characteristics that distinguish themselves from other students on campus. Honors students are described as the *best and brightest*, the academically gifted—the community of scholars who *think differently*. They are identified as highly motivated, and high-achievers who are engaged in their own learning and relish the challenging experiences college has to offer. The honors community of scholars respects intelligence, both individually and in respect to others; these learners participate in serious intellectual work, engage in new and different life experiences, and resolve to achieve future success in college and life. The

Honors Program at the University of Nevada Reno (UNR) is one of hundreds of honors programs rooted in campuses across the country. In fact, it is estimated that over fifteen hundred institutions offer honors educations nationwide (Scott and Smith).

The origins of honors study at UNR is traced back to the early 1960s when the University made its commitment to meet the high expectations of the academically gifted students by providing an honors degree to students who completed a number of honors credits that included a research component and the completion of a senior thesis. Over the years, honors students at UNR experienced the University at its best, studying with expert professors, engaging in advanced learning, and maintaining meaningful relationships. Great efforts were made to expand college access to diverse low-income, underrepresented, and first-generation students (Valentine). This excerpt describes the hallmark characteristics of the honors environment at the University that sustain high academic standards and help support an intellectual environment that lead to fulfilling scholarly, professional, and social success.

The Origins and Beginnings of Honors Education

The first signs of honors within the context of a university system date back to the sixteenth-century Oxford educational model whereby selected academically able students were offered individualized and direct study through the tutorial system of learning. Valuing this style of British scholarship, in the late nineteenth century, the principles and practices of Oxford teaching and learning were transferred to the ivied halls of Harvard University, Princeton University, Columbia University and the University of Michigan. In 1922, however, Swarthmore College in Pennsylvania established what is recognized as the first honors program in the US. Within a hundred years, by the twenty-first century, over fifteen hundred honors programs and honors colleges with wide variability were established transnationally in all types of institutions of offering quality education to the academically talented student. Today, two-year community colleges, four-year universities, publicly supported and privately-owned schools, faith-based colleges, co-educational and single-sex institutions, small liberal arts colleges, technical schools, and research and teaching institutions boast of honors programs and colleges throughout the country. In fact, the entire issue of JNCHC celebrated the fiftieth anniversary of the National

Collegiate Honors Council (NCHC) by publishing the "Forum on the Value of Honors" in higher education presented through the eyes of thirty nine university presidents throughout the nation (Long and Mullins). Moving beyond the shores of the US, the last few decades have witnessed the spread of honors education to other regions of the world that include Chile, China, the Netherlands, Brazil, Mexico, and Qatar, with each country fashioning their own brand of honors approaches and models to fit their institutional needs (Long and Mullins).

According to the NCHC mission, an honors program should provide a "distinctive learner-directed environment and philosophy" that promotes "measurably broader, deeper, or more complex" learning experiences typically found at institutions of higher education (About NCHC). In other words, the honors enterprise is designed to offer the highly motivated student distinctive, rigorous educational opportunities beyond that of other students by providing the gifted student with challenging experiences by way of special academic and extracurricular benefits and a personalized learning experience. Honors is offered not only as a magnet for attracting and retaining the academically motivated candidates, but also for the goal of enhancing the intellectual and academic experiences of all students and faculty as well as for the purpose of elevating the academic reputation of a university and improving its standing among institutions of higher education. Not all arguments are in favor of providing special benefits to a small segment of the student body. To counter, honors is often criticized as a style of education for students of "privilege, pedigree, and promise" and one that promotes a superior group of "elite niche" learners (Valentine 78). Advocates of honors education argue, however, that honors has claimed the ideal space, and it is "one of the few spaces left within the context of mass education where students have the opportunity to experience a transformational education . . . honors becomes a site of resistance to an otherwise utilitarian education" (Stoller 10).

The National Collegiate Honors Council (NCHC), the professional recommending body of collegiate honors education, adopted The Basic Characteristics of a Fully Developed Honors Program in 1994, which endorses seventeen best practices that should be shared by honors programs. To guide the development of honors programs and colleges and to determine their strengths, weaknesses, and outcomes, this instrument of standards is widely accepted as a set of practical criteria typically characterized by organizational structure, budgetary consideration, resources and facilities, admissions and completion standards, curricular offerings, and distinctions and recognition. Depending on the mission of the university, the mission and vision of the honors program, the student composition, administrative structure, institutional support, budgetary constraints and other academic and social factors, each honors program sets up its own model to fit the institution and the high academic-achieving student population. In other words, no one model or one-size-fits-all standards of honors education. To gain a better understanding of the path that honors education has taken in the US and the current state of honors across all types of institutions in the US, research in honors has surveyed and tracked the population of institutions that deliver honors education and described the honors landscape in terms of size, structure, resources, distribution of student populations, and other aspects (Scott and Smith; Sederberg). Only through such research, can we advocate for a robust honors education throughout the US. This paper asks the questions:

- How does an academically motivated student achieve success in college?
- How does the honors student participate in his/her own success?
- How does an honors student take ownership of his/her destiny?
- How does the Honors Program at UNR meet the expectations of academically gifted students?

Honors Education at the University of Nevada, Reno

The concept of an honors education at UNR was conceived in 1962 during a time when universities across the nation responded to the panicked mandate to improve the quality of education throughout the American university system. In particular, responding to the perceived threat of the launch of Sputnik by the Soviet Union in 1957, governmental efforts focused on developing competencies in technological, scientific, and global study in math, the sciences, engineering, and foreign languages into the university and college systems. Feeling the pinch of losing outstanding Nevada high school seniors to out-of-state programs, at the recommendation of a program review, the current structure of a University-wide honors program was established in 1989, as the premiere academic program to help recruit and retain Nevada's best and brightest undergraduates in all majors of study. The primary mission of the University Honors Program was to offer "talented students additional opportunity for developing their skills and training their powers of observation, thought, and expression. Successful participation in the program gives superior students the personal satisfaction of having met and mastered the most innovative and challenging program the University offers" (UNR General Catalogue 1988–1989). Attaining a culture of academic achievement, the UNR Honors Program attained acclaim for offering Ivy League quality at state school prices (Nemko), and was rated one of the 55 Best Honors Programs at State Universities Nationwide (Sullivan & Randolph). In INSIDE HONORS 2018–2019, the University of Nevada, Reno Honors Program was ranked in the top half of outstanding public honors programs in the nation.

Originated to enhance growth, learning, and development, and to graduate highly educated and skilled individuals who could handle the foreseeable complex, multifaceted problems and issues in the global era, the mission of the UNR Honors Program states its goals as "to prepare leaders who effectively engage our complex and rapidly changing world, a university education must go beyond the provision of a strong fund of professional knowledge and skill. It is the mission of the Honors Program at the University of Nevada, Reno to provide strong support for the development of students' capacities to think deeply and critically and to act in ways that promote the betterment of all citizens." Designed to inspire, empower, and transform, the vision of the UNR Honors Program seeks: "to provide students who are both academically talented and highly motivated with an undergraduate education that nurtures and promotes students' capacities to think competently, understand deeply, and act ethically" (UNR Honors Program). Drawn to an honors environment, presently the number of national merit and presidential scholars has reached unprecedented numbers, and the Honors Program has grown to approximately 500 members, graduated over 1,000 students, and channeled hundreds of UNR graduates into graduate school, professional school, international scholarship exchanges, and employment in their fields. Today the UNR Honors Program attracts more and better students from a wider range of disciplines and retains highly qualified undergraduates in the Honors Program at a higher rate than that of the University. The Honors Program increases the academic standards and reputation of the University, and enhances the quality of life across the state through the contributions of honors graduates. The academically talented students in the Honors Program raise the level and quality of intellectualism on the campus, increase the retention, persistence, and graduation rates, broaden opportunities for social engagement, service enrichment, and academic enhancement for the entire campus, and contribute to the institution's undergraduate academic and research plan. Since the 1960s, honors education at UNR has provided a high-quality and meaningful undergraduate experience to promising students. It has established itself as the center of campus attention for academic excellence helping to build a strong learning community and culture across campus and among faculty. The Honors Program has established itself as a first-class academic program that carries out the tradition of excellence by providing a quality learning experience through intellectual inquiry, scholarly community, innovative engagement, and celebratory achievement.

Hallmark Features of the UNR Honors Program

In the past fifty years, honors programs have embraced the twenty-first century philosophy of a learner-centered practice of immersing students in high-impact practices (HIPs) to help attract, retain, and ensure the academic and professional success of outstanding student scholars—practices that emphasize impactful, powerful, and active learning experiences and activities that complement student engagement and achieve deep learning (Kuh; Cobane and Jennings). The university-wide Honors Program at the University of Nevada also embraces the HIP philosophy of high intensity experiences, deep engagement, high performance standards, authentic learning instruction, experiential problem solving, strategic partnerships, and high-level critical thinking. The Honors Program at UNR has designed and characterized its system of honors education around hallmark features to energize student success initiatives. The pathway to the goal of academic and personal success includes a high impact agenda that includes a first-year seminar that addresses critical global issues; a common curriculum of high-level courses taught by top faculty; writing-intensive courses, collaborative assignments and team-based projects; intellectual engagement and an interactive community; undergraduate research, entrepreneurial ventures, and creative activities that result in a senior thesis; a living learning residential community; global and multicultural curricula that lead to international study; service and civic engagement in the local community; mentoring programs, internships and field experiences; and access to nationally competitive fellowships—outcomes that underlie the mission of the Honors Program and the academic, professional, and personal success of honors graduates (Valentine).

The Honors Program at UNR provides the foundational conditions necessary to make academic achievement and personal success happen. If a member of the Honors Program claims the honors space and takes advantage of building these competencies, then the student is well prepared for the next stages in his/her life. As one Honors Program graduate put it: "During my time at the University of Nevada, I have found the Honors Program an essential part of my academic and personal success. Especially with the recent increases in student population, it is critical for incoming students to find a niche where they are recognized as individuals and where their aspirations are understood and supported."

The Honors Program at UNR gives dedicated and motivated students opportunities to demonstrate their knowledge, competence, and interest in diverse subject areas, to acquire new abilities by becoming a part of an active learning network, and to engage in new and different life experiences. To meet the needs of such students, the Honors Program provides enriched educational opportunities and enhanced student learning through international education, undergraduate research, civic involvement, socialization, and fellowship opportunities. Moreover, the Honors Program builds a learning community and culture across the campus and student body that shares the mission and vision of excellence in learning and excellence in teaching.

What works in honors programs can be viewed as an innovative site of learning within the context of the wider university. The distinct characteristics of honors students help shape their college experience and influence the pathways to success; honors students take responsibility for their way of thinking about learning, exploring comparative perspectives, and executing a strategic planning model. With this in mind, experimentation, exploration and creativity form the cornerstone of honors education at UNR, and the structure of the Honors Program is organized around the following competencies of deep learning and teaching experiences. Honors is a journey, an experience that a student embarks on, rather than a final destination.

The following discussion outlines five predictive factors for success that help honors students gain a competitive edge to shape their future, lead a productive life, and develop into a whole person: academics; research and creative scholarship; service learning and civic engagement; international engagement and global citizenship; social connectedness and campus involvement; and national competition and risk taking. Taking a more holistic perspective of student development leads students to a more positive and successful future.

Competency 1: Academics

The scholarly community of honors programs expects unusually high standards of scholastic excellence and intellectual rigor to develop academic socialization, critical thinking, reflection, and personal and intellectual growth (Bedetti; Bell; Bleicher; Kaplan; Kelly; Quay and Damico). Upon completion of the Honors Program at UNR, students will have demonstrated master of an intellectually changing, enhanced honors curriculum. Students will become active learners and informed global citizens. To meet the expectations and abilities of this high achieving population and to advance intellectual pursuit, the Honors Program enriches the academic experience with the defining characteristics of an honors curriculum of courses, discussion-based seminars, and individualized study that actively engages the student and promotes sophisticated thinking, collaborative exploration, and independent learning skills. Academic opportunities outside the classroom complement the in-class experience by emphasizing experiential coursework, applied learning exercises, co-curricular activities, civic engagement, social cohesion, and faculty interactivity. Exposure to interdisciplinary and disciplined-based skills and tactical perspectives leads to accomplishing certain student learning outcomes through self-discovery, active learning, and intellectual curiosity. The honors mantra is "not more work, but deeper work." Whether responding to newsworthy articles on the refugee resettlement crisis from the *New York Times*, developing a professional poster on the Rhodes scholarship, attending a presentation on the prehistoric ichthyosaur, Nevada's state fossil, or performing meaningful public service with the Reno-based nonprofit teaching farm *Urban Roots*, students are profoundly engaged in learning and leveraging their faculties to pave the way for future success. By applying and evaluating varied modes of academic inquiry, creative expression, and research analysis historically and in the contemporary global contexts, students make connections among multiple perspectives in order to better understand real-world issues, demonstrate responsibility to their local communities and beyond, and practice global awareness and diversity sensitivity.

Through small class sizes and top-notch teaching, honors students develop high-level thinking skills to gain proficiency in professional quality written, oral, reading, presentational, and graphic skills applicable to a liberal arts education in general and to the students' disciplines in particular upon which they can refine and reflect on their personal and educational goals. A student's capacity to learn is reflected in the substantial number of advanced and accelerated honors courses and credits taken over four years, in the student's strong academic performance, and on the student's academic transcripts and diplomas, specifically coursework that satisfies the required qualifications to pursue competitive fellowships and scholarships, graduate school, and post-graduate employment. The Honors Program delivers both discipline-based and interdisciplinary educational experiences, and opportunities for students to be a member of a community of scholars who interact with the learning process at their pace, initiate self-discovery, and design a path for the future. To quote a chemical engineering graduate: "The Honors Program was the University's directory and facilitator of my scholarly endeavors. As a graduate with fifty percent of my coursework as honors credits, I have experienced what it means to receive an honors education at the University of Nevada, Reno."

Competency 2: Research and Creative Scholarship

A lengthy body of research demonstrates the value of an honors education that prepares student scholars for lifetime skills and engagement (Banks: Buckner; Cundall; Lacey; Mariz; Walsh-Dilley; Walshe). Conducting independent research and supervised research leads students into the academic world of scholarship and professional life. No other aspect of a student's college years is more challenging, yet rewarding, to a student than conducting original research, following in the footsteps of scholars in the student's field, sharpening writing and research techniques, and forging mentoring relationships with faculty and professionals in their major field. From the time an honors student enters the Honors Program at UNR, the student is exposed to the significance of research through an introduction to the annual faculty lecture series, exposure to mini-research projects, and enrollment in the librarian-led course *Research Across the Disciplines*. By the time the student finishes the four-year honors journey, the student has identified a research problem, developed an extensive bibliography, sustained an argument from upwards of forty pages to over a hundred pages, and produced a high quality undergraduate written project and oral defense.

The University of Nevada, Reno has held a strong commitment to the tradition of an honors thesis since the program's days designated as "honors study." Today, to complete the Honors Program, all students must register for a minimum of six thesis credits under the supervision of a faculty mentor, complete a research-based thesis/project in his/her major, orally prepare the argument as a defense, presentation, or poster, and submit a written manuscript following the guidelines of the University Graduate School and the Honors Program submission guidelines as outlined in the *Honors Senior Thesis Handbook*. To support undergraduate honors research, the Honors Program provides financial support for travel, equipment, and supplies through the Honors Undergraduate Research Award (HURA), a token mentor stipend, personal reference librarians, professional writing consultants, and stationary and supplies to bind the final product. Up-to-date, over a thousand honors students have accepted the greatest challenges well beyond what traditional undergraduates achieve. Over a thousand students have met the challenges of the thesis process working alongside a leading faculty researcher for minimally two semesters—research that leads to innovative on-going research, international presentations, and professionally recognized publications in highly respected scholarly journals. With pride, the UNR Honors Program boasts of a number of NCHC Portz Scholars for outstanding theses that exhibit intellectual breadth, depth, and rigor, sophisticated reasoning, originality, high quality writing, intellectual independence and creative and intellectual risk. Moreover, students more often than not prepare their honors research work for publication, graduate school writing samples, professional presentations, and national fellowship applications (Buckner).

"Critical pedagogies seek not simply to transmit what is known about the world but to empower the creative capacities of students" (Stoller 13).

Whether a creative or traditional thesis, students evaluate the literature and scholarly works within their discipline and seek to advance a topic. Senior thesis work is an ideal place for students not only to apply their disciplinary methods, skills, and knowledge to real world social problems or issues, but also to inspire social responsibility and develop citizenship (Kaplowitz). Depending on the field, students have the freedom to approach the honors thesis from different directions: field research, examination of primary documents, analysis of literary texts, experimental designs, statistical studies, surveys, engineering-based projects, theoretical investigation, qualitative analysis, community-based research, educational curriculum, laboratory-based experiment or study of original work in fiction, art, or music. As long as the student produces a written component on the conceptual issues and the writing reflects research conducted by the student, students can approach the answer to their research question using a quantitative, qualitative, or multimethod research approach (University). In no other academic space can an honors-level undergraduate perform good work when they have the freedom to experiment with different approaches and direct attention to solutions to a social issue and, at the same time, benefit from such an experience equivalent to that of a master's-level student. "One of the features that distinguishes honors education is the opportunity for undergraduate students to take on greater independence in pursuing their own research and intellectual projects" (Cognard-Black and Savage 109).

At UNR, the Honors Program-approved senior theses/projects satisfy the University capstone requirement. Fulfilling the capstone requirement through research and the thesis process is expected of all honors graduates and will benefit them for life. By the end of the research experience, students should be able to acquire the following knowledge and skills, and apply them in all facets of their lives:

- Identify an original research question within the disciplinary academic framework and formulate a hypothesis
- Identify and demonstrate appropriate research methodologies
- Have command of library resources and other search tools to search for existing body of research relevant to the topic
- Evaluate and synthesize the existing body of research relevant to the topic
- Productively and responsibly collaborate with a faculty member and relevant professional community or engage in networking with the academic and professional communities
- Engage in the thesis/project development independently and effectively
- Identify and practice research ethics and responsible conduct in research
- Reflect on feedback as part of the peer review process and

incorporate into the research process; demonstrate proficiency (command of academic writing as appropriate for the discipline) in professional quality written, oral, reading, presentational, and graphic skills
- Effectively explain the research to others in the field and to broader audiences by an oral defense and written product
- Demonstrate an understanding of the scholarly research process: proposal, prospectus, final thesis
- Reflect constructively on the research experience in making decisions about academic and professional future

Accomplishing the above objectives, students are able to apply academic knowledge, skills, techniques, and abilities to a worldly setting; develop specialized competencies and relationships in an expert environment; identify, assess, and develop personal and professional strengths; evaluate career choices and further define career goals, and develop a capacity for collaborative work and leadership potential. As one student highlights her research experience:

> The Honors Program opened my eyes to the research opportunities at the University of Nevada. In the summer of my first year of college, I conducted research in nanotechnology. As a junior, I worked in an electrophysiology and pharmacology lab at the medical school where I investigated potential drug targets for ischemic strokes. This research complemented my honors coursework in electrical engineering beautifully as I prepared for a career in medicine.

Competency 3: Service Learning and Civic Engagement

According to forty years of research, a study published by the American Psychological Association shows that the younger generation is less likely than any other generation to engage in the political process, show concern for others, and have an interest in saving the environment; this generation is more materialistic and individualistic (Twenge, Freeman, and Campbell). Studies conducted on honors students, in particular, show similar results. High academic achieving students tend to be traditional-college aged, white, single, and female; parents hold higher-levels of education and higher family incomes (Brimeyer, Schueths, and Smith). They represent traditionally served populations who focus on tangible, extrinsic goals like earning top grades, winning national competitions, and gaining acceptance to graduate and professional schools (Hawkins and Kaplan). Developing empathy, community feeling, and collective change among honors students presents a challenge to honors education. Where universities are increasing focus on service learning and community engagement efforts and encouraging civic learning as part of students' core curricular requirements, honors programs across the US have long considered it their responsibility to promote public service and prepare students for social citizenry through civic-mindedness programs among their students (Buckner et al.; Hawkins and Kaplan; Jacobs and Walsh-Dilley; Kaplowitz; Holman, Smith, and Welch). The Honors Program at UNR, too, expects students to participate in structured service-learning activities and be civically engaged. It is committed to student diversity, service, and public responsibility, and it has long advocated for community-based programming as a means to developing engaged citizens, community relations, and effective change agents among the honors community.

The UNR Honors Program places great emphasis on applied learning, creating opportunities for students to apply their disciplinary skills to public service to build civic character, self-esteem, diversity awareness, and leadership skills. The Honors Program promotes civic engagement by offering students several opportunities to promote a more caring, community-oriented environment, and a healthy view of their place and responsibility to the communities around them. For example, since the beginning of honors education at the University, the Honors Program has offered students the opportunity to earn honors service credits by combining civic engagement with learning beyond the classroom. Honors students use their abilities and talents to demonstrate a commitment to an ethic of civic responsibility by engaging in a community-based activity that benefits both the student and the Reno community. Students are awarded honors service points for up to 190 hours of community service for mentoring underserved young populations in middle and high schools, organizing donation drives for refugee families at international centers, and providing ESL instruction to new English learners. Honors students also engage in meaningful, reciprocal action on campus or in the local community by volunteering with nonprofit organizations, medical centers, government agencies, and other community partners. Hundreds of hours of service are recorded by honors students who pursue careers in health and medical sciences, environmental science and management, and the education field.

Also implemented is a plan that requires all honors students to participate in service learning and civic engagement in the community setting throughout their four years of undergraduate study. A required learning outcome for all students in the Honors Program is participation in structured service-learning activities in the first semester honors seminar on global perspectives, where students engage in leadership development and community service through fifteen hours of volunteer and community service with a Nevada-based partner pre-approved by the Honors Program and the University Service Learning and Civic Engagement office. Students affiliate with the community in a meaningful way early in their undergraduate careers that provides an avenue for them to continue their service beyond their four-year college career. Over 2,000 hours of civic service are logged annually by each first-year honors class alone.

More recently, in response to the challenges of empathy and community feeling, the Honors Program designed the Honors Bonner Leaders Program (HBLP) that supports the Bonner Foundation's mission "to provide diverse low-income, under-represented, and first-generation students with the opportunity to attend college, while engaging their talents and educations in building and supporting communities" and build a strong and diverse community of scholars on and off campus (Goals). The four-year developmental program provides a financial award to students with a lifelong orientation to service in exchange for 140 hours of service each semester. Beginning with a service-oriented first-year experience providing ongoing training and enrichment over eight semesters, the program guides students in assuming progressively responsible roles within their chosen service organization and prepares them for engagement in the nonprofit, government, and private sectors. As expected, the Bonner Scholars become excellent candidates for the Truman Scholarship, a graduate fellowship that supports graduate education for students who demonstrate leadership potential and a commitment to public service leadership.

Service is extensive in the Honors Program: capstone courses draw on the knowledge of the student's understanding of their discipline; service internships involve the student in an experience that benefits both the community and the student; and independent studies train students to be advocates for their communities. After students leave college, it is hoped that by showing students the "way" of helping others, showing feeling for other groups, contributing to their local community, and working toward collective change in the public sphere, the Honors Program has played a role in cultivating empathetic and engaged citizens. For they are the next generation of leaders, change agents, and motivators in their areas of study and community who not only will positively impact the lives of others, but will prepare themselves for endless professional and personal possibilities.

Competency 4: International Engagement and Global Citizenship

Honors programs throughout the US have long been at the forefront at promoting international education and global citizenship. They support study abroad experiences and value service learning, research, and scholarship in academic exchanges around the world (Killinger et al.; Levy; Skews et al.). Research shows that honors students who study abroad graduate at a higher rate, with a higher GPA, with greater functional knowledge of cross-cultural and linguistic systems and with a greater capacity for mutual understanding through civic engagement, social entrepreneurship and volunteerism (Dean and Jendzurski). And the Honors Program at the University of Nevada is no exception. Its mission is "to encourage students to engage in real-world issues, discover new learning in diverse contexts, and prepare to compete in a global environment." The Honors Program engages students in international study at a rate of 15 percentage points higher than the overall University student rate. And commissioned by the University, that number will increase across campus. What better way to understand one's self and one's culture, than to leave the comforts of home to study in another country to promote their cultural sensitivity and global awareness? One international experience touches the hearts and souls of these young people. As one honors student highlights:

> I have long been a supporter and advocate of international education. I have encountered first-hand the transformative learning experience of international engagement. From the time I was an undergraduate I had a strong interest in language variation and cultural hegemony. After years of Hindi language study, I was awarded a junior fellowship to study for one year in New Delhi. This experience impressed upon me the importance of undergraduate study abroad, international educational partnerships, and critical language study; and it led to a career of research and scholarship in South Asian areal linguistics. In retrospect, I realize that the foundation for an

> honors undergraduate experience had been laid: undergraduate research, national fellowship application, international travel, and civic engagement. From that time forward, I became active in the fields of language equity, English in multilingual, multicultural global contexts, language teaching, and international education. And now, through my honors directorship, teaching, and research mentoring, I can offer students what I experienced: the freedom, responsibility, and power to choose what I wanted to learn and how I wanted to learn it in order to make informed choices and appropriate decisions in this world. Returning from years of study and travel to India, Lithuania, Costa Rica, Japan, and most recently from academic exchange in France on the Fulbright Commission Franco-Américaine grant for International Education Administrators, I realize how important a feeling of global connectiveness is toward the development of a whole person who can make decisions critically and independently, who will become an active, productive member in society, and who will become a citizen of the world.

The Honors Program is heavily involved in international education initiatives at the University of Nevada. Working closely with other campus partners, it oversees the campus-wide nationally competitive fellowships office and works closely with the University Study Abroad Consortium, Office of International Scholars and Students, and the Northern Nevada International Center. In addition, the Honors Program proposes a curriculum that offers credit for international study abroad, international service learning, and the study of global issues; guides students through the application process of national scholarship competition programs such as the Fulbright, Rhodes, Marshall, and Boren; hosts fellowship workshops, receptions and lecture series; and does so much more to promote the value of international engagement. The Honors Program presents these students with challenges to increase cross-cultural understanding, to expand the capacity for meaningful international engagement, to develop a deeper understanding of global issues, and to build a cultural repertoire necessary to identify as a global citizen.

Competency 5: Social Connectedness and Campus Involvement

It has been well established that social and campus involvement promotes college students' sense of connectedness and belonging (Elkins et al.). By participating in campus activities and co-curricular programming, honors students cultivate a level of community or place that complement their course of learning and increase their satisfaction with the college experience. Honors programs emphasize an engaged community and work to provide ample engagement opportunities to its members to foster social connectedness. Characterized by engaged learning and academic determination, students thrive when they develop and maintain positive and meaningful relations with others (Schreiner). According to Cuevas et al., Honors students at all class levels report higher levels of involvement in campus leadership activities, student organizations, and community service than the non-Honors sample, and this involvement is a more significant pathway to their thriving in college. It appears that high achieving students are willing not only to accept the challenges of advanced and accelerated academic work, but also to undertake additional sorts of engagement that involve their peers, faculty members, community partners, and international contacts—essential elements that promote academic, psychological and social wellbeing (Cuevas et al.; Kampfe et al.).

Upon completion of the University Honors Program, students will have contributed to the development of a community of scholars across the campus. In addition to a robust honors curriculum of special classes that includes a first-year honors seminar, first-year advising and academic support, a long-standing two-day honors retreat at Lake Tahoe, and an Honors FIT (Freshman Intensive Transition) program, the Honors Program offers incoming students the opportunity to live, work, study, and socialize with other honors students in a residential setting. Honors living learning communities have proven to have a positive impact on students' cognitive and psychosocial development, combining peer interactions, living arrangements, and co-curricular activities (Daffron and Holland). In the Fall of 2006, the Honors Program, in partnership with Residential Life, offered its first communal Living Learning Community (LLC). Renamed the Honors Residential Scholars Community, the Honors LLC established an instant community of scholars that has continued for almost fifteen years sealing friendships for life (Valentine). In addition, to promote a sense of community among honors students, the Honors Program offers engagement opportunities that include an annual faculty lecture series, an honors student ambassador program, and an honors alum chapter. Instruction and presentations on health and wellness, social gatherings at sports events, and excursions off campus bring honors students at all levels together to develop a sense of community. Through participation in academic, social and campus activities, honors students' lives are enriched by building a circle of friends and scholars and gaining a feeling of belonging (Dinan).

Expressed below is an honors student's experience of increasing her community of friendships:

> As an incoming freshman, I did not imagine I would be part of such a strong Honors community. Living with other Honors students in the Honors Residential Scholars Living Learning Community led to my sharing college "firsts" with a cadre of friends who remained my supporters until the completion of my senior thesis. I am happy I have formed and retained relationships with my honors friends and professors. I know they are the support system I can always fall back on as I head to graduate school for speech-language pathology.

Competency 6: National Competition and Risk Taking

In 2005, the Honors Program at UNR took it upon itself to hang a sign outside its door that read "Office of Undergraduate Fellowships." Prior to this year, faculty members associated with the Honors Program stepped up to guide and advise potential applicants who "heard" about some scholarships that might win them some money and recognition. Of course, these students were inquiring about the most prestigious nationally competitive awards, the Rhodes, Goldwater, Truman or Fulbright—scholarships that students have, according to Suzanne McCray "a five to six percent chance of winning and a ninety-four to ninety-five percent chance of losing" (p. 50). But, the goal is not necessarily to win, but for students "to think strategically about their future and position themselves for success well beyond graduation" (Cobane and Jennings). Applying for national competitions is a part of the model of high impact learning practices that lead to personal satisfaction and professional success. "The process teaches students strategic planning and expands their ability to write about their disciplines, goals, and aims—all skills that are crucial in the professional world" (Cobane and Jennings 41).

The Office of Undergraduate (and Graduate) Fellowships at UNR follows the mission of the National Association of Fellowship Advisors (NAFA) "to promote the full potential of fellowship candidates through the application process" ("Mission and Code of Ethics: The National Association of Fellowship Advisors (NAFA)"). The office provides as much support and assistance as possible to increase fellowship exposure and develop competitive candidates.

At UNR, honors students are exposed to national scholarships in their first-year seminar. Not only are students required to learn about each of the major scholarships, but they delve deeply into one scholarship as an expert and present a professionally produced poster to a student audience. It is important that students recognize their potential and seek out opportunities and new learning experiences early on, then begin the application process as soon as possible to build their resumes, develop personal statements, and prepare for mock interviews.

In addition, the Honors Program offers sophomores and juniors the opportunity to get the feel of the scholarship process. It offered its first scholarship advising class to twelve qualifying students in 2011. A former Marshall scholar and physics Ph.D. proposed a one-credit course for students who had a serious interest in entering highly selective national or international scholarship competitions such as the Rhodes, Marshall, Gates Cambridge, and Fulbright for graduate study abroad, or the Goldwater, Truman, and Udall for undergraduate study in the US. Building on the leadership development and societal aspirations associated with each of these scholarships, the course proceeded through a series of discussions and assignments to help students learn more about who they are, what they do, and why. Through these exercises, after assessing their strengths and weaknesses, students determined which of these national scholarships were most compatible with their personal and professional aims. In the process, students acquired the necessary skills in thinking, planning, and execution that could help them become deep conversers, active listeners, contrarian thinkers, effective organizers, and disciplined players. Students developed confidence in telling their stories, both in written and oral presentational formats. While focused on the enumerated national scholarship competitions, the skills, knowledge, and experience acquired in this class prepared students for a variety of life situations that requires principled leadership, persuasive argument, quick wit, empathy, attention to detail, and sacrifice for an unknown outcome (Gupta). And a challenge it was, indeed. That first class produced a number of winners: a Marshall scholar, a Marshall and Rhodes finalist, a Goldwater, a Truman, a Udall, and a Fulbright; among these class members, winners were selected for the Phi Kappa Phi fellowship and Critical Language Scholarship. Through the years to follow, many more students have entered the ranks of candidates and winners.

To expand interest in national fellowship competitions campus-wide, the Honors Program offers a series of informational sessions each semester focusing on nationally competitive fellowships and scholarships with the hope of opening students' eyes to their potential and the benefits of candidacy that extend beyond graduation. The process is grueling. It takes true grit and determination. It takes time, confidence, and self-reflection. Whether the applicant is awarded a prestigious scholarship or not, the student has gained life-changing skills, and prepares them for future success.

As one engineering graduate paid tribute to honors:

> I am just reaching out to all of you to let you know things are good for me at Stanford. It was a rough start being in this environment, but I eventually figured it out as I was prepared for rigorous academics, and today I am on track to graduate with a master's degree next year as well as have the opportunity to take qualifying exams for candidacy for a Ph.D. in aeronautics and astronautics next spring.I want to thank you for all your guidance and support during my time at UNR and to the Honors program for allowing to get involved in research, advanced mathematics courses and national competitions that have helped me so much as a graduate student. This was the key for my admission to graduate school and eventual admission to the Ph.D. program. There is still a long path ahead of me, but I wanted to share this accomplishment with you.

Conclusion

Success is measured by how well we as educators address the needs of the next generation of learners, citizens, and leaders. High achieving students represent the highly educated work force who will be faced with the challenges of adulthood, resolving complex problems, and critically thinking through solutions in the time of rapid globalization (Bedetti 130). We can equip students with the tools necessary to achieve positive thinking, to meet these challenges, and to engage as productive citizens, but it is up to these capable students to pick up these tools and use them constructively and positively. Cobane and Jennings argue that the success of growing scholars in their honors program is the four-year scholar development plan (SDP) "as an organizing principle that both shapes student experiences and guides cross-unit collaboration" (40). Students "develop short-term targets that move them toward long-term achievements" (40).

In my first-year seminar years ago, the class helped me develop a list of short-term targets that once achieved would prepare them for a life of distinction (Duban). Each student was required to design a four-year plan for him/herself with specific details on how each learner was going to accomplish the short term to achieve the long-term of personal and professional goals. They responded with the following list, not in any particular order:

- Maintain high grades
- Develop competence in a certain area of study
- Make a contribution to their field of study
- Cultivate an aptitude for innovation, exploration, and creativity
- Take responsibility for self-learning
- Gain experience in their field of interest
- Begin professional networking
- Target specific jobs for postgraduate employment
- Be campus involved
- Engage the community
- Acquire leadership skills
- Improve communication skills
- Uphold good work and study habits
- Take risks and step out of one's comfort zone
- Expand social circles
- Identify as a global citizen

A comprehensive honors curriculum, research and scholarly activity, an engaged honors community, global and diverse experiences, and scholarship preparation provides the foundation necessary for honors student to achieve academic, professional, and personal success, and realize a meaningful honors experience. Building on a tradition of honors education more than half a century long, the Honors Program at the University of Nevada, Reno offers academically talented students meaningful academic experiences and enriched educational opportunities beyond that of the traditional student. All colleges students can participate in high impact learning practices, but it is honors students who proactively seek out engaged opportunities and take full advantage of what a university has to offer. In other words, when high achieving students enter college, it is vital that we encourage them to be engaged in a variety of high impact activities to meet their end goals. The Honors Program at UNR is designed to help make that happen.

REFERENCES

About NCHC. National Collegiate Honors Council, 2019. https://www.nchchonors.org/about-nchc.

Banks, H. K. "A tradition unlike any other: Research on the value of an honors senior thesis." *Journal of the National Collegiate Honors Council*, vol. 17, no. 1, 2016, 23–29.

Bedetti, G. "Academic socialization: Mentoring new honors students in metadiscourse." *Honors in Practice*, vol. 13, 2017, 109–135.

Bell, J. "Expand the honors curriculum: Teach entrepreneurship, risk-taking, and change across the curriculum." *Honors in Practice*, vol. 1, 2005, 93–101.

Bleicher, E. "The last class: Critical thinking, reflection, course effectiveness, and student engagement." *Honors in Practice*, vol. 7, 2011, 39–51.

Brimeyer, T., Schueths, A., and Smith, W. "Who benefits from honors: An empirical analysis of honors and non-honors students' backgrounds, academic attitudes, and behaviors." *Journal of the National Collegiate Honors Council*, vol. 15, no. 1, 2014, 69–83. http://digitalcommons.unl.edu/nchcjournal/420.

Buckner, E., Shores, M., Sloane, M., Dantzler, J., Schields, C., Shader, K., and Newcomer, B. "Honors and non-honors student engagement: A model of student, curricular, and institutional characteristics." *Journal of the National Collegiate Honors Council*, vol. 17, no. 1, 2016, 191–217.

Buckner, E. "Ten steps to honors publication: How students can prepare their honors work for publication." *Honors in Practice*, vol. 3, 2007, 149–155.

Cobane, C., & Jennings, A. "Lessons from honors: National scholarships, high-impact practices, and student success." *Journal of the National Collegiate Honors Council*, vol. 18, no. 1, 2017, 39–44.

Cognard-Black, A., & Savage., H. "Variability and similarity in honors curricula across institution size and type." *Journal of the National Collegiate Honors Council*, vol. 17, no. 1, 2016, 93–113.

Cuevas, A., Schreiner, L., Kim, Y., and Bloom, J. "Honors student thriving: A model of academic, psychological, and social wellbeing." *Journal of the National Collegiate Honors Council*. vol. 18, no. 2, 2017, 79–119.

Cundall, M. "How to develop and promote an undergraduate research day." *Honors in Practice*, vol. 2, 2006, 49–57.

Daffron, E., and Holland, C. "Honors living-learning communities: A model of success and collaboration." *Honors in Practice*, vol. 5, 2009, 197–209.

Dean, K., and Jendzurski, M. "Using post-study-abroad experience to enhance international study." *Honors in Practice*, vol. 9, 2013, 99–111.

Dinan, S. "The importance of the first semester experience: Learning communities and clustered classes." *Honors in Practice: Breaking barriers in teaching and learning*, edited by J. Ford & J. Zubizaretta. Lincoln, NE: NCHC, 2018.

Duban, J. "Be a college achiever: The complete guide to academic stardom." Trafford: Victoria, BC, 2005.

Elkins, D., Forrester, S., and Noel-Elkins, A. "Students' perceived sense of campus community: The influence of out-of-class experiences." *College Student Journal*, vol. 45, no. 1, 2011, 105–21.

"Goals." The Corella & Bertram F. Bonner Foundation. http://www.bonner.org/goals.

Gupta, Vipin. "Fellowship prep seminar course syllabus." University of Nevada, Reno, 2011.

Hawkins, L., and Kaplan, L. "Helping the me generation decenter: Service learning with refugees." *Journal of the National Collegiate Honors Council*, vol. 17, no. 2, 2016, 157–175.

Holman, D., Smith, T., and Welch, E. "Honoring experiential education." *Honors in Practice*, vol. 5, 2009, 211–218.

Jacobs M., and Walsh-Dilley, M. "Cultivating empathy: Lessons from an interdisciplinary service-learning course." *Journal of the National Collegiate Honors Council*, vol. 19, no. 1, 2018, 15–23.

Kampfe, J., Chasek, C., and Falconer, J. "An examination of student engagement and retention in an honors program." *Journal of the National Collegiate Honors Council*, vol. 17, no. 1, 2016, 219–235.

Kaplan, L. "Innovative discussion-based pedagogy." *Honors in Practice: Breaking barriers in teaching and learning* edited by J. Ford & J. Zubizaretta. Lincoln, NE: NCHC, 2018.

Kaplowitz, C. "Helping with the 'how': A role for honors in civic education." *Journal of the National Collegiate Honors Council*, vol. 18, no. 2, 2017, 11–17.

Kelly, S. "Assessing success in honors: Getting beyond graduation rates." *Journal of the National Collegiate Honors Council*, vol. 14, no. 2, 2013, 25–30.

Killinger, M., Spies, K., & Runyambo, D. "A global endeavor: Honors undergraduate research." *Honors in Practice*, 12, 2016, 109–121.

Kuh, G. D. *High-impact education practices: What they are, who has access to them, and why they matter.* Washington, DC: Association of American Colleges and Universities, 2008.

Lacey, J. "The senior honors thesis: From millstone to capstone." *Honors in Practice*, vol. 4, 2008, 143–144.

Levy, G. "Sweden in the summer: Developing an honors study-abroad program." *Honors in Practice*, 4, 2008, 121–126.

Long, A., and Mullins, D. (Eds.). "Honors around the globe." *Journal of the National Collegiate Honors Council*, vol. 13, no. 2, 2012.

Long, A., and Mullins, D. (Eds.). "Forum on the value of honors." *Journal of the National Collegiate Honors Council*, vol. 16, no. 2, 2015.

Mariz, G. "An agenda for the future of research in honors." *Journal of the National Collegiate Honors Council*, vol. 17, no. 1, 2016, 3–8.

McCray, S. *Nationally competitive scholarships: Serving students and the public good.* Fayetteville: University of Arkansas Press, 2007.

"Mission and Code of Ethics: The National Association of Fellowships Advisors (NAFA)." National Association of Fellowships Advisors, 2015. https://www.nafadvisors.org/mission-and-code-ethics.

Nemko, M. *How to get an ivy league education at a state university.* Avon Books, 1988.

Quay, S., and Damico, A. "Cultural studies as the foundation for an honors program: Documenting students' academic and personal growth." *Honors in Practice*, vol. 4, no. 3, 2008, 43–57.

Schreiner, L. "The 'thriving quotient': A new vision for student success." *About Campus*, vol. 15, no. 2, 2010, 2–10.

Scott, R., and Smith, P. "Demography of honors: The national landscape of honors education." *Journal of the National Collegiate Honors Council*, vol. 17, no. 1, 2016, 73–91.

Sederberg, P. "Characteristics of the contemporary honors college: A descriptive analysis of a survey of NCHC member colleges." *Journal of the National Collegiate Honors Council*, vol. 6, no. 2, 2005. http://digitalcommons.unl.edu/nchcjournal/180.

Skews, J., Sampaio, C., and Conway, F. "Honors in Chile: New engagements in the higher education system." *Honors in Practice*, 14, 2012, 69–83.

Stoller, A. "Theory and resistance in honors education." *Occupy Honors Education*, edited by L. Coleman, J. Kotinek, and A. Oda. Lincoln, NE: NCHC, 2017.

Sullivan, R., and Randolph, K. *Ivy league programs at state school prices: The 55 best honors programs at state universities nationwide.* Wiley and Sons, 1994.

Twenge, J., Freeman, E., & Campbell, W. "Generational differences in young adults' life goals, concern for others, and civic orientation, 1966–2009." *Journal of Personality and Social Psychology*, vol. 102, no. 5, 2012, 1045–1062.

"University of Nevada, Reno Honors Program." *Honors senior thesis handbook.* University of Nevada, Reno, 2014.

"UNR Honors Program." University of Nevada, Reno. 2019. https://www.unr.edu/honors.

Valentine, T. "Lessons learned from Nevada's honors residential scholars community." *Honors Housing*, edited by In L. Frost, L. Kay, and R. Poe. Lincoln, NE: NCHC, 2015.

Valentine, T. "Access to a quality education: First-generation students reach for college honors education." *Success for All: Programs to Support Students Throughout Their College Experience.* Edited by Choroszy, M., & Meek, T. University of Nevada Press: Reno & Las Vegas, NV, 2020.

Walsh-Dilley, M. "Research in, on, or about honors." *Journal of the National Collegiate Honors Council*, vol. 17, no. 1, 2016, 31–34.

Walshe, E. "Conducting research in honors." *Honors in Practice*, vol. 6, 2010, 17–55.

CHAPTER 26

Student Media Drive Journalism Student Success

MADELINE PURDUE

Madeline Purdue is a recent graduate of the University of Nevada, Reno. She graduated from the Reynolds School of Journalism in May 2019. For three years she reported for The Nevada Sagebrush, the University's student newspaper, and served as editor-in-chief during her senior year. In addition to being a loyal protector of the First Amendment, she helped with campaigns both on campus and in the wider public to highlight issues facing student media, including #SaveStudentNewsrooms. Madeline has bylines in national publications including *USA Today* and *Eat This, Not That!* health magazine.

At the University of Nevada, Reno (UNR), student media consists of *The Nevada Sagebrush* student newspaper, *Insight Magazine*, Wolf Pack Radio, *Brushfire Literary Journal*, and the Inkblot marketing team. Out of all of the student-run media organizations, the *Sagebrush* has been around the longest and has produced many successful students and professionals. Application of journalistic studies outside the classroom have led to increased opportunities with internship programs, fellowships, and employment with some of the best and most notable media organizations around the world. Those who have not gone into journalistic practices have also been successful in other areas, such as business and government. The *Sagebrush* has long held a commanding respect among journalists, especially in Northern Nevada. However, the *Sagebrush* is not immune to the challenges facing all newspapers and media outlets today.

The *Sagebrush* started in 1893 by a group of students rebelling against the Board of Regents, who had declared a newspaper too much of a responsibility for students to run. The students met at the top of the mining building on the University of Nevada, Reno, campus and unanimously decided they were going to publish one anyways, assembling it in the basement of the Congressional Church. The first issue of the publication then known as the *Student Record*, was published on October 19, 1893. The *Student Record* became the *Sagebrush* in 1910 after future Rhodes Scholar and then editor Stanley M. Wilton decided the name of the paper should better describe the spirit of Nevada (Clifton 3). "Any college or prep-school can have a 'Student Record,' but only Nevada can have a Sagebrush," said Robert Farrar, *Sagebrush* editor from 1912 to 1914 (Clifton 3). Since that defiant day, the *Sagebrush* became known for its boldness regarding University subjects and issues that others would rather keep quiet and became the most feared publication on campus (Ali).

In October 2018, the *Sagebrush* celebrated its 125th year in publication. In that time, its alumni have gone on to become important and influential members of the Nevada community, and the country as a whole—Nevada Governor Emmett Boyle, U.S. Senator Alan Bible, director of the United States Mint Eva Adams, state Supreme Court Justice and Lt. Governor Myron Leavitt, and Reno mayor Francis Smith, to name a few. *Sagebrush* alumni also include four Rhodes scholars, six Pulitzer Prize winners, and at least seventeen Nevada Newspaper Hall of Fame inductees.

The *Sagebrush* itself has been recognized by college media organizations for its work, including seven Pacemaker Awards from the Associated Collegiate Press, one of the most prestigious awards given to student publications in the country. As much as *Sagebrush* alumni brag about the student newspaper, others recognize its value as well. However, the *Sagebrush* is not just published to be recognized and win awards, but to help grow journalists of the future.

An important aspect of student media is that it allows journalism students to apply the skills they learned in the classroom to a real-life publication, giving them time to harness their reporting skills while gathering article "clips" for future internship and job opportunities. Often times, the current *Sagebrush* staff members are considered and even accepted to the best internship programs offered through the University and around the country. In just the last few years, Sagebrush staff have interned with national media outlets such as *USA Today*, *The Los Angeles Times*, *ABC News*, *The American Society of Magazine Editors*, KUNR and iHeart Media. Former staff have gone on to work at the *Las Vegas Review-Journal*, the *Nevada Independent*, the *Post Register*, the *Reno Gazette-Journal*, and a number of broadcast news stations around Nevada, in addition to stations around the country. For example, a *Sagebrush* alumnus was recently named the executive editor of the RGJ. The *Sagebrush* has a legacy of success that continues on with every generation of new bylines.

Internships are generally considered the way to measure journalism student success, and often when recent graduates apply for jobs, the quality and quantity of their internships, as well as the work performed as an intern, are considered during the hiring process. On top of the resume submission, hopeful journalists also send in "clips" to showcase the work they have produced. Journalism has become an intensely competitive field, so the quality of the internship and the work produced over the course of the internship is crucial when it comes to securing a job after graduation. According to a *Forbes* interview with Jonathan Jones, the Head of Investment Talent Development at Point72 Asset Management, student participation in internships not only shows the student's seriousness and commitment to their field of study, but also that at least one other organization saw enough credibility in the student to employ them for a given amount of time. Jones states "If you show up in your final year of college—let alone beyond—without meaningful, relevant internship experience or something comparable, the odds are very, very slim that you will secure an attractive opportunity. It's competitive out there, and that's just the way it is" (Quora).

However, student publications—where students go to publish work and make themselves attractive to internships and eventually employers—are at risk and facing severe adversity from the universities with which they are affiliated. Just over ten years ago, a former *Sagebrush* editor negotiated with the Associated Students of the University of Nevada (ASUN), the student government at the University, to allow the *Sagebrush* to become financially independent from the University and ASUN. This independent label may seem arbitrary to outsiders, but it is vital yet rare for student media to be independent from the University they cover. Independence allows student journalists to cover University issues, especially ones the University does not want to become known, without fear of repercussions or prior restraint. The *Sagebrush* is the only student media at the University that is independent from the University, and has taken advantage to report on it in good times and bad, fairly and accurately. The University values the privileges the First Amendment awards to all journalistic publications, and to my knowledge, has not tried to censor any publications that use ASUN money to fund their operation. Student media at many other universities are not in that position and depend heavily on their university, and therefore make editorial decisions based on that dependence.

In 2018, issues of independence, budgeting, and censorship caused student journalists from across the country united and organized to form a movement called #SaveStudentNewsrooms to raise money for underfunded student publications and raise awareness of the challenges all publications face. In group discussions on social media, student editors highlighted the horrors they had to overcome to avoid being shut down. They talked about having to sue their student government for the money that was allocated to them, about administrations threatening to pull all funding from the newsroom if they published a certain story, about administrations censoring the stories they wanted to publish before they were made publicly available—all these issues which would be abhorrent and fiercely opposed in a professional newsroom. These issues are not overly exaggerated by these students.

The largest issue student media faces is their operations budget. As printing and employment costs skyrocket, the budget dwindles faster every year. Just in my three years at the *Sagebrush*, our budget has decreased 30 percent. Since the *Sagebrush* is independent from the University, it relies on advertising revenue to pad the budget and allow it to continue to print year after year. However, the print industry as a whole is declining and advertisers are looking less often to print publications to reach their intended audience. The *Sagebrush* does have a website, but the main profit comes from in-print advertising. The declining print business is causing printers to charge more each year to print a product, putting publications in a bind. Reno is a small community with the University at its center, and more often than not, businesses will come to the school to advertise their product. This leaves University organizations that rely heavily on advertising revenue to compete with each other for advertisements within the campus ecosystem. Advertising is an old funding model for publications that has largely gone out the window with the technology boom and print increase, but student publications don't have access to other sources of revenue—such as sponsored content—that national publications do. Such a strategy also brings ethical questions into play as to whether publications should write sponsored content at all, increasing their appearance of bias. Therefore, we have had to cut positions, extra newspaper copies or pages—anything that is not absolutely vital to the operation. However, I do not know how much more there is to cut with barely a dozen employees to put together our newspaper week to week. The system in place is not always reliable and largely depends on who is selling advertising year to year to determine the budget.

The *Sagebrush* has a long and continued history of bringing its student employees success beyond their college career. However, this legacy stands tested year to year as it tries to remain ethically sound by not being attached to the University while working on a minimal budget to see the next day. "*The Nevada Sagebrush* is a symbol of freedom among student journalists, a group of journalists left out of the equation when it comes to editorial independence." (Ali 57). Students at the *Sagebrush* are some of the best the University has to offer, and they see success because of the work they produce for the paper. Without these kinds of opportunities for student journalists available at the University, they are less likely to succeed—at the very least, the number of opportunities to succeed significantly lowers.

REFERENCES

Ali, O. "125 Years of Independence." *Nevada Silver & Blue*, October 2018, 56–57.

Clifton, G. "An independent voice for students for 125 years." *The Nevada Sagebrush*, October 16, 2018, 3.

Quora. "How Valuable Are Internships To College Students' Future Careers?" *Forbes*, November 13, 2017. https://www.forbes.com/sites/quora/2017/11/13/how-valuable-are-internships-to-college-students-future-careers/#7f3366ca1b14.

PART VI

Success with the UNRSOM

The University of Nevada, Reno School of Medicine demonstrates success by enhancing the medical workforce of the state of Nevada and through establishing programs for those who aspire to become M.D. students as well as those who are currently enrolled in the M.D. program. With over 50 years of serving the community, the program has grown and changed to meet the health needs of Nevada. This section highlights the School of Medicine's Post-Baccalaureate Program, the Multi-Tiered Systems of Support Program, and the wellness initiatives from the School of Medicine. The Post-Baccalaureate Program encourages students from underserved backgrounds who want to attend medical school to obtain certification for early assurance admission into the School of Medicine. The Multi-Tiered Systems of Support Program helps current medical students by structuring instruction and intervention need through various intensities (tiers). The School of Medicine's dedication to the health and wellness of its students promotes to create a culture and environment that supports it.

CHAPTER 27

School of Medicine's Post-Baccalaureate Program

ZACHARY WALKER, M.S.

Zachary Walker is the coordinator of Educational Outreach and Pipeline Programs at the University of Nevada, Reno School of Medicine (UNRSOM), where he oversees the Post-Baccalaureate, BS-MD Direct Entry, and TRIO Pre-Med programs. Through these programs, Zachary assists and supports pre-med students from all backgrounds in developing themselves into qualified, competitive medical school applicants. He has more than eight years of experience working in higher education, focusing on reducing barriers and increasing access to college and professional programs for disadvantaged student populations. Zachary earned his bachelor's degree in Mathematics from California State University, Monterey Bay followed by a master's degree in Educational Leadership at Portland State University. He is currently pursuing a Ph.D. in Equity and Diversity in Education at the University of Nevada, Reno.

Introduction

Approximately 40 percent of students applying to medical school for the first time will be accepted into a program (Association of American Medical Colleges, 2018). While these statistics are not in favor of the applicant, the likelihood of being accepted to medical school declines rapidly for those who apply from non-traditional and underrepresented backgrounds, such as first-generation, low-socioeconomic status, underrepresented in medicine, and rural candidates (Association of American Medical Colleges, 2018). In an effort to address this discrepancy in medical school matriculants, the University of Nevada, Reno, School of Medicine (UNR Med) has developed and implemented the Post-Baccalaureate Certificate Program (Post-Bac Program). Eligibility requirements for this program were built in order to provide an opportunity for students who, historically, would not be successful in applying through the general applicant pool due to lower academic metrics. In addition, students accepted into the Post-

Bac Program come from backgrounds often underrepresented, with stories and experiences that enrich the make-up and diversity of future medical school cohorts.

The vision statement at UNR Med is "A Healthy Nevada", with a focus on increasing the physician pool serving the state of Nevada. However, the institution does not simply aim to increase the number of physicians practicing in Nevada. There is a focus on providing Nevadans with physicians who represent them; physicians who look like their patients, speak their language, and have shared backgrounds and experiences with their patient populations. In order to meet this goal, traditional and non-traditional applicants alike must matriculate, graduate, and remain in Nevada to serve in urban and rural settings, large hospitals and small clinics, and provide care in areas of medicine ranging from family medicine to highly specialized fields. In this chapter, we will further explore the physician shortage issues facing Nevada, how UNR Med aims to addresses this issue in an inclusive manner, and the longitudinal impact of the Post-Bac Program.

Problem

According to the Nevada State Office of Rural Health, twelve of the sixteen counties in Nevada are considered to be rural (Griswold, Packham, Etchegoyhen, Marchand, & Gunawan, 2015). Between 2004 and 2014, the number of licensed Medical Doctors (MDs) per 100,000 population in Nevada increased from 150 to 172.3—an increase of 14.9 percent (Griswold et al., 2015). However, the number of MDs per capita in rural and frontier counties decreased by 9.6 percent in the same period of time (Griswold et al., 2015). The state of Nevada ranks forty-seventh in the country for the number of active patient care physicians per capita (Dill, 2017). In Nevada, 11.1 percent of licensed MDs and 14.5 percent of rural and frontier MDs completed their undergraduate medical education (UME) at UNR Med (Griswold et al., 2015). UNR Med's initiatives to increase the physician pool within Nevada is only one part of the problem, and a thoughtful, inclusive approach in supplying UNR Med with a more diverse applicant pool is necessary to provide the state with a workforce of healthcare practitioners. With potential future physicians serving the state of Nevada graduating from UNR Med, the University intends to ensure these physicians understand and represent the population they aim to provide care for in the future.

While there is a physician shortage in Nevada, and especially in rural environments and within certain specializations in medicine, the problem is multifactorial. According to the most recent population estimates in the US Census data for the state of Nevada, 74.6 percent of the population identifies as White (U.S. Census Bureau, 2018). With 1.7 percent of the population identifying as American Indian and Alaskan Native, 9.8 percent identifying as Black or African American, and 28.8 percent identifying as Hispanic or Latino, UNR Med focuses on ensuring adequate representation from these groups in its medical school applicant pools (U.S. Census Bureau, 2018). In 2010, the same year of the implementation of the Post-Bac Program, the graduating medical school class at UNR Med contained no students from Native American and Alaskan Native backgrounds, only one Black or African American (1.6 percent) student, and five Hispanic or Latino (8.1 percent) graduates. Falling far short of the demographics of the state, UNR Med aimed to bridge this gap through the Post-Bac Program, which quickly became a critical pipeline program brining more diversity to the applicant pool considered for matriculation into UNR Med. This discrepancy between the demographics of the state of Nevada, and the demographics of those matriculating into UNR Med has been reduced, but there remains work to be done. In the most recently accepted medical school class (the class of 2023), UNR Med brought in two Native American and Alaskan Native students (2.9 percent), five Black or African American (7.1 percent), and fifteen Hispanic or Latino (21.4 percent) students onto the UNR Med campus to begin their studies.

There are a number of challenges and barriers facing the pre-medical student population regardless of background. The socio-economic status of an applicant can heavily impact the type of resources and support programs available to help navigate the process of preparing for and applying to medical school. Pre-medical students with a physician in their immediate or extended family have much stronger access to the medical community, allowing for stronger networking in gaining clinical experience, physician shadowing, and in the pursuit of quality letters of recommendation for their application. These same pre-medical students are more likely to receive quality pre-professional advice guiding them towards the most appropriate experiences in gaining the important elements necessary for a medical school application. While the specific pre-medical experiences are important in an application process, participation in these activities also provides students with content and lived experience aiding in their performance in the medical school interview process, allowing for an additional stronger metric to exist in their application profile.

Students with the proper financial means are able to pay for structured academic support programs and systems, such as hiring a paid tutor for course support or paying for a commercial Medical College Admissions Test (MCAT) preparatory program. These two elements of an application—MCAT and GPA—are the two traditional metrics medical schools utilize in order to assess the "academic horsepower" of an applicant. For many medical schools, a lower GPA or MCAT score will result in an applicant never making it to the interview process. For other programs, when comparing two similar applicants for admission, the raw metric scores in GPA and MCAT can provide an easy method of filtering between applicants. When looking at MCAT performance nationally between 2015 and 2017, White test takers score, on average, nine points higher than their Black or African American counterparts, seven points higher than their Hispanic or Latino counterparts, and six points higher than their American Indian or Alaskan Native counterparts (American Association of Medical Colleges, 2018). The American Association of Medical Colleges (AAMC) has attempted to address this discrepancy through facilitating a full restructuring of the exam and the implementation of various resource access programs, but these discrepancies have not improved over time. When medical schools fail to recognize the systemic contributing factors to these differences in MCAT performance, otherwise qualified applicants fall through the cracks.

It is difficult for an admissions committee member to differentiate premedical experiences and narratives within a personal statement as compared to academic metrics on a piece of paper. However, data provided by the AAMC shows small differences in academic success of students in their first two years of medical school for those obtaining average GPA and MCAT scores when compared to those in the upper-tier metric ranges (American Association of Medical Colleges, 2018). In order to provide an opportunity for students with lower traditional academic metrics, but by all other means are prepared and competitive medical school applicants, the Post-Baccalaureate Program was implemented at UNR Med.

Program History

It is the philosophy of UNR Med that there is not one way to pursue a career in medicine, but rather many routes a pre-medical student may take in achieving their dream to become a physician. The Post-Bac Program "offers a structured, one-year certificate program designed for students who need GPA improvement, MCAT preparation, or additional upper division science coursework to be competitive for medical school admissions" (University of Nevada, Reno School of Medicine, 2018). Preference for admission into the Post-Bac Program is given to Nevada residents who identify as a member of an underserved or underrepresented population in medicine, including first-generation (defined as neither parent holding a bachelor's degree), underrepresented minority, low-income, rural, and military veteran applicants.

The program began as a collaboration between UNR Med and the University of Nevada, Reno (UNR) in the fall of 2010. Six students were brought onto the UNR campus for the first pilot cohort participating in the year-long program, and since then the collaboration has expanded to the University of Nevada, Las Vegas (UNLV), and Nevada State College (NSC). In the current 2018–2019 academic year, the Post-Bac Program supports 14 students along with one participant in an accelerated iteration of the program, designed for those who have applied to UNR Med and were required to address certain elements of their application profile.

Since the start of the program, additional components and support services have been added, including a year-long MCAT Preparation Program offered for course credit, pre-med workshops ranging from personal statements to math techniques, and a peer mentorship program to aid in the transition into the Post-Bac Program and into medical school. To date, seventy six students have completed the Post-Bac Program through UNR Med along with forty students in their second term within the program.

As the Post-Bac program grows in competitiveness, UNR Med recognizes that not every applicant to the Post-Bac Program will matriculate. In order to support those who are not invited to join the program, UNR Med is one of the few institutions with a Post-Bac Program who provide feedback and pre-professional advising for denied applicants. The hope is to guide these applicants in how to best improve their application for the following cycle or to provide advising on what their next step may be in pursuing a career in medicine. This practice aligns with the program ideology—there are many pathways into medicine, and any student matriculating into a health professions program contributes to the healthcare needs facing Nevada and the country as a whole.

Program Overview

Once accepted into the Post-Bac Program, a prescribed academic schedule is provided to students, which places them into a total of 32 credits of upper-division science coursework over their academic year. With roughly 16 credits in each term, students face a rigorous academic load balancing four to six advanced biology, chemistry, and psychology courses alongside their preparation for other elements of the medical school application process. These courses are specifically tailored to each student in order to provide support in their preparation for the MCAT and critical pre-med coursework which aids in the transition into medical school curriculum. For example, a student may take a grouping of classes in their fall semester including: Introduction to Biochemistry, Organic Chemistry II, Metabolic Regulation, Abnormal Psychology, and Immunology. Table 1 below shows a sample schedule of an average Post-Baccalaureate schedule.

In addition to the academic component of the program, participants often seek out additional pre-med "activities", including gaining additional experiences shadowing physicians, working directly with patient

TABLE 1.

Fall Semester		**Credits**
CHEM 342	Organic Chemistry 2	3
BCH 400	Intro to Biochemistry	4
BIOL 453	Immunology	3
MED 461	Medical Student Admissions Test Foundations	3
Semester Credits		16
Spring Semester		**Credits**
PSY 441	Abnormal Psychology	3
BIOL 315	Cellular Biology	3
BCH 405	Molecular Biology	3
MICR 425	Virology	4
MED 461	Medical Student Admissions Test Foundations	3
Semester Credits		16
Total Program Credits		**32**

populations, participating in community service, and spending time conducting research in labs throughout the University.

Participants of the program take thirty two credits of upper division coursework, complete the MCAT exam, apply to medical schools, and interview with UNR Med all in the same year. The majority of these components are completed in the summer months, with the American Medical College Application System (AMCAS) application being submitted in June, the MCAT taken in July-August, and interviews taking place in August. Post-Bac Program students apply as an early-assurance applicant, providing them with their UNR Med acceptance in mid-October, whereas their general application pool counterparts would not find out the results of their applications until mid-December at the earliest. In order to successfully matriculate into UNR Med from the Post-Bac Program, students must maintain a 3.5 GPA and obtain a pre-determined MCAT and interview score. Once accepted into the medical school class, students have a "gap year" before they start at UNR Med, offering an opportunity to continue investing in the medical community of Nevada through clinical volunteering or employment, additional research opportunities, or alternative employment before beginning their medical school training.

Beginning with the 2017–2018 cohort of Post-Bac students, all program participants have a reserved seat in their future medical school class at UNR Med. This program change came out of observations from administrative faculty and staff who support the program, citing a detrimental competitive nature within previous Post-Bac cohorts. Prior to this change, the ten to fifteen Post-Bac students enrolled each year were all vying for one of the coveted seven medical school reserved seats. The competitive nature born out of this structure did not allow for a supportive, collaborative environment in the year-long MCAT preparation program, and also resulted in some Post-Bac Program graduates ultimately matriculating at other medical schools due to not receiving an early seat. The administrative faculty and staff made the recommendation to UNR Med's Admissions Executive Committee (AEC) to provide the same number of spots in our medical school class as we accept into the Post-Bac Program. As the institution itself is investing time, energy, and resources into these Post-Bac students, the decision was made to provide the best environment and structure for retaining these applicants. Since this change was implemented, those working with cohorts of students have cited a more collaborative and supportive environment where each student is invested to see the entire group succeed. This results in a stronger connection to UNR Med, a stronger sense of community within program participants, and better retention rates of those who successfully complete the program.

While we strongly recommend program participants not work during their Post-Bac year, due to the particular student population and financial investment in tuition costs, many students take on part-time jobs. This dynamic often results in lower-than-desired academic performance and an inability to address other weaknesses within their "pre-medical profile" of program participants. Our institution balances this recommendation with the understanding that remaining unemployed during their program year could create access barriers for low-SES students and limit participation to only those who have the financial means to either pay for the tuition outright or take on additional student loans.

Unlike many Post-Bac Programs across the US, UNR Med does not currently charge a program fee for participation, and only asks for a small ($35) application fee which supports academic resources for students. With other programs around the country charging fees between $500 and $20,000 for enrollment into a Post-Bac Program, our institution is committed to keeping access to the program as open and equitable as possible. However, there still remains a financial burden on program participants due to the increasing tuition costs associated with taking the required thirty two credits of coursework. One potential solution to address the financial burden of the program is offering a scholarship to program participants through grant and external funding sources in order to support the financial impact on students. However, efforts to keep sustainable funds available to Post-Bac students have fallen short. Any program or institution interested in implementing a similar program to combat the inequity and access issues facing medical schools should identify consistent, sustainable funds to support students in their academic journey.

Impact of Program

There are a number of different ways to measure success within program participants. Initially, UNRSOM aims to support each accepted student in meeting their goal of maintaining a 3.5 GPA, successful MCAT attempt, and multiple mini-interview (MMI) score. We consider it a "success" if program participants ultimately matriculate into any medical school or health professions program. The program's strongest success metric is in our Post-Bac Certificate Program graduation rates, with a year-to-date program completion rate of 88 percent, which is defined by meeting the GPA requirement upon completion of the program. To date, 95 percent of students participating in the Post-Bac Program identified with one or more of the UNRSOM Mission-Based Diversity Group categories, defined by UNRSOM as: African American/Black, Hispanic/Latino, low SES (Pell Grant and/or Fee Assistance eligible), rural (have had significant experience living in or serving in a non-metropolitan area) and first generation (neither parent nor guardian has attained a Bachelor's degree or higher). Historically, Post-Bac students have an average undergraduate GPA of 3.09 prior to their year-long program, while achieving an average of 3.72 GPA throughout the rigorous thirty two credit academic load.

The largest barrier to matriculation into UNRSOM's future medical school class is the MCAT score requirement, and this exam is arguably one of the largest barriers for any prospective medical school applicant. Since the implementation of the year-long structured MCAT Preparation Program at UNRSOM, 68 percent of program participants achieved the program required score for the MCAT on their first attempt. Post-Bac Program support faculty and staff are constantly updating and adding elements and offerings to students aimed to increase retention and successful exam completion rates. However, there is an inherent challenge in achieving this goal, as the majority of student demographics and academic profiles within the program align with pre-medical student populations are traditionally at a disadvantage in taking this exam and achieve lower MCAT scores when compared to their more traditional pre-medical counterparts.

Comparing the number of Post-Bac students with a program-required successful MCAT score to the number of students who matriculate into UNRSOM, we see a 72 percent matriculation rate—indicating there were more qualified applicants applying through the Post-Bac Program than there were available seats in the early assurance designation. If the program year where each accepted Post-Bac student with acceptable MCAT score had a reserved seat at UNRSOM, there would be a 100 percent matriculation rate. Lastly, our institution keeps track of any program participants who ultimately matriculate into any medical school or health professions program. Including matriculation rates into UNRSOM, since the beginning of the program, 77.7 percent of program participants have matriculated into medical school or other health professions programs.

Conclusion

The data indicates UNRSOM's Post-Bac Program supports the increased diversity of future medical school graduates and contributes to the applicant pool of non-traditional students. However, there is additional work that remains to be done. We, as an institution, fall short of ensuring our graduating physicians adequately represent the demographics of the state of Nevada. Interventions must be made early and often, not only through initiatives like the Post-Bac Program, but in the support and preparation of younger Nevadan's from all backgrounds and environments in order to increase the diversity of future medical school applicants. If outreach and recruitment programs provided future pre-medical students from disadvantaged backgrounds with the advising, support, and guidance necessary to remain competitive throughout their academic career, the need for structured GPA and MCAT repair pipelines like the Post-Bac would not exist. In the meantime, UNRSOM aims to increase and improve the resources and support necessary for current and future Post-Bac students in order to improve retention and graduation rates, further increasing the diversity of future medical school classes. Through collaborative initiatives in the K-12, undergraduate, and pre-professional healthcare programs environments, we aim to improve the status of the forty-seventh ranked state in the country for the number of active patient care physicians per capita (Dill, 2017). It is not enough to simply increase the physician pool within the state of Nevada; UNRSOM must ensure that future medical school graduates represent the population they aim to provide care for and inspiring the next generation of future physicians to pursue a career in medicine.

REFERENCES

American Association of Medical Colleges (2018, November 9). *Applicants and Matriculants Data.* Retrieved from: https://www.aamc.org/data/facts/applicant matriculant/.

American Association of Medical Colleges (2018, June 1). *Using MCAT Data in 2019 Medical Student Selection.* Retrieved from: https://www.aamc.org/download /462316/data/mcatguide.pdf.

Bureau of Health Professions, Health Resources and Services Administration. (2010). *Shortage Designation: HPSAs, MUAs, and MUPs.* Washington DC: US

Department of Health and Human Services. Retrieved from: http://hpsafind.hrsa.gov/HPSASearch.aspx.

Dill, M. (2017). *2017 State Physician Workforce Data Report, AAMC*. Retrieved from: https://members.aamc.org/eweb/upload/2017%20State%20Physician%20Workforce%20Data%20Report.pdf.

Griswold, T., Packham, J., Etchegoyhen, L., Marchand, C., & Gunawan, A. (2015). *Nevada rural and frontier health data book—seventh edition*. Reno, NV.

University of Nevada, Reno School of Medicine (2018, October 1). *Post-Baccalaureate Program Overview*. Retrieved from: https://med.unr.edu/admissions/how-to-apply/special-programs/post-bac.

U.S. Census Bureau (2018). *QuickFacts, Nevada*. Retrieved from: https://www.census.gov/quickfacts/nv.

CHAPTER 28

School of Medicine's Multi-Tiered Systems of Support (MTSS) Program

RANNA NASH, M.A.

Ranna Nash, MA, is the coordinator for Student Development and Academic Enrichment at the University of Nevada, Reno School of Medicine where she oversees the Learning and Wellness Resource Center housed within the Office of Admissions and Student Affairs, and oversees all programming in regards to academic support and wellness support or learners served by UNR Med. She earned her bachelor's degree in Biological Sciences from the University of Nevada, Las Vegas. She earned her master's degree in Educational Leadership: Higher Education Administration from the University of Nevada, Reno. She obtained post-master's degree graduate certificates in Adult Learning Disability Assessment from Sacramento State University. She is currently earning her Ph.D. in Special Education and Disability Studies with a focus in Medical Education from the University of Nevada, Reno.

Introduction

Background

Medical students are considered to be the best and the brightest of student learners and engage in a rigorous process in order to be accepted into medical school. They go through hours, weeks, months, and years of volunteering and community service. They achieve high GPAs and high standardized test scores. They perform well in their medical school interviews and are chosen to matriculate into medical school. Fifty-four percent of applicants are rejected to every medical school they apply to. Getting into medical school is becoming more difficult each year. According to the Association of American Medical Colleges, medical school applicants within the United States increased by more than 35 percent over a 10-year span (Kowarski, 2017). There is a high demand nationally for an increase in competent medical practitioners which some contribute to the increased application number.

However, when students are accepted into medical school, it does not mean the expectations lower; they have to maintain a high level of motivation and still perform on exams while being subjectively measured. Students are then mixed in with other high achieving students, which can often be intimidating for some, and for the first time they are not the top achievers in every class. The graduation rate for MD students dropped from 96 percent in the 1990s to 81 percent in 2010 (Association of American Medical Colleges, 2014). There are many reasons why students struggle, which can include: under preparedness, family stress, burned bridges, illness, and the decision that medicine was the wrong career choice. Due to some of these reasons, medical schools have looked at ways to initiate interventions to aid students who struggle before dropping out or dismissal can occur.

There are many intervention models in medical education. Different schools have processes and procedures in place that work with students once they are identified as a struggling or remediating learner. One of the issues with identification is that it tends to happen too late to be able to help the student not fail a component of their medical education. When students fail a course, or "block", they undergo remediation of that block or content. Remediation programs differ throughout medical education, however students are generally identified at this time to need extra support. For this reason, students can be placed on probation, asked to repeat the year, or be dismissed from medical school. When these situations occur, students' future career choices are often limited, and students tend to not completely build skills to allow them to progress further.

Problem

These initiatives, which have recently started including learning specialists, have increased over the past few years. The goal is to best help students as they progress through medical school. Content retention levels of learners have been an ongoing problem and can be problematic when students are in their clinical years and medical education (Custers, 2007). With diversity and inclusion initiatives increasing nationally, it gives medical schools a diverse population of learners. These diverse populations (minority and economically disadvantaged students) are often at higher risk for academic challenges, with a higher rate of medical school withdrawal and dismissal as well as lower pass rate on the United States Medical Licensing Exam (USMLE) Step 1 test (Miller, 2014). Early identification and support of students that are at risk in medical education is generally recommended in the research literature, though very little is described about the longitudinal interventions and progress monitoring of medical students in preventing failure long term along with little evidence indicating best practices in remediating medical learners (O'Neill, Mette Morcke & Eika, 2016).

Significance

There are many models that try to catch struggling learners early; for example, pre-matriculation programs have been set up during the summer before medical school to give students skills in anatomy and histology (Miller, 2014), which are some of the higher failed subjects in the first year of medical school. Students learn study strategies, test-taking skills, and are introduced to a small cohort of their peers at an early time before the stressors of medical school overcome them. However, these "programs" are not longitudinal and retention of study habits are not examined throughout medical school, specifically not monitoring the "at risk" student population who gets invited to these programs (Miller, 2014). Miller (2014) also indicated it would be beneficial in the future to examine the same topic from a faculty and administrative viewpoint.

There are also classroom interventions that have students utilizing active learning, or case-based learning in hopes of students retaining content faster. Most medical schools administer multiple choice question assessments for the first two years of their programs (Kosobuski et al., 2017). Depending on how these assessments are measured, students are expected remember an unrealistic amount of content and perform at a high standard to get high scores. There has recently been a push for wellness initiatives in medical education to aid in high burnout and suicide rate amongst students, residents, and physicians. Behavioral issues have been correlated to increased rates of burn out amongst medical students. These initiatives correspond to access to counselors, disability services, and often ACT training or mindfulness practices.

There are also policies in the form of interventions in place that students must guide their required expectations. These interventions are often not well planned and piecemealed together and the authorities behind these interventions are unknown. The literature indicates that the intervention players do not exactly communicate with each other; they are often in "silos". If intervention players came together, they could better help students as can be seen by the multi-tiered system (MTSS) model in the K-12 system (Rodriguez, Loman, & Borgmeier, 2016). The multi-tiered system eliminates silos and brings everyone together (McIntosh, Horner & Sugai, 2009). The purpose of the MTSS model was to communicate and develop data driven plans based on expertise to help students meet their needs whether they are behavioral or academic and meets them at their individual levels (McIntosh, Horner & Sugai, 2009).

Within the K-12 system nationally (and in Washoe County), MTSS frameworks have helped achieve a commitment to academic, personal, and college entry success(McIntosh, Horner & Sugai, 2009). A Multi-Tiered System of Support (MTSS) is a school wide problem-solving prevention model with widely proven effectiveness (Graden, Stollar, & Poth, 2007; Kansas Multi-Tier System of Supports and Alignment, 2015). MTSS uses data-based decision making to inform academic and behavioral instruction and intervention. The instruction and intervention are delivered to students varying intensities (multiple tiers) based on student need. "Need-driven" decision-making helps to ensure that school and district resources reach the appropriate students at the appropriate levels to accelerate the performance of ALL students to achieve college and career readiness (Florida Department of Education, n.d.).

MTSS: Academics and Behavior

MTSS is designed to provide both academic and behavioral services to improve for all students (Glover & Vaugn, 2010). "All students" includes every student on the performance continuum (i.e., high achieving, grade-level, low achieving, English as second language learners, and students who are special education eligible).

Program History

The University of Nevada, Reno School of Medicine is committed to creating an education system where all students achieve academic success, develop personal and civic responsibility, and achieve clinical career readiness for current times. UNR Med has had an intervention program in place for many years. In 2012, the remediation program was created, and in 2013 the Letter of Concern intervention was put into place. The purpose of the Office of Medical Education (OME) Letter of Concern (LoC) was to allow for UNR Med's Learning Specialist to have earlier interventions with students in hopes to prevent remediation caused by block failure and the overall prevention of a USMLE Step 1 failure. Other schools, such as Arizona, UCLA, and UC Davis (from whom we have mirrored our remediation program), all notify students when they fall below a certain academic threshold and are put on "watch lists". This process was implemented in the fall of 2013 for the Class of 2017. Based on performance on Step 1 and block performance for the Class of 2016, it was decided that any students who scored below 72 percent on a given exam would receive a LoC encouraging the student to seek help from the Learning Specialist.

There was conversation whether or not the LoC was working, and consequently, if interventions were working. A committee formed in April 2018 further looks at historical data of LoC and serves as a working group to develop a MTSS model for medical education. The committee determined that the current intervention model was not accomplishing student success outcomes as original intended.

About 80 percent of our students do well academically and professionally (Tier 1). Fifteen percent of students receive LoC and have professionalism concerns (Tier 2). Students in Tier 2 receive interventions to help them move to Tier 1 where 80 percent of students are. Those who are not successful in the Tier 2 system move to the Tier 3 system for remediation. See the following diagram:

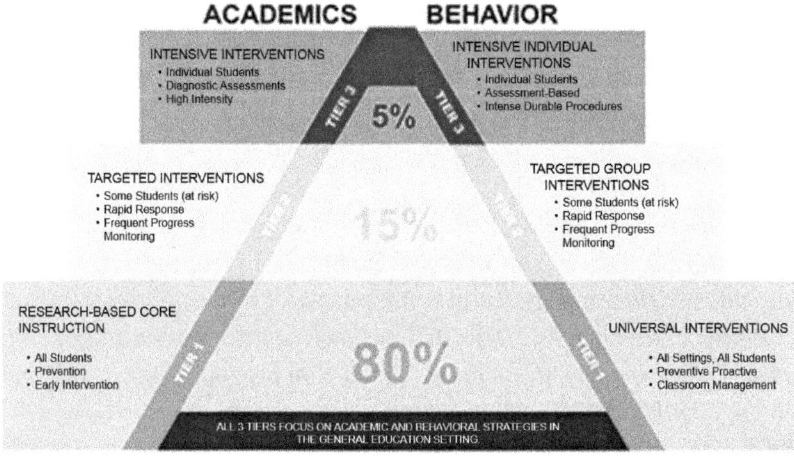

The above is the K-12 Tier system that is used, which means that students of this generation are used to this type of intervention system.

Response to Intervention Proposal (Multi-Tiered System of Support)

What is "Tier 2"?

This is where the LoC would have a role. The conversation will be to discuss why we use the threshold of 75 percent to send letters to students and our intervention systems to see what is working. These targeted interventions would target academic and behavioral issues (see fig. 1).

Program Overview

What the committee has developed thus far—this working group will continue to be in development as we start collecting data

Utilizing the problem-solving model, the following Tier system was established:

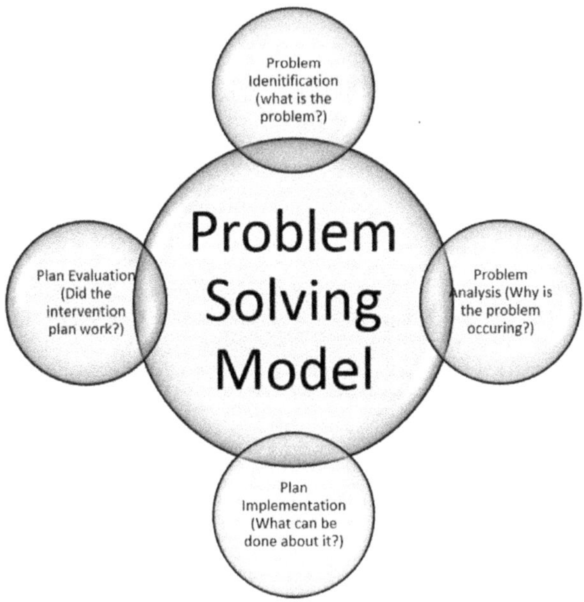

The number of letters will determine "Tiers." A total of three Tiers are in our given system (see figure below).

1. **Proficient**—80 percent of the student population
2. **Attention/Concern**—15 percent of the student population
   a. **Attention**—1 Letter of Support—PLC consists of the Learning Specialist, Block Directors, and a Counselor. Point of contact will be the Learning Specialist who will work with the other members to develop a plan for the student.
   b. **Concern**—2 Letters of Support—PLC consists of Learning Specialist, Block Directors and Counselor with heavier intervention.
3. **Warning/Remediation**—5 percent of the student population
   a. **Warning**—three or more Letters of Support (but no failures)—PLC consists of Coordinator for Student Development and Academic Enrichment, Learning Specialist, Block Directors, and Counselor.
   b. **Remediation**—Failure of a Block—PLC consists of Coordinator for Student Development and Academic Enrichment, Learning Specialist, Block Directors, Counselors, and Associate Dean for Admissions and Student Affairs.

Student profile reports will be developed to help with tracking successful interventions. Quantitative data regarding a student's exam score, the overall class average on any given exam, and overall block scores are readily available and should be included in any student profile. In addition, it was noted that data contained in a Strengths and Opportunities report, which

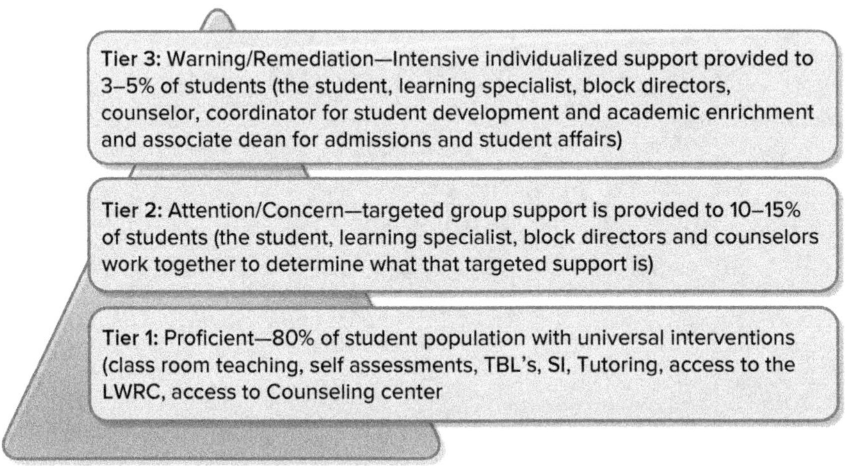

can be easily pulled from ExamSoft, will provide content specific detail that will let intervention team members know which subject(s) and/or category(ies) a student had difficulty with on any given exam. Qualitative data will also be collected.

Sample Student Profile: (Universal screenings of *all* students will be conducted three times per year to proactively and objectively identify which students are potentially in need of educational supports/enhancements to supplement the core curriculum):

University of Nevada, Reno
School of Medicine
Learning & Wellness Resource Center

Class of: Class of 2022

Graduation Date: May 2022

Application Type: «Application_Type»

First Name: **«First_Name»**

Last Name: **«Last_Name»** Gender: **«Gender»** First Gen: «First_Generation»

Rural: **«Rural»** Race: **«Race»** Ethnicity: **«Ethnicity»**

SES: ________ MMI Score: **«MMI_Score»**

Undergrad College: **«College»** Major: **«Major»**

Degree: **«degree»** Total GPA: **«GPA_Total»** GPA BCPM: **«GPA_BCPM»**

Graduate College: ____________________ Major: ____________________

Degree: ________________ Total GPA: ________

MCAT 2015 Score: **«Entry_MCAT_2015_Score»** MCAT Numeric 1: **«MCAT_Numeric»** MCAT Numeric 2: **«MCAT_Numeric1»** MCAT Numeric 3: **«MCAT_Numeric2»** Number MCAT Attempts: **«M__MCAT»**

Years 1 & 2:

	Ex 1	**Ex 2**	**Ex 3**	**Ex 4**	**LP 1**	**LP 2**	**LP 3**	**Overall**
Block 1								
Block 2								
Block 3								
Block 4								
Block 5								
Block 6								
Block 7								
Block 8								
Block 9								
Block 10								

Step 1:

	Score
Practice 1	
Practice 2	
Practice 3	
Step 1 Score	

MTSS:

Comments: **«Comments»**

Student Profile Rev. 7/12/18 1

University of Nevada, Reno
School of Medicine
Learning & Wellness Resource Center

Class of: Class of 2022

Graduation Date: May 2022

Application Type: «Application_Type»

First Name: **«First_Name»**

Last Name: **«Last_Name»** Gender: **«Gender»** First Gen: «First_Generation»

Rural: **«Rural»** Race: **«Race»** Ethnicity: **«Ethnicity»**

SES: __________ MMI Score: **«MMI_Score»**

Undergrad College: **«College»** Major: **«Major»**

Degree: **«degree»** Total GPA: **«GPA_Total»** GPA BCPM: **«GPA_BCPM»**

Graduate College: ________________________ Major: ___________________________

Degree:____________________ Total GPA: __________

MCAT 2015 Score: **«Entry_MCAT_2015_Score»** MCAT Numeric 1: **«MCAT_Numeric»** MCAT Numeric 2: **«MCAT_Numeric1»** MCAT Numeric 3: **«MCAT_Numeric2»** Number MCAT Attempts: **«M__MCAT»**

Years 1 & 2:

	Ex 1	**Ex 2**	**Ex 3**	**Ex 4**	**LP 1**	**LP 2**	**LP 3**	**Overall**
Block 1								
Block 2								
Block 3								
Block 4								
Block 5								
Block 6								
Block 7								
Block 8								
Block 9								
Block 10								

Step 1:

	Score
Practice 1	
Practice 2	
Practice 3	
Step 1 Score	

MTSS:

Comments: **«Comments»**

Student Profile Rev. 7/12/18 1

Grade Cut-Off Criteria for Letters of Concern

It was determined that a flat grade cut-off of 75 percent would be best with the option to increase that to 77 percent in Block 1 (at the discretion of the Block Directors).

Intervention Implementation Per Tier

It was determined that the LoC for Blocks 1 and 2 should be treated differently as they both deal with a transition in some form or another, so consequently the interventions for those two blocks will also need to be conducted differently. It is still uncertain as to what the content of any Letter of Concern should be in these two blocks, but any such Letter (whether printed or via email if that is decided to be the best form of communication) should not become part of the student's permanent file. The goal is to encourage the student to seek the intervention.

If available and possible, this first intervention should include counseling. A complete plan for interventions will need to be created, detailing which interventions to use for each of the possible academic and behavioral issues a student could be facing, with the student being present and used as a resource for their intervention plan. It was noted that most students need assistance with study plans, question decoding, concept mapping, and test-taking strategies.

The Implementation Phase Typically Involves a 5-Step Process

1. *Measuring the integrity of MTSS implementation*: Checking integrity means that the schools are measuring and reviewing how well the school is adhering to their implementation of MTSS, including both systemic and individual plans. School teams can use surveys to plan and monitor the implementation of MTSS. The results are used to identify the degree to which MTSS systems and procedures are in place and focus school's teams on action planning. An initial survey is administered to serve as a baseline measure, and the same survey is used periodically throughout the year to monitor progress towards full implementation.
2. *Ensuring the "continuum of support" meets the needs of all the students*: Schools will need to continually check their support systems to ensure that they are appropriate for their students. Doing so will prevent students from "falling through the cracks."

3. *Revisiting the problem-solving framework*: Schools must ensure that problem solving remains at the forefront of conversations about students' needs. Regularly-scheduled, systemic data review focused on determining student benefit response to intervention plans are essential. Interventions should be adjusted promptly when data indicate students are not making sufficient gains to meet their goals.
4. *Cerebrate!* Celebrations and reflections time are vital to achieve our goals.
5. *Collaborate and share experiences*: Schools benefit when they take time to share their successes, lessons learned, ideas, and strategies with each other.

Impact of Program

The impact of the MTSS program has proven to be successful as students who fail a given block has reduced from previous years. The amount of letters to students has also reduced in comparison to previous years.

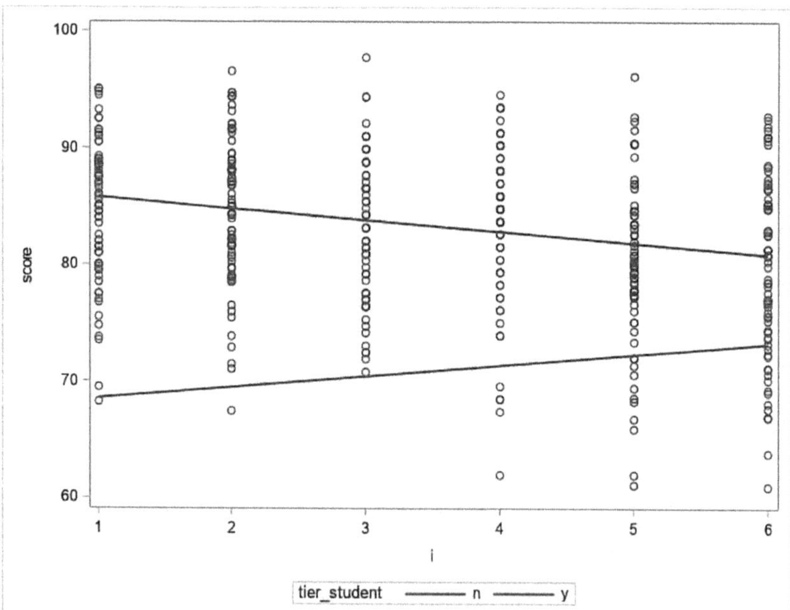

* The above figure compared students who have received Tiered intervention compared to the rest of the class population. As indicated by the graph, students who receive interventions increase in exam scores while other decreased.

Intervention plans were created with each student that moved up the Tier system. Interventions consisted of tutoring, weekly monitoring, supplemental instruction, small group review sessions, test taking strategies practice, note taking strategies, participation in wellness activities, video viewing of lectures, counseling, disability resource center, mindfulness-based stress reduction, cognitive testing, and meeting with specific faculty.

Current MTSS model after first semester:

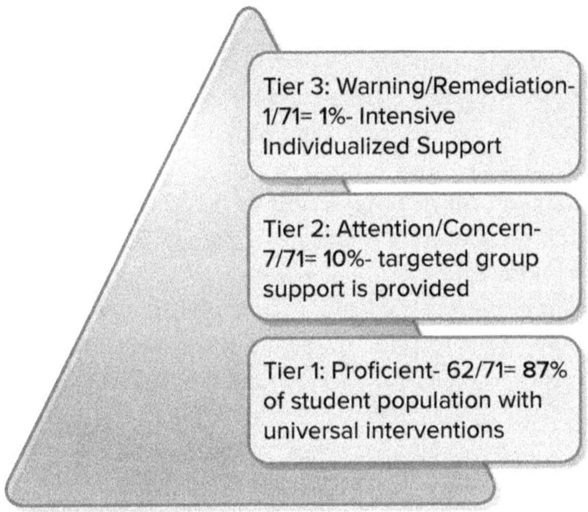

* Decreased from previous year (Tier 1: 75%, Tier 2: 15%, Tier 3: 9.6%)

Conclusion

Currently, the preliminary data indicates that students are getting the help that they need faster due to the implementation of the MTSS model. Early identification of students with a learning disability or mental health needs are seeking these services faster which helps their progression throughout medical school. Students intervention plans and follow through are measured as they complete exams. Students who complete increased levels of their given intervention plan tend to be more successful than those who do not.

However, this model is new and the population size of the UNR Med School is small so there needs to be more years of data to further indicate success.

REFERENCES

Albritton, Kizzy (2014). Professional development to increase problem-solving in a response to intervention framework. *Contemporary Psychology*. 18*(1)*. 44–58.

Association of American Medical Colleges. (2014). Analysis in brief. Association of American Medical Colleges, 14. Retrieved from https://www.aamc.org/download/401814/data/.

Burns, Matthew K. Egan, Andrea M. Kunkel, Amy K. McComas, Jennifer. Peterson, Meredith M. Rahn, Naomi L., Wilson, Jennifer. (2013) Training for generalization and maintenance in RtI implementation: front-loading for sustainability. learning disabilities research and practice. *Learning Disabilities Research & Practice*. 28*(2)*. 81–88.

Cilliers, Francois, Schuwirth, Lambert W.T., Herman, Nicoline, Adendroff, Hanelie J., van der Vleuten, Cees P.M. (2012). A model of the pre-assessment learning effects of summative assessment in medical education. *Advances in Health Sciences Education*. 17*(1)*. 39–53.

Cowan, Carolina, Maxwell, Gerri (2015). Educators' perceptions of response to intervention and impact on student learning. *Journal of Instructional Pedagogies*. 16.

Florida Department of Education (n.d.). Florida's Multi-Tiered System of Supports. Retrieved from http://www.florida-rti.org/floridaMTSS/index.htm.

Graden, JL., Stollar, SA., Poth, RL. (2007). The Ohio Integrated System Model: Overview and Lessons Learned. *Handbook of Response to Intervention*. Pp 288–299.

Harkins, Sylvia (2016). Response to intervention for student success in higher education: is it possible? *Journal of Instructional Research*. 5. 79–82.

Harlacher, Jason E., Siler, Chelsea E., (2011). Factors related to successful RTI implementation. *Comunique*. 39*(6)*. 20–22.

Harvey, Michael W., Yssel, Nina., Jones, Rueth E., (2015). Response to intervention preparation for preservice teachers: what is the status for Midwest institutions of higher education. *Teacher education and special education*. 38*(2)*. 105–120.

Hayes, Lindsey., Lillenstein, Jennifer. (2015). Framework for coherence: College and career readiness standards, multi-tiered systems of support, and educator effectiveness. *Center on Great Teachers and Leaders*.

Helle, Laura., Saljo, Roger (2012). Collaborating with digital tools and peers in medical education: cases and simulations as interventions in learning. *Instructional Science: An International Journal of the Learning Sciences*. 40*(5)*. 737–744.

Hortsch, Michael., Mangruklar, Rajesh S. (2015). When students struggle with gross anatomy and histology: a strategy for monitoring, reviewing, and promoting student academic success in an integrated preclinical medical curriculum. *Anatomical Sciences Education*. 8*(5)*. 478–483.

Hu, Yinin., Martindale, James R., LeGallo, Robin D., White, Casey B., McGahren, Eugene D., Schroen, Anneke T. (2016). Relationships between preclinical course grades and standardized exam performance. *Advances in Health Sciences Education*. 21*(2)*. 389–399.

Kansas Multi-Tier System of Supports and Alignment (2015) Retrieved from https://www.ksdetasn.org/mtss.

Kosobuski, AW, Whitney, A., Skildum, A., & Prunsuke, A. (2017). Development of an interdisciplinary pre-matriculation program designed to promote medical students' self efficacy. *Medical Education Online*. 1087–2981.

Kowarski, I. (2017, October 31). Getting Into Medical School Is Becoming Harder. *U.S. News and World Report*. Retrieved from https://www.usnews.com/education/best-graduate-schools/top-medical-schools/articles/2017-10-31/getting-into-medical-school-is-becoming-even-harder.

Machera, Robert P. (2017). Teaching intervention strategies that enhance learning in higher education. *Universal Journal of Educational Research*. 5*(5)*. 733–743.

McIntosh, K., Horner, RH., & Sugai, G. (2009). Sustainability of systems-level evidence-based practices in schools: Current knowledge and future directions. Handbook of Positive Behavior Support. Pp 327–352.

Miller, Cynthia J. (2014). Implementation of a study skills program for entering at-risk medical students. *Advances in Physiology Education*. 38*(3)*. 229–234.

Rodriguez BJ., Loman, SL., & Borgmeier, C., (2016). Tier 2 Interventions in Positive Behavior Support: A Survey of School Implementation. Preventing School Failure: Alternative Education for Children and Youth. 60 *(2)*.

CHAPTER 29

Wellness Initiatives to Support Student Success in Medical Schools

MEGAN ALMANSOORI, M.A.

Megan Almansoori is the learning specialist for the University of Nevada, Reno School of Medicine (UNRSOM). She works specifically with students in their first and second year of the medical degree program, as well as students in the physician assistant program. She has more than twenty years of experience working in education and has focused on supporting students from economically and educationally disadvantaged backgrounds. Almansoori is currently working on a Ph.D. in equity and diversity in education at the University of Nevada, Reno.

Suboptimal Wellness as a Barrier to Success

It is common for the demands of medical school to cause students to question whether the admissions committee made a mistake. The requirements for acceptance to medical school necessitate students to have met high standards throughout their prior educational career, and it favors applicants who set very rigorous expectations for themselves. After matriculation, these students must continue to meet the high standards set by the curriculum (Henning et al.), only this time, they are not the only high-achiever in the room. The perfectionism which many students enter medical school with, in combination with the severity of new challenges and comparison to others, can trigger extreme self-doubt, anxiety, and depression which has been found to be prevalent in medical education due to an environment that relies on high-stakes evaluation (LaDonna et al.).

Through a systematic review of studies focusing on U.S. and Canadian medical schools, it was found that medical students exhibited higher prevalence of anxiety and depression when compared to similar-aged peers. Even more concerning was the finding that 11 percent of medical students in a longitudinal study cohort from seven medical schools disclosed having had suicidal thoughts in the past year (Seritan et al.). As educators, we might hope to see performance insecurities and anxiety decrease as medical training and experience in the field progresses. Unfortunately, Villwock et al. discovered the opposite to be true, combining information from multiple studies which collectively showed that "while medical students begin their training with similar rates of depression as their nonmedical counterparts, their mental health declines as their education progresses" (367).

Unfortunately, due to perceived societal pressures for physicians to appear invincible and concerns about "Wounded Healer" stigmatization, medical students and practitioners are notorious for their low levels of help-seeking behaviors when it comes to their own mental health (Hankir et al.). The fear of appearing weak can result in these students feeling that they have to hide their problems, further exacerbating both the causes and effects of mental health issues, the ramifications of which can reach beyond the individual who is suffering. Not only could poor mental health care negatively impact an individual's medical training and career advancement, it may also cause them to underperform and inhibit the health outcomes of their patients.

Gone untreated, low mental quality of life and burnout have been found to be independent risk factors of suicidal ideation in the healthcare provider population. "These risk factors for suicide translate into medical practice where male physicians are twice as likely, and female physicians three times as likely, to commit suicide than the general public (Villwock et al.).

In response to the alarming national and institutional statistics relating medical training and mental health, medical schools all over the country have begun implementing wellness programs. Unfortunately, while the studies demonstrate a clear issue with medical student wellness, there lacks a concrete and comprehensive understanding of what factors may be affecting student wellness, resulting in high variability of implementation and success of such programming (Seritan et al.). However, with interest in medical trainee mental health and wellness on the rise over the past twenty years, research results are beginning to emerge, schools are attempting to utilize ensuing recommendations, and many are committed to broadening the already expanding research base in this area.

Wellness at the University of Nevada, Reno School of Medicine

Our vision at the University of Nevada, Reno School of Medicine (UNRSOM) is to create a healthy Nevada, starting with a healthful and positive environment that promotes excellence in clinical care and education. Realization of our vision requires an environment in which medical students feel safe and supported academically, emotionally, and physically. We see students holistically, as people first and students second. We recognize and appreciate how academic and professional success can be impacted by experiences beyond our classrooms and clinics, and seek to implement the most effective programming to support the well-being of our students by providing a culture of care.

Since 2011, UNRSOM has been integrating wellness programming, beginning with simple activities such as social events, free yoga, and other stress reduction opportunities. The program has evolved to include more longitudinal initiatives like N-ergy, which encourages students to adopt and maintain healthy behaviors, the Mindfulness, Breathing, and Stress Reduction (MBSR) curriculum, as well as a vital collaboration with UNR counseling services. We have also created a Student Wellness Committee to oversee the planning and implementation of wellness programming and have established the UNRSOM Learning and Wellness Resource Center to provide students a physical space to seek support and unwind.

While the medical students are reporting high levels of satisfaction with the wellness offerings, the combination of low engagement in many of the activities and continued reports of high stress feelings is telling an alternate story—a story which is being echoed by many medical schools across the country. With a rigorous curriculum and high expectations necessitating extreme levels of preparation, medical students are viewing wellness as just "one more thing to do" in an already packed schedule. Many do not view wellness activities as having a correlation to improved performance in their academics in the same way that studying does, while others may have their own ways of attending to their physical and emotional health.

Emerging trends in medical trainee wellness research are calling for an approach which is more integrated into the culture and curriculum, and less supplemental:

> The current wellness model focuses on reducing the manifestations of student stress rather than addressing its underlying sources, which are often environmental, interpersonal, or cultural in nature

> [...] a paradigm shift is needed in the current wellness movement. By recognizing wellness as a philosophy, not an activity, a culture instead of a program, we can begin to generate lasting solutions that will truly promote and sustain the well-being of our nation's next generation of physicians (Gaw 899).

In keeping with Gaw's sentiments, UNRSOM is looking at how to modify our current supplemental wellness programming structure to, instead, catalyze and sustain larger culture changes. We are doing our own research to identify the social-emotional needs of our learner community and developing a strategic plan for how to address these needs at an institutional and curricular level.

In a population that is often known for self-sacrifice, it is not easy to cultivate an environment where students and faculty are self-aware, practice balance, and seek appropriate help for themselves (Seritan et al.). To this end, UNRSOM is dedicated to our vision of a healthy Nevada, and are continuing our work toward improvements in medical trainee wellness, modeling a culture of care, and providing the state with a competent and compassionate healthcare workforce.

REFERENCES

Gaw, C. E. "Wellness Programs in Medical School: Reevaluating the Current Paradigm." *Academic Medicine*, vol. 92, no. 7, 2017, 899. https://doi.org/10.1097/ACM.0000000000001749.

Hankir, A. K., Northall, A., & Zaman, R. "Stigma and mental health challenges in medical students." *BMJ Case Reports*, 2014. https://doi.org/10.1136/bcr-2014–205226.

Henning, K., Ey, S., & Shaw, D. "Perfectionism, the impostor phenomenon and psychological adjustment in medical, dental, nursing and pharmacy students." *Medical Education*, vol. 32, no. 5, 1998, 456–464. https://doi.org/10.1046/j.1365-2923.1998.00234.x.

LaDonna, K. A., Ginsburg, S., & Watling, C. "'Rising to the Level of Your Incompetence': What Physicians' Self-Assessment of Their Performance Reveals About the Imposter Syndrome in Medicine." *Academic Medicine*, vol. 93, no. 5, 2018, 763. https://doi.org/10.1097/ACM.0000000000002046.

Seritan, A., Hunt, J., Shy, A., Rea, M., & Worley, L. "The State of Medical Student Wellness: A Call for Culture Change." *Academic Psychiatry*, vol. 36, no. 1, 2012. https://doi.org/10.1176/appi.ap.10030042.

Villwock, J. A., Sobin, L. B., Koester, L. A., & Harris, T. M. "Impostor syndrome and burnout among American medical students: a pilot study." *International Journal of Medical Education*, vol. 7, 2016, 364–369. https://doi.org/10.5116/ijme.5801.eac4.

Afterword

College Success Community College Student Perspective

Melanie Purdy, PhD, NCC

Melanie Purdy, Ph.D., NCC has been a Professional Counselor and Academic Faculty member at Truckee Meadows Community College, Reno, Nevada, since September 2007. Her areas of interest and specialty in counseling include health and wellness; spirituality; life transition issues; academic confidence and success; and motivation. In addition to providing personal counseling, she created and facilitates Academic Success Kit (ASK) workshops for students on academic probation and provides crisis intervention. She is a certified Quality Matters online educator, and teaches EPY 101: Educational, Career, and Personal Development and has developed an online Suicide Prevention Intervention Training for first responders, medical and mental health professionals. All of her educational degrees are from the University of Nevada, Reno, beginning with a bachelor's degree in Journalism; followed years later by a master's degree in Counseling and Educational Psychology/College Student Development specialty; and then a Doctorate in Counseling and Educational Psychology.

College success is defined in interesting ways. According to the National Center for Education Statistics, the keeper of Integrated Postsecondary Education Data System (IPEDS) data, which gathers data on all higher education institutions that participate in federal student aid programs; as of 2015, the students who REALLY count are the "four degree/certificate-seeking undergraduate student cohorts: 1) Full-time, first-time, 2) Part-time, first-time, 3) Full-time, non-first-time, and 4) Part-time, non-first-time. The reported data are for two points in time: six-years and eight-years after a cohort enters an institution." (https://nces.ed.gov/ipeds/about-ipeds). This seems comprehensive; however, what is assessed is the number of awards conferred upon these degree-seeking populations IF they graduate in a predetermined amount of time. Going deeper and investigating success from the community college student perspective is a critical step in rounding out the definition of the meaning of college success.

In Nevada, a state with a small network of public institutions, the Nevada System of Higher Education (NSHE), and the NSHE Board of Regents, clearly believe that success is also predefined in "measurable" ways that primarily mean graduation. In a statement extracted from the NSHE *Six Strategies to Success Summit*, held in February 2019, Board of Regents Chair Kevin Page said, "It's not enough to get students to go to college; we have to refocus our efforts, from presidents to professors, on getting students to graduate. By graduating, a student creates a pathway to the middle class and a better future." In the same article, System Chancellor Thom Reilly concurred that "These strategies will help guide our institutions toward increasing graduation rates."

So what do students think? In an informal qualitative assessment of students at Truckee Meadows Community College (TMCC) in 2019, students responded to the statement: "Define what your personal success points in college are. This can certainly include graduating, but please include any other definitions and/or stories that apply to you." They overwhelmingly agree—graduation is important to them. One student, age twenty six, says, "College success to me is exceeding all expectations and receiving that rolled up piece of paper that will help me to achieve my biggest goal of becoming a Registered Nurse." This student is not the only one to believe that graduating is important. Another returning student, age twenty nine, identifies success as "Graduating with good grades, taking everything I learned with me and then continuing it furthermore." Sub themes tied to graduating are getting good grades, and surprisingly, "gaining knowledge," or "learning and taking in information and knowledge." Though students do see the value of graduating, to most of the twenty three students who responded, overwhelmingly college success means more than just an increase in the "graduation rate."

According to the 44 percent of students who do mention graduation as a measure of success, it is important primarily because they truly believe it will lead to a practical end, or to quote a younger, female, age twenty two, "College success to me is getting my degree and my dream job." One student stated it like this, "College success to me is graduating with a degree that actually means something, and what I mean by that is, graduating in a field that I can actually get paid in," age thirty three. Others who identify success as the importance of learning what their career path will be, also think their success is tied to learning the applicable skills for that profession. A student, age thirty nine, says, "To me it is taking what I have learned and applying it to my future job and to my personal life."

A second year student, age twenty three, too says that "Graduating is the big success that we are constantly aiming for; however, there is so much more to college success than just graduating." What ARE those other things that contribute to success? A seventeen-year-old high school/college student identifies the next common theme by saying "College success to me is to succeed and become someone." This thread of purpose and meaning comes through vividly in the student responses. Though for some students, the purpose and meaning is tied to finding a meaningful career, it also means providing for family; financial security; opportunity; and finding self-worth. "College success to me is being able to find a purpose or something that lights a fire in your soul," says an older male returning student, age thirty nine.

This just scratches the surface. The students who responded, some fresh into the college experience, many returning after living other "professional" lives, were completing a college level communications/human relations course, and were offered a small incentive of "bonus points" if they responded. The whole process was optional. As may be expected, the students have a robust, broad sense when it comes to defining college success for themselves, specifically as relates to college as providing purpose and meaning. The respondents ranged in age from seventeen to fifty one, were two thirds female, one third male. They identified thoughtful, multilayered definitions of success and how it ties to gaining self-worth.

The emergent themes that tie to "becoming someone" or "feeling more accomplished" related back to development of "soft skills," "becoming confident in my own learning abilities," and completing difficult tasks. One twenty year old says "College success to me is getting good grades on your assignments, while also keeping a good mind set." Another, parent/student says success is "being able to be a wife, mother, and college student . . . I am already learning that I am better at math than I originally thought."

However exciting it is to see students celebrating these important tasks as successes, looking even deeper, we see that for many students, just being in college or being a college student, represents that purpose, and meaning, and success. "College was always my 'golden ticket,' my plan on how I was going to get out of that rut that so many were in"—a graduating (May 2019) thirty-eight-year-old. She goes on to say "College success is setting an example. My nineteen-year-old daughter, now a dual major at UNR, has seen me struggle, and seen me win." A twenty-five-year-old working student, describes how now, in her THIRD attempt at college, after failing out in 2012 and in 2015, she is finding success because she "...grew up, had a daughter and wanted to prove to her that she can do anything she wants. That nothing could stop her from getting in the way of what she wants to become."

Purpose and meaning as measures of success are closely followed by the concept of college success as being tied to learning for life, and developing life skills. "My experiences in college will help me with my personal hobbies, my children, and my overall personal view of life in general. Success in college assures me that I have the ability to become an organized, detail oriented and well-rounded individual who can support my opinions from known facts and experiences." Other life skills like resiliency and interdependence are important. A twenty-three-year-old identifies that, "Establishing positive friendships with those who push me to be better and offer growth is considered success to me. Learning how to redirect negative and stressful circumstances into positive ones by being a creator even in hard times is success to me. Conquering the challenges of college and everyday life combined is college success to me. Lastly, but not least, never giving up after experiencing failure is college success to me." Another students adds "...it is also proving I CAN do anything I put my mind too. This is very important to me because I have always struggled with school and it has been one of the hardest things I have dealt with. So by accomplishing school it would mean that my options are limitless. I can accomplish anything if I put my mind to it."

According to a forced career change male student, age fifty one, "Going to school is challenging." Perhaps celebrating some of these other successes is honoring these students. Community college students are unique, they juggle many tasks, and they have to stop going to college for a while. For example, a thirty year old working mother, who said, "Even though I have moved on to a full time job elsewhere ... I have put my final goal of nursing school on hold for the time being because of the needs of my family...

but I feel great with what I have already accomplished at TMCC and I can't wait to be able to go back to finish my dream!" It is important to allow college success to be all these things, not just a "rolled up piece of paper." By honoring the labor and the successes of all of our students and not just those who contribute to "increasing graduation rates," we truly demonstrate the depth and value of students and education.

REFERENCES

https://nces.ed.gov/ipeds/.

https://nshe.nevada.edu/2019/02/nshe-identifies-six-strategies-to-improve-student-success/.

Index

Page numbers in *italics* refer to figures and tables.